# The Michigan Womyn's Music Festival: An Amazon Matrix of Meaning

# The Michigan Womyn's Music Festival:
## An Amazon Matrix of Meaning

Laurie J. Kendall, Ph.D.

Second Printing, 2013
SECOND EDITION

First Edition © 2008
Laurie J. Kendall
The Spiral Womyn's Press

Library of Congress Cataloging-in-Publication Data

Kendall, Laurie J., 1961-
        The Michigan Womyn's Music Festival: An Amazon Matrix of    Meaning / Laurie J. Kendall.
        Includes bibliographical references.
        **ISBN 978-0-6152-0065-1**
        1. Lesbians.   2. Lesbian Culture.   3. Amazon Consciousness.
        4. The Michigan Womyn's Music Festival.
        5. Ethnography - Research

# Dedication

For my wife, Bobbie. Thank you for your love and faith. I love you all the way to heaven and back. I also want to remember the womyn who fed me with their words – Kay Gardner, Maxine Feldman, June Jordan, Ruth Ellis, and Gloria Anzaldua.

# Acknowledgements

First I want to offer a special thanks to Lisa Vogel for envisioning and building a place that welcomed me home. I would also like to thank all of the womyn who took the time to share their stories with me at the festival. Without your generosity this work would have been impossible. I would also like to express my appreciation and love for the womyn who lovingly shared their lives with me and welcomed me into their families: Cindy Avery, Marnie Keifer, Beth Bitner, Lorraine Alexis, Kathy Davis, Connie Marks, Julianne Meyerle, Kip Parker, Patricia Lay-Dorsey, Ruth Barrett, and Falcon River.

I would also like to give a special thanks to my undergraduate research team: Lauren Wethers, Maryam Gbadamosi, Marissa Corwin, Kate Thom, and Diana Davis. Your assistance helped capture the richness and diversity of the Festival.

# Content Disclaimer

The information contained in this text was not provided by, nor endorsed by Lisa Vogel, the We Want the Music Corporation, or any employee of the Michigan Womyn's Music Festival. The views, attitudes, and interpretations contained in this text are those of the author and the women who participated in this study, and do not necessarily reflect those of any other woman who attends the festival. In no event shall Lisa Vogel, the We Want the Music Corporation, or the Michigan Womyn's Music Festival be responsible or liable for any damage or loss caused by the content of this text.

# Table of Contents

# ⚔ Introduction ⚔
## From the Liminal to the Land:
## Building an Amazon Consciousness and Culture

Every year in August, thousands of women from around the world make a journey that transforms their consciousness. This journey takes women from a world of patriarchal marginalization, oppression, and violence, to the *safety* of a Land where they build a matriarchal culture of *families*, *homes*, and *sacred traditions*. This journey binds them to each other as a people, and to the homeland and culture they love. This book is an ethnographic study of "womyn" who create their own culture at the Michigan Womyn's Music Festival. It should not be read as representative of *all* women or *all* lesbians, or even of *all* individuals who attend the Festival. Rather, it is an exploration of 32 women's journeys in consciousness and the physical work they do to create a material world that places their minds and bodies, their values and experiences, and their relationships and traditions at the *center* of a unique culture specific to the Michigan Womyn's Music Festival. This unique culture is what I refer to as "Amazon culture."

I was first introduced to the Michigan Womyn's Music Festival in a women's studies classroom, through a film titled *Stolen Moments.*[1] In the opening frames of the Festival segment, the stage announcer shouted, "Welcome home women. Welcome home." Suddenly, hundreds of women with painted faces and bare breasts were drumming their way across the screen. A moment later Rhiannon took the stage and began singing "Amazon." Her voice rang out strong and clear:

> I am, I was called Amazon. Now I am called Lesbian.
> Oh, you know the matriarchy ruled back then.
> Oh sister, you know the matriarchy's gonna rule again.
> Amazon women rise. Amazon women weavin' rainbows in the sky.[2]

Martin Stokes, an ethnomusicologist, argued that music is socially meaningful because it "provides means by which people recognize identities and places, and the boundaries which separate them."[3] When I first heard the song "Amazon," I was stunned by its power. Tears streamed down my face as a wave of intuitive

---

[1] *Stolen Moments.* Margaret Westcot, dir. Documentary. Videocassette. Icarus Films, 1999.
[2] Maxine Feldman. *Amazon.*
[3] Martin Stokes, ed. *Ethnicity, Identity and Music: The Musical Construction of Place.* (New York: Berg, 1997), 5.

recognition flowed over me, filling me with a warm sense of connection to the living Amazons that drummed out their hypnotic rhythms on the Land. Somehow I knew what the song meant, and though I had never heard of the Michigan Womyn's Music Festival before, I suddenly felt (like a salmon) an instinctual drive to swim upstream and find my way *home*.

A second later, the film narrator described the Michigan Womyn's Music Festival as the largest women's community gathering in the world. Each year since 1976, women from around the world have made their pilgrimage to Michigan, where "womyn are sacred and girls are safe."[4] This pilgrimage takes them away from the *everyday liminality* they experience in the male centered and homophobic world to a Land where they build a city from the ground up; a city that safeguards the sanctity of children and institutionalizes the sacredness of women. The Festival is a "utopia" that Bonnie Morris describes as "an entire city run by and for lesbian feminists. Utopia revealed. An Eden-built by Eves."[5]

In the woods of Michigan, women come together to construct roads, footpaths, community centers, kitchens, and medical facilities. They lay plumbing pipes and hook up electrical systems that support populations of up to ten thousand women and children. They create their own communication, transportation, and waste disposal systems. They build three childcare centers, two easy access living areas for disabled women, a crafts bazaar, basketball and volleyball courts, and a network of educational spaces. They construct an R.V. park, an orientation facility, a movie theater, two snack shops, a general store and a clothing store. In addition to all of this, they also erect four stages complete with their own lighting and sound systems. Michigan is proof, as Bonnie Morris claims, "…that women can perform every job required in the construction and administration of a city."[6] Then, because these women consider the Land sacred, and believe that it should be allowed to return to its natural state, after the Festival is over the whole city is torn down and packed away in storage, where it waits for the women to return to Michigan and rebuild it the next summer.

However, just because the city is disassembled and women leave the Land does not mean that their experience of the Festival was liminal. On the contrary, like people living in a diasporic country, returning to Michigan is like returning to an Amazon homeland where the landscape and culture are familiar and comfortable. Furthermore, just because people leave their homelands and return to the diaspora does not mean that they leave behind their cultural traditions or family structures. Cultures do not spring forth naturally from the ground, nor do they remain rooted in particular landscapes. People build

[4] Michigan Womyn's Music Festival. [online]. Accessed 30 October 2000. Available from www.michfest.com.
[5] Bonnie J. Morris. *Eden Built By Eves: The Cultural History of Women's Music Festivals.* (Los Angeles: Alyson Books, 1999), 60.
[6] Ibid., 59.

2

cultures to structure and give their lives meaning, and they carry those meanings across geographical borders. The Amazon culture created at the Michigan Womyn's Music Festival transcends the boundaries of the Land, providing women with a constant source of loving support and connection that helps them survive their liminal lives in the patriarchal culture of America. After seeing "Stolen Moments," I realized that somewhere in Michigan women were building a new culture that narrated a new meaning of womanhood and lesbian identity, and that was a story I longed to hear.

This study began with two large questions. First, what is the culture of the Michigan Womyn's Music Festival, and second, in what ways do women make their experience meaningful? I began by asking my working-class friends if they had ever heard of the Michigan Womyn's Music Festival. Like me, none of them knew anything about it. So, I asked lesbian friends at the university if they had ever heard of the Festival. "Ah, Michigan," they sighed with pleasure. "There's no place like it." Not only did they all know about "Michigan," but most of them had been to the Festival. It seemed that among well-educated, middle-class lesbians, "Michigan" held legendary status and was even used as a code word for lesbian recognition. These friends told me, "the music is wonderful, and the women are great! You should go! It will blow your mind!" When I asked for more details, they just smiled and said, "You have to experience it for yourself. There are no words to describe it."

Yet, during my fieldwork I discovered that there are words women consistently use to describe their experience. Between 2001 and 2005, I interviewed 32 women at the Michigan Womyn's Music Festival. Of the 32 women who participated in my study, roughly 75 percent identified as lesbians. The other 25 percent included one gender queer, one bisexual, and six heterosexuals. Ethnically, approximately 25 percent were women of color, including one Hispanic, one Native American, and six African American women. The other 75 percent were white women, and included one Australian woman and two Jewish women. Although all 32 of the womyn's narratives are heard in this text, 21 became primary participants because of their experience and knowledge of the festival, or because of the depth and quality of their interviews. Over and over again, these women consistently used concrete words like "home," "family," and "sacred" to describe their experience and the Amazon culture they created; words that seemed to challenge the theoretical framing of lesbian cultural spaces as "liminal."

In his study of festivals, Victor Turner theorized that they were "liminal" time periods "betwixt and between" the structures of everyday life.[7]

---

[7] Victor Turner's work on the relationship between symbol, myth, and ritual and the liminal spaces of festivals and other celebrations is well documented in: *Celebration: Studies in Festivity and Ritual*, (Washington: Smithsonian Institution Press, 1982), *From Ritual to Theatre: The Human Seriousness of Play*, (New York: PAJ Publications, 1982), *The Anthropology of Performance*, (New York: PAJ Publications, 1988). *The Anthropology of Experience*, (Chicago: University of Illinois Press, 1986), *Ritual Process: Structure and Anti-Structure*, (New York: Aldine De Grauyter, 1995).

Turner borrowed the term "liminal" from the French ethnologist Arnold van Gennep, who used the concept to describe "rites of passage." However, Turner used the concept of liminality to describe a process whereby individuals go through a "ritual marginalization" that strips away, inverts, or otherwise incapacitates the normal social structures of everyday life, and where the "communitas" is freed to explore new forms of relationships and develop "generative symbols and metaphors and comparisons; art and religion are their products rather than legal and political structure."[8] The process of "ritual marginalization" transforms diverse social actors into a group that Turner called "communitas." In communitas, social roles and social bonds are relatively unstructured, undifferentiated, and non-hierarchal. In communitas, "normal" social roles are reversed or turned upside down, thereby creating an "antistructure" capable of "redressing" the injustices and oppressions of everyday life. Turner suggested that the communitas entering the antistructure of liminal space/time are "threshold people" who "are necessarily ambiguous, since this condition and these persons elude and slip through the network of classification that normally locate states and positions in cultural space. Liminal entities are neither here nor there; they are betwixt and between the positions assigned by law, custom, convention, and ceremonial."[9]

Masquerades, shifting realities, and status reversals are all qualities of the liminal time/space. As Turner suggested, when the communitas enters the liminal period, "we find performances about performances about performances multiplying. . . . We play roles, occupy statues, play games with one another, don and doff masks, each a typification."[10] During Mardi-Gras for instance, men often perform feminine roles and women perform masculine roles, and the fool becomes king for a day. Turner argued that this donning of masks and performing role reversals conceals "a process of structural realignment."[11] During the liminal period, these reversals work to redress social injustices in a playful way, as "authority is now wielded by communitas itself masquerading as structure."[12]

Yet these periods of reversal do not fundamentally change the dominant social structures, for when "making the low mimic the behavior of the high, and by restraining the initiatives of the proud, they underline the reasonableness of the everyday culturally predictable behaviors between the various estates of society. . . . Not only do they reaffirm the order of structure; they also restore relations between the actual historical individuals who occupy positions in that structure."[13] In other words, for culturally dominant groups who go through ritual marginalization and role reversals, who don masks and

---

[8] Turner, *The Ritual Process: Structure and Anti-Structure*, 127-128.
[9] Ibid., 95.
[10] Turner, *The Anthropology of Performance*, 107.
[11] Turner, *The Ritual Process*, 173.
[12] Ibid. 185.
[13] Ibid., 177.

4

masquerade as the marginalized, the liminal period is not permanent, nor does it fundamentally alter the power structures and privileged positions of the dominant group. The liminal period is entered into voluntarily and with the attitude of playfulness in contemporary Western cultures.

Yet, drawing on Victor Turner's theory of liminality, many scholars insist on describing lesbian and gay cultural spaces as "liminal." For instance, in *Lesbian Rule: Cultural Criticism and the Value of Desire*, Amy Villarejo described a lesbian bar as "a liminal space, oscillating between visibility and invisibility, wherein we find ourselves secretly knowing that to which others remain oblivious."[14] Scott Thumma and Edward Gray also described the "Gospel Hour," an Atlanta drag show that mixes drag performance with evangelical gospel music, as a "performance [in] a liminal time and space set apart from the everyday."[15] Steven Kates and Russell Belk also frame their five-year study of Gay Pride festivals as "liminal" because "such celebrations are consistent with Turner's observation..." of ritual, excess, and power inversion that the communitas experiences.[16] Likewise, Boden Sandstrom argued that Turner's theory of liminality was "appropriate to the analysis of the Michigan Womyn's Music Festival because the Festival attempts to redress the oppression of women through a cultural performance."[17]

However, I would argue that it is paradoxical when theories of liminality are used to describe the cultural spaces of an *already* marginalized people. How are women in general, and lesbians in particular, "transformed" through the liminal period and made ready to "integrate" into the social structures of everyday life? What "rite of passage" does the liminal time/space offer lesbians? How are women or lesbians "ritually marginalized" by the institution of the Michigan Womyn's Music Festival?

Granted, the Michigan Womyn's Music Festival does appear to contain "liminal" elements when women produce the costumes, symbols, arts, and religions that Turner claimed "redress" social injustices and inequalities. The paradox is that by ritually marginalizing people, liminal times and spaces counteract the normality of everyday life. Yet, for an already marginalized group like the women who attend the Michigan Womyn's Music Festival, the liminal is not so *temporary*, and their costumes, symbols, arts, and religions form the concrete foundation of Amazon culture, a culture that normalizes their identities and experiences.

---

[14] Amy Villarejo. *Lesbian Rule: Cultural Criticism and the Value of Desire.* (Durham: Duke University Press, 2003), 1.

[15] Scott Thumma and Edward R. Gray, eds. "The Gospel Hour: Liminality, Identity, and Religion in a Gay Bar," in *Gay Religion*, (Walnut Creek, CA: Alta Mira Press, 2005), 286-287.

[16] Steven M. Kates and Russell W. Belk. "The Meaning of Lesbian and Gay Pride Day: Resistance Through Consumption and Resistance to Consumption." *Journal of Contemporary Ethnography.* Vol. 30 No. 4, August 2001, 403.

[17] Boden Sandstrom. *Performance, Ritual and Negotiation of Identity in the Michigan Womyn's Music Festival.* (University of Maryland: Dissertation, 2002), 184.

Liminality is a flawed concept for describing lesbian cultures. It is a concept that has been blanketed onto lesbian and gay cultural spaces because it describes something different or something "other" than normal. By continuing to use the concept of liminality to describe lesbian events and spaces, it hides the actual culture building processes going on in these spaces and it actually works to maintain lesbian "otherness." However, my use of the word is meant to signify what lesbians experience outside the Festival. Like Gloria Anzaldua and Chela Sandoval, who use words like "borderlands" and "interstitial" to describe the reality of their everyday experience, I use the word "liminal" to describe the nuances of everyday ritual marginalizations that many lesbians experience in their everyday lives. In other words, I am inverting the concept of liminality, and relocating it to the everyday social world as a way to better describe lesbian experience in American culture. Outside the Festival, many lesbians live in an "anti-structure" where the normal social structures do not include them. Turner claimed that the liminal was "betwixt and between" the social rules of normal life, yet everyday life is where lesbians are systematically marginalized and caught "betwixt and between" the ideologies and institutions of American culture.

For instance, lesbian couples often veil their relationship or masquerade as something other than what they really are, loving marriages in every sense of the word. Furthermore, lesbians often experience ritual marginalization within their own homes, and by families, churches, employers, and by public servants who fail to protect them. Many lesbians become consummate actors, playing the "appropriate" relationship roles associated with female gender in the dominant culture; lovers become sisters or cousins, or mothers and daughters. Some even masquerade by living in "drag" or "passing" as men in order to escape the oppression of the normative sex/gender system. While dominant groups voluntarily enter the liminal time/space with an attitude of playfulness, the ritually marginalized are forced to masquerade in perpetual liminality.

Constantly masquerading and living in a perpetual state of liminality leaves many women feeling exhausted, orphaned, and homeless within their own cultures and countries. Gloria Anzaldua expressed this feeling of homelessness eloquently when she wrote of women living in borderlands. Yet her words seem to hint at the many ways lesbians are dealing with their feeling of "homelessness." Anzaldua wrote:

> As a Mestiza [and lesbian] I have no country, my homeland cast me out; yet all countries are mine because I am every woman's sister or potential lover...I am cultureless because, as a feminist, I challenge the collective cultural/religious male-derived beliefs of Indo-Hispanics and Anglos; yet I am cultured because I am participating in the creation of yet another culture, a new story to explain the world and our

participation in it, a new value system with images and symbols that connect us to each other and to the planet.[18]

Understanding Anzaldua's concept that women create new stories, cultures, and value systems through images and symbols has helped me interpret the things I have experienced and the stories I have heard at the Michigan Womyn's Music Festival. As Kip said to me during an intense interview, "This is my *home*! Even when I'm out there, I know where my *home* is, where my people are."[19] For Kip, and many women like her, the Michigan Womyn's Music Festival is far from a liminal time/space. It is a culture more "real" to them than the dominant culture. It is a culture they have built from a consciousness of difference, an Amazon consciousness born of ritual marginalization in the dominant patriarchal, sexist, and homophobic world. This Amazon consciousness has used love as a building tool to construct *homes*, *families*, and *sacred* traditions into an Amazon culture that sustains them, their values, and their relationships throughout the entire year.

Therefore, a more adequate framework for understanding the culture women build at the Michigan Womyn's Music Festival is Chela Sandoval's *Methodology of the Oppressed*. Sandoval argued that the methodology of the oppressed was developed in the writings of "feminists of color [who] exist in the *interstices* between normalized social categories."[20] Her work makes clear the processes marginalized groups go through to empower themselves and their social movements. According to Sandoval, marginalized people combine "semiotics, deconstruction, meta-ideologizing, and democratics through differential movement."[21] Differential movement is made possible by what she calls the "apparatus of love." "Together, these processes and procedures comprise a hermeneutic for defining and enacting oppositional social action as a mode of 'love' in the postmodern world."[22] These technologies enable an oppositional consciousness to engage in several emancipatory social movements, including "equal rights," "revolutionary," "supremacist," and "separatist," and to *tactically* shift between them using the "apparatus of love."[23] In this sense, love is not a private or romanticized emotion, but rather an act of will and a crafting tool for building a new consciousness and culture.

For Gloria Anzaldua, this "oppositional consciousness" manifests in what she called a "Mestiza consciousness," and develops in interstitial spaces like "borderlands." According to Anzaldua, the Mestiza consciousness "puts history through a sieve, winnows out the lies, looks at the forces that we as a

---

[18] Gloria Anzaldua. *Borderlands/La Frontera: The New Mestiza*. (San Francisco: Aunt Lute Books,1999), 102-103.

[19] Kip Parker. Personal interview. 8 Aug. 2003.

[20] Chela Sandoval. *Methodology of the Oppressed: Theory Out of Bounds*. (Minneapolis: University of Minnesota, 2000), 46.

[21] Sandoval, 3.

[22] Ibid., 147.

[23] Ibid.

race, as women, have been a part of. This step is a conscious rupture with all oppressive traditions of all cultures and religions."[24] Anzaldua argued that the Mestiza consciousness "reinterprets history and, using new symbols, shapes new myths. [The Mestiza] adopts new perspectives toward the darkskinned, women and queers. She strengthens her tolerance (and intolerance) for ambiguity."[25] The "Mestiza consciousness" takes shape when the self is recognized as existing *between* worlds (male/female, brown/white, hetero/homo, liminal/institutional), and acquires the situated knowledge to resist these oppressive structures.

Like women of color who live in borderlands or interstitial spaces, lesbians live "betwixt and between" the social institutions and ideologies of American culture, where they develop their own "oppositional consciousness" and use these same "technologies" to build an Amazon culture. Using the "apparatus of love," lesbians deconstruct dominant categories and images, and use the tool of *love* to craft new symbols, arts, and sacred traditions into a meaningful cultural matrix. Thus, the Michigan Womyn's Music Festival is a space beyond the liminal, where *Amazon consciousness* rejects essentialized definitions of "woman" and "lesbian," and refuses the "neocolonizing forces of postmodernism" that fragment identity.[26]

Similar to the concept developed in Chela Sandoval's methodology of the oppressed, the culture of the Michigan Womyn's Music Festival "allows survival and more, [because] it allows practitioners to live with faith, hope, and moral vision in spite of all else."[27] When womyn move from the Liminal to the Land, they move into a culture that places their experiences, values, and definitions of family, home, and the sacred at the *center*. During an interview at the 2002 Festival, Ro said to me: "We call it just 'Michigan.' The poor people who live in this state! We just say we're going to 'Michigan,' and we're supposed to know what that means. And we do! We do."[28]

When womyn like Ro say "Michigan," they are not just talking about a music festival for womyn. Rather, they are talking about the loving and nurturing *homes, families*, and *sacred* traditions they have built into a cultural matrix that helps them survive in a world hostile to their very existence. This cultural matrix connects them to each other, the Land, and to a shared history through an imaginative network of symbols, myths, and rituals that provide them with the strength to fight against oppressive ideologies and institutions of American culture. By sifting history, winnowing experience, and reinterpreting myth, the *Amazon consciousness* empowers womyn not only speak their oppositional narratives of home, family, and the sacred, but to embody them on the Land and in the liminality of their everyday lives. In other words, Michigan becomes more than an alternative home or family, or a symbolic landscape in

---

[24] Anzaldua, 104.
[25] Ibid.
[26] Sandoval, 3.
[27] Sandoval, 7.
[28] Rosemary Rasmussen. Personal Interview. August, 2002.

interstitial space. Michigan is a place where womyn, by the sweat of their brows and the blisters on their hands, literally build a matriarchal culture that stands in stark contrast to the patriarchy. This is what womyn like Ro mean when they say "Michigan." Not only is it the place womyn construct to offer each other the warm greeting of "welcome home," it is also the ground on which they stand to mount their fight against the patriarchal, racist, homophobic, and sexist ideologies and institutions of American culture.

*Tree in the Night Stage Bowl*

# ⚒ 1 ⚒

## It's Absolutely a Culture of Its Own

On the morning Bobbie and I left for our first Michigan Womyn's Music Festival, all we really knew was there would be food, music, and about six thousand lesbians camping in the woods together. Yet, the thought of a week among thousands of women like ourselves was irresistible; a whole week where we could be open about our relationship and not have to pretend to be anything other than what we were. But on that hot August morning back in 2001 we had no idea that we were about to take a journey in consciousness that would transform the material reality of our lives. Nor did we know the feeling of safety and homecoming we would experience as we entered that womyn-only community.

Bobbie shoved the last of our camping gear in the van while I checked our packing list one last time; lantern, water cooler, camp stove, coffee pot and coffee, propane tank, flash lights, extra batteries, camp potty, suitcase, briefcase, notebook, camera, folding chairs and table, ice chest, first aid kit, and sleeping bags. Everything was in the van, along with several "just in case" items; tool-chest, emergency gallon of water, flares, and junk food. As usual we over-packed, but we are lesbians, so of course we were loaded for bear and ready for any contingency. Little did we know that our gear paled in comparison to the amount of equipment and material goods other women hauled to Michigan to share with the community.

About ten miles outside of Baltimore, Bobbie asked, "you've got the envelope with the tickets and the directions, right?" "Yup," I replied, "it's in the glove box with the map." She flipped open the glove box, pulled out the map and began tracing her finger along a green line that ran from the border of Maryland through Pennsylvania, Ohio, Indiana, and up into Michigan. "You know, it's going to take us about fourteen hours to get there," she said. Looking back on that moment, I should have said, "What's fourteen hours? We had to wait nearly 20 years to learn that the Festival even existed."

Even though Bobbie and I had been together nearly 20 years, never once during that time had anyone ever told us about the Michigan Womyn's Music Festival. I only learned about it by chance, in a women's studies classroom when the instructor showed a film on lesbian cultures from around the world. The film was over an hour long, with segments on German lesbian experience, French lesbian experience, Canadian lesbian experience, and so forth. Yet buried within the hour of footage was a small nugget of information that changed my consciousness and the course of my life. In the short four-minute segment on the Michigan Womyn's Music Festival, the film's narrator said:

> The post-Stonewall era saw the concurrence of women's liberation and gay liberation propel large numbers of lesbians into emancipation and the dream of a lesbian nation. The Michigan Womyn's Music Festival has become a tradition reflecting that vision. Since the mid 70s, each summer thousands of lesbians from around the world attend this five-day celebration. During the 70s and 80s, dykes established many alternative institutions for themselves. They created women only living spaces, set up viable economic institutions, became publishers of their own books and magazines. They founded women's health care systems, managed to get clean and sober, and became an important force in the environmental movement. They found themselves capable of doing things never before dreamed possible. The entire setup for this festival is done by women. And they manage and operate the largest kitchen in the world, providing hot meals for ten thousand women at a time, come rain or shine. One of the triumphs of the lesbian feminist movement was the creation of a women's music industry, which has been instrumental in the success of many of today's mainstream artists.[29]

This nugget of information not only set me on the road to Michigan, but it also propelled me into the exploration of lesbian feminist herstory and the building of the Lesbian Nation.

## The Lesbian Nation

During the 1970s lesbians found themselves multiply marginalized in various social justice movements. Lesbians of color experienced racism in the National Organization for Women and homophobia in the Black Nationalist movement. Audre Lorde wrote, "Black women who once insisted that lesbianism was a white woman's problem, now insist that Black lesbians are a threat to Black nationhood, are consorting with the enemy, are basically un-Black. Their accusations, coming from the very women to whom we look for deep and real understanding, have served to keep many Black lesbians in hiding, caught between the racism of white women and the homophobia of their

---

[29] *Stolen Moments.* Margaret Westcot, dir. Documentary. Videocassette. Icarus Films, 1999.

sisters."[30]  A couple of the womyn interviewed for this project talked about their own experiences and the tension they felt in the women's movement.

Van: "My experience with white women is that they tend to be politically conscious on a different level.  Which is fine, I have no problem with them.  My mom and I did volunteer work for NOW [National Organization for Women] in Chicago.  But as I walk by the table and the group that's representing NOW here [at the Festival], in the craft area – they have two boards of pictures and there's no women of color in those pictures!  So what does that say?  We don't exist?  So that tends to bother me."[31]

Akosua: "In the world of feminism, in the world of lesbianism, in the world of politics, Black women don't see the need to join.  Traditionally, we haven't felt part of the wider women's community – the wider activist community.  And the term 'feminist,' there's always been this debate about whether or not Black women are feminists, and if there's any kind of common ground there – and I don't use the term 'feminist' a lot.  But I also recognize that without those women, be whatever race they are, there are a lot of things that I wouldn't have, and you wouldn't have, if those women didn't step forward.  And so, I can use the term feminist in appreciation.  I think, as Black women, we have to come to terms with some of that.  It has been largely a white movement, but we have a place there as well."[32]

One place Black women articulated their feminist consciousness was in the Combahee River Collective.  In 1974 women of color formed the collective as a way to think through the connections between gender, race, sexuality, and class.  The Combahee River Collective issued "A Black Feminist Statement" in which they wrote:

> The most general statement of our politics at the present time would be that we are actively committed to struggling against racial, sexual, heterosexual, and class oppression, and see as our particular task the development of integrated analysis and practice based upon the fact that the major systems of oppressions are interlocking.  The synthesis of these oppressions creates the conditions of our lives.  As Black women we see Black feminism as the logical political movement to combat the manifold and simultaneous oppressions that all women of color face.[33]

When Black women began articulating oppression as an interlocking system of race, class, gender, and sexuality, white lesbians were still articulating their own

[30] Audre Lorde. Age, Race, Class, and Sex: Women Redefining Difference." In *Feminist Theory: A Reader.* Wendy Kolmar and Frances Bartkowski, eds. (Mountain View: Mayfield Publishing, 2000), 288.
[31] Van. Personal Interview. August, 2005.
[32] Akosua. Personal Interview. August, 2005.
[33] Combahee River Collective. "A Black Feminist Statement." (1977). In *Feminist Theory: A Reader.* Wendy Kolmar and Frances Bartkowski, eds. (Mountain View: Mayfield Publishing, 2000), 272-273.

oppressions in the National Organization for Women (NOW) and the Gay Liberation Front (GLF) as a two dimensional problem.

In the Gay Liberation Front, lesbians argued that gay men were "not sufficiently sensitive to sexism and issues of particular concern to lesbians."[34] They argued that the GLF was essentially a patriarchal organization concerned with fighting for the rights of gay men to have sex. Lesbians in GLF were frustrated because they felt the organization should make the conscious connections between sexual oppression and gender oppression.

Likewise, in the National Organization for Women, Betty Friedan dubbed lesbians the "lavender menace" and tried to purge them from NOW because she feared that accusations of "lesbianism" would destroy the women's movement.[35] In 1973, after Friedan told the *New York Times* that "lesbians were sent to infiltrate the women's movement by the CIA as a plot to discredit feminism," Rita Mae Brown's writing group took over the opening night of the Second Annual Congress to Unite Women.[36] Killing the lights in the auditorium, lesbians donned "Lavender Menace" t-shirts and when the lights came on again they were standing in the isles holding signs that read: "Take a Lesbian to Lunch," "Superdyke Loves You," and "The Women's Movement is a Lesbian Plot."[37] That night the "Lavender Menace" held the stage as members of the audience joined them in discussing their lives as lesbians.[38] Later, the Lavender Menace formed a consciousness-raising group called the Radicalesbians. Together, they wrote an article titled "The Woman Identified Woman," in which they asked the question, "What is a Lesbian?" They answered with the following statement:

A lesbian is the rage of all women condensed to the point of explosion. . . . Lesbian is a label invented by Men to throw at any woman who dares to be his equal, who dares to challenge his prerogatives (including that of all women as part of the exchange medium among men), who dares to assert the primacy of her own needs. . . . A lesbian is not considered a "real woman." And yet, in popular thinking, there is really only one essential difference between a lesbian and other women: that of sexual orientation – which is to say, when you strip off all the packaging, you must finally realize that the essence of being a "woman" is to get fucked by men. . . . By virtue of having been brought up in a male society, we have internalized the male culture's definition of ourselves. . . . As

---

[34] Neil Miller. *Out of the Past: Gay and Lesbian History from 1869 to the Present.* (New York: Vintage Books, 1995), 374.
[35] Ibid.
[36] Lillian Faderman. *Odd Girls and Twilight Lovers: A History of Lesbian Life in Twentieth-Century America.* (New York: Penguin Books, 1991, 212.
[37] Miller, 375.
[38] Ibid., 376.

long as we are dependent on the male culture for this definition, for this approval, we cannot be free.[39]

This same year, Jill Johnson's book, *Lesbian Nation: A Feminist Solution* became a rallying cry for lesbian feminisms.[40]   The term "lesbian nation" was an important symbol for lesbians who dreamed of transforming the patriarchal culture into a matriarchy.  Across the country, lesbians began creating the art, music, and literature of their new culture.  They also formed collectives rather than hierarchical power structures to oversee their cultural projects.

One of the women I interviewed told me about her first attempt to go to a NOW meeting, and how that experience propelled her into the Lesbian Nation.

Falcon: "In 1975, I walked out of the bars and right into the feminist movement.  And I tried to go to my first NOW meeting, but I was met at the door by a man who told me that I couldn't come in.  And, I'm like, 'well, I'm a woman.  What are you doin' here?'  But I didn't go in, because I looked in there and I didn't see anybody that looked like me.  So instead, I got involved with a local lesbian feminist organization called the 'Lesbian Feminist Union.'  We started a collective, and started a bar.  The bar was called Mother's Brew.  We had all the big name women performers come in.  We had Meg [Christian].  We had Holly [Near].  We had Robin Flowers.  Maxine Feldman did a fundraiser for us.  She helped us get our bar started.  We had women's art shows.  We had a safe space in the back for battered women.  In fact, I think we may have been the first battered women's shelter there.  And then we went up to the first National Women's Music Festival, and someone gave me one of these little mimeographed flyers, and it had a full moon in the center and a gathering of women in woods, or something like that, and it was the first flyer for this festival [Michigan Womyn's Music Festival].  And so a bunch of us loaded up in the van, 29 years ago, and we drove up here from Kentucky.  And we didn't have a clue how in the hell we were gonna find this place, but we found it, and I've been comin' every since."[41]

Falcon's narrative demonstrates the differential consciousness involved in lesbian feminism, particularly as it was concerned with the "equal rights" of women as well as creating "revolutionary" spaces like battered women's shelters and creating "supremacist" forms of women's art and music, all within "separatist" spaces like lesbian bars.  According to Arlene Stein, lesbian feminism "was founded on the belief that women could retrieve a self that had been denied to them by the dominant culture."[42]  Men had the power to define women and to lock them into institutionalized roles that men controlled.  What

---

[39] Radicalesbians. "The Woman Identified Woman." In *Feminist Theory: A Reader.* Wendy Kolmar and Frances Bartkowski, eds. (Mountain View: Mayfield Publishing, 2000), 195-196.

[40] Jill Johnson. *Lesbian Nation: A Feminist Solution.* (New York: Simon and Schuster, 1973).

[41] Falcon River. Personal Interview. August, 2004.

[42] Arlene Stein. *Sex and Sensibility: Stories of a Lesbian Generation.* (Berkeley: University of California Press, 1997), 89.

the patriarchal culture denied lesbians was the right to exist; to be active and visible participants in the social order. What lesbian feminism offered was the power for lesbians to define themselves politically. This meant redefining the liminal space between the Civil Rights, women's liberation, and the gay liberation movements, and building a unified lesbian feminist movement that empowered women to redefine themselves according to their own definitions and value systems. Lesbian feminists believed that "such unity seemed easy to attain, since there appeared to be a consensus among them about what the broad configuration of the Lesbian Nation would look like: a utopia for women, an Amazon dream."[43]

*The Michigan Womyn's Music Festival – 2002*

However, women from different social locations and educational backgrounds had very different ideas about what the Lesbian Nation would look like, what lesbian feminism was, and who could define themselves as a lesbian. For instance, Charlotte Bunch led a separatist writing collective called the Furies. The Furies intended to "recast lesbianism as a political strategy that was the outcome of feminism"[44] Likewise, Ti-Grace Atkinson argued,

---

[43] Faderman, 218.
[44] Stein, 113.

"feminism is the theory and lesbianism is the practice."[45]  And Adrienne Rich's concept of a "lesbian continuum" was meant to "include a range – through each woman's life and throughout history – of woman-identified experiences, not simply the fact that a woman has had or consciously desired genital sexual experience with another woman."[46]  Ideas like these began reshaping what it meant to be a lesbian because it suggested that *every* woman had a lesbian within, and that all women's relationships were lesbian in nature.  Suddenly, as Arlene Stein noted, previously heterosexual women were claiming to be lesbians because "lesbianism was a matter of identification, not simply a matter of desire."[47]

Once lesbianism was recast as a political, rather than a sexual identity, lesbian feminists began building rigid boundaries around that identity.  For example, they drew boundaries around lesbian attire, which meant adopting the androgynous lesbian feminist uniform - flannel shirts, jeans, and desert boots. Lesbian Feminists also drew boundaries around lesbian sex, which they argued should not be penetrative because that would reflect male values.  Furthermore, many lesbian feminists adopted "separatism as a strategy… to ensure the survival of lesbian institutions and organizations."[48]  In essence, if lesbian feminism was the philosophy, then separatism was the practice.

From the beginning, some critics of lesbian feminism believed that its supporters faced somber challenges.  Lillian Faderman wrote that lesbian feminism was "doomed to failure because of [its] youthful inexperience and an inability to compromise."[49]  Because many collectives were idealistic young women with little business experience, few had the skills to manage their projects.  And because middle-class lesbian feminists tried to declass themselves by de-emphasizing making money or profiting from their projects, many collectives simply could not sustained themselves economically.  In addition, because lesbian feminists felt the need to define themselves in absolute opposite terms from the patriarchal culture, the Lesbian Nation became just as restrictive and oppressive in terms of class division, language, dress, sexual expression, and political ideologies.  There was also the problem of race.  In their eagerness to unify the Lesbian Nation, many lesbian feminists failed to recognize the fact that white lesbian perspectives dominated the movement and that the tools used to oppress women and lesbians were the same tools used to oppress women of color.  Just as the larger women's movement had not wanted to take on "lesbian issues," lesbian feminists had not thought to take on "race issues."

Finally, as sexually identified lesbians watched heterosexual women

---

[45] Miller, 377.
[46] Adrienne Rich. "Compulsory Heterosexuality and Lesbian Existence." In *Feminist Theory: A Reader.* Wendy Kolmar and Frances Bartkowski, eds. (Mountain View: Mayfield Publishing, 2000), 305.
[47] Stein, 24.
[48] Wendy Kolmar and Frances Bartkowski, eds. *Feminist Theory: A Reader.* (Mountain View: Mayfield Publishing, 2000), 163.
[49] Faderman, 220.

claim lesbian identities, they began questioning the authenticity of the new political identity. Life-long lesbians argued that just because a woman was privileged enough to shed her patriarchal shackles by joyously bursting out of the closet as a lesbian feminist, this did not mean that she knew anything about the oppression that "real" lesbians carried on their shoulders and in their consciousness.[50]

On the other hand, new political lesbian feminists argued that by smashing sexual categories, they were creating an authentic self-defined lesbian identity rather than remaining oppressed within the old patriarchal category of lesbian.[51] New politically defined lesbian feminists "broke down not just the boundaries between heterosexual and homosexual worlds but also the elaborate, gendered organization of secretive lesbian sub-cultures."[52] Lesbian feminists tended toward "fanaticism" in defining themselves in opposition to butch-femme lesbians, feminist lesbians who were comfortable in their middle-class lifestyles, and any other lesbians who did not practice their asexual, politically correct brand of loving women.[53] Ultimately though, new political lesbians learned that "smashing the categories was a much simpler task than remaking the self."[54] Nor did smashing the categories change the oppression women who loved women experienced in their everyday life. In fact, smashing the categories created a new sense of liminality for life-long lesbians within the movement.

Even today, womyn at the Festival question the categories and terminology for what they see as an authentic "lesbian" space and culture. Although bisexual and straight women are welcome at the Festival, the life-long lesbians I interviewed claim "Michigan" as their culture and debate the wisdom of calling it a "women's festival," fearing that the terminology promotes the idea of assimilation.

Lorraine: "They really tried to make a big issue of this being a 'women's' festival, not a 'lesbian' festival. They were really trying to root out the lesbian image because they wanted it open to all women. I don't know why. Maybe they thought it would be a good socialization experience for women, or maybe it was more of a marketing thing because then they could bring in more people, because it is a money making endeavor now. But it dilutes our community down, because now it's almost like we don't need to be 'other,' because we are going to be assimilated within. So it really dilutes out our whole ethnicity. Every year there's evolution good and evolution bad, and I noticed this year that they got away from calling it the 'cunt'ree store. In the brochure now, it has 'general store.' And then under the workers area, it has 'country store.' So what's that about? Give us back our culture. We're taking back the

---

[50] Stein, 89.
[51] Ibid., 46.
[52] Ibid.
[53] Faderman, 217.
[54] Stein, 46.

words and the language, and using them for our own endeavors!"[55]

Van: "Susanne said something the other day in the Womyn of Color Tent, 'No matter what you call yourselves, you're still a bunch of dykes, so get over it.' And I firmly believe that. I mean, look at me, I'm totally fem. But technically, I'm butcher than Sarah [Van's partner]. She can't even drive a nail in the wall. But my mother made sure we could all take care of things like that. So, I just put on a pair of gloves to protect my nails."[56]

Clearly, smashing the categories was not a goal for lesbians who wanted a recognizable culture of their own; one where they recognized their own experiences in the music, art, literature, spiritual traditions, and politics, and that also institutionalized their socialist, egalitarian, communal, and ecological values. Lesbians of this mindset began distancing themselves from the androgyny of lesbian feminism and joined with other women interested in building "womyn's culture."

## Womyn's Culture

As Lorraine's narrative suggests, it seems ironic that lesbians at the Festival would name their culture "womyn's culture." But the spelling of the word was meant to signify the rejection of patriarchal definitions of both "woman" and "lesbian." For Linda Shear, one of the early Festival performers, the goal of womyn's culture was not to redefine heterosexual women as lesbians, or to redefine lesbians as androgynous asexual women, but rather to build an authentic culture based on lesbian values and experience. In a letter to *Lesbian Connection*, Shear argued against mixing the two identities at her concerts because, "Mixed concerts create androgynous energy, and androgynous energy will create androgyny, not Dykes and Amazons."[57] Shear used the terms "dykes" and "Amazons" to reclaim the sexual meaning of lesbianism, and artists, musicians, and writers of womyn's culture were working day and night to provide the images of a new utopian womyn's culture. Maxine Feldman's "Amazon" is just one musical example, but there were also a plethora of feminist utopian fictions written in the 1970s. These cultural workers were influential because they not only provided imagery of strong capable women, but they experimented with various ideas for structuring womyn's culture.

In the years between 1969 and 1985, there was an explosion of feminist utopian literature. Diane Crowder noted that, "in the five-year span between 1975-1979, twenty-four utopias by women were published in the U.S. alone."[58] Utopian literature is the literature of hope that often accompanies revolutionary, supremacist, and separatist movements. Feminist utopian fictions were popular

[55] Lorraine Alexis. Personal Interview. August, 2002.
[56] Van. Personal Interview. August, 2005.
[57] *Lesbian Connection.* 2.1 (Mar., 1976):7.
[58] Diane Griffin Crowder. "Separatism and Feminist Utopian Fiction." In *Sexual Practice, Textual Theory: Lesbian Cultural Criticism.* Susan J. Wolfe and Julia Penelope, eds. (Cambridge: Blackwell Publishers, 1993), 237.

in the early years of the womyn's cultural movement because they articulated the systematic oppression of all women, and gave voice to the "deep-seated rage such oppressions caused."[59]  They also provided images of women who were quite capable of defending themselves against male oppression.  In additions, they provided critical analyses of the sex/gender system and created alternative systems and worlds that were superior to those created by men.  Yet how women in these utopias expressed their rage, and how they went about creating alternative worlds fell into two broad categories that reflected the different theoretical perspectives and experiences in the lesbian feminist and the womyn's cultural movements.

An example of the first category was Monique Wittig's *Les Guerilleres*.[60] In this novel women employed violence and acted collectively to make actual war on all men who would not fight for women's liberation.  Wittig described women using guerilla tactics to destroy their enemies.  She wrote:

> Their favourite [sic] weapons are portable.  They consist of rocket-launchers which they carry on the shoulder. . . . It is possible to run and change position extremely quickly without loss of fire-power.  There is every kind of rifle.  There are machine-guns and rocket-launchers.  There are traps with jaws in ditches pitfalls hollows lined with rows of slicing bamboo-blades driven in as stakes.  The manoeuvres [sic] are raids ambushes surprise attacks followed by a rapid retreat.  The object is not to gain ground but to destroy the greatest number of the enemy to annihilate his armament to compel him to move blindly never to grant him the initiative in engagements to harass him without pause.[61]

At the end of the war, the only men left were those who had relinquished authority to women, and whom women had kept alive for their "spermatozoa." In Wittig's post-patriarchal world, women took over the institutions of men, recreating them as they "worked, made love, sang, and played as a group."[62]

Likewise, in *The Female Man*, Joanna Russ painted a world where a literal war raged between the sexes.[63]  What *The Female Man* and *Les Guerilleres* had in common was that both evoked the rage of the reader, both were explicitly lesbian and separatist, both employed violence, and both responded to "a desire for a concrete plan of action."[64]  Both Wittig and Russ named "men" as the literal enemy rather than impersonal social structures, and both advocated

---

[59] Crowder, 238.
[60] Monique Wittig. *Les Guerilleres*. Translated by Peter Owen, and published by the Viking Press in 1971. (Boston: Beacon Press, 1985).
[61] Ibid., 95.
[62] Crowder, 239.
[63] Joanna Russ. *The Female Man*. (New York: Bantam Books, 1975).
[64] Crowder, 239.

armed revolt.[65]  Yet, as Crowder noted, neither author embraced a notion of female superiority, but rather offered "a clear-eyed analysis of the cultural basis of male supremacy."[66]

The second category of feminist utopian novels reflected the shift in lesbian thought.  The characters in novels published between 1975 and 1985 were generally pacifists, and did not advocate for violence in any form.  An example of this type of feminist utopian fiction was Charlotte Perkins Gilman's *Herland.*  In *Herland,* men were dispatched through the natural disaster of an earthquake, which left women to build a culture in harmony with the natural environment.  The women of *Herland* evolved naturally into self-procreating women, whose primary philosophy was to create better people in each generation.  Most of the novels in this second category shifted the present patriarchal world into a distant past, where characters encountered sexism and male supremacy through "remembering rooms," "time-travel," "dreams," and their "imaginations," thus giving these novels a science fiction flavor.  Novels like *Wanderground* by Sally Miller Gearhart, *Walk to the End of the World* by Suzy McKee Charnas, and *Woman on the Edge of Time* by Marge Piercy tended to shift criticism from the contemporary world to the dystopia of the past.[67]  Crowder speculated that, "perhaps the superficial progress toward feminist goals in our real culture made writers think our world would not seem bad enough."[68]

What writers of feminist utopian fictions had in common was that none of them could imagine a world where men were not sexist and violent.  All of the writers seemed to agree that utopia could only be built by women, and that it would be lesbian, communal, egalitarian, and separate from men.  Where the newer writers differed from their predecessors was in their theoretical framework.  Writers like Gearhart, Charnas, and Piercy left the social constructionist standpoint of Wittig and Russ for more essentialized concepts of gender.  Gearhart, Charnas, and Piercy painted men as "naturally" violent and oppressive, whereas women were "naturally" humane, communal, and nurturing.  Furthermore, they differed in the way they eliminated men.  While Wittig and Russ chose armed revolts and open warfare, Gilman, Gearhart, Charnas, and Piercy chose "natural" disasters like plagues and earthquakes.  Crowder argued that although the second category of "separatist utopias provided a fictional space for imagining what a world based upon female values might look like," because they adopted essentialized concepts they left "little hope that we in the real world can achieve the kind of society shown."[69]

---

[65] Ibid., 239.
[66] Ibid., 240.
[67] Sally Miller Gearhart. *Wanderground: Stories of the Hill Women.* (Denver: Spinster Ink Books, 1979).  Suzy McKee Charnas. *Walk to the End of the World.* (New York: Ballantine Books, 1978).  Marge Piercy. *Woman On the Edge of Time.* (New York: Fawcett Crest, 1976).
[68] Crowder, 241.
[69] Ibid., 243.

What is important to recognize in both categories of feminist utopian fiction is the way they were shaped by lesbian experience and how lesbians used them as imaginative sources for building their own culture. Crowder argued, "Separatism in lesbian and feminist utopian fictions thus reflected the evolution of lesbian experience, from the explosion of anger and hope in the early 1970s to the dreams of lesbian community of the late 1970s."[70] For women like Crowder, these novels helped express their anger, provided them with the hope that women could build a better world, and fueled their desire to "live in a utopian world."[71] Arlene Stein noted the power of these novels when she wrote, "listening to women's music, reading lesbian fiction, and thinking 'like' a lesbian feminist" was enough to make any woman a lesbian feminist or a member of womyn's culture even if she did not desire women sexually.[72] Likewise, Bonnie Zimmerman wrote, "A woman becomes a citizen of the Lesbian Nation, a lesbian feminist, through the books she reads, the music she listens to, the heroes she identifies with, the language she speaks, the clothes she wears – even if at times she resents the required codes."[73]

These utopian fictions not only crafted the imagery of lesbian experience, but they also provided a generation of lesbians with the inspiration and reference points for building womyn's culture. During the 1970s womyn were actively building their own versions of utopia. They joined collectives to buy land and build women-only communities. Members of these collectives were often active participants in the environmental movement, and saw themselves as caretakers of Mother Earth. Most land collectives concerned themselves with maintaining healthy ecological systems. Some even drew up contracts between their members to ensure each womyn understood her responsibility to the land, as well as to the other womyn in the collective. For instance, the 20 womyn of Maud's Land signed an "Ecological Agreement" that began with the statement, "We need to live gently on the land with all our sister creatures. We agree that everything that is alive has the right to live. In order to live on this land, I agree to abide by the following policies."[74] Some of the twenty ecological policies for Maud's Land included protecting water resources, not using pesticides and herbicides, not cutting living trees, requiring biodegradable household cleaners, and restricting the use of outside utilities.

Womyn in land collectives often experimented with earth-friendly building techniques such as straw bale and adobe construction. They also experimented with recycling aluminum cans and bottles into building materials, and planned roads and walking paths designed to reduce soil erosion. They experimented with alternative sources of energy such as solar power, and as animal rights activists and avid gardeners who grew much of their own food,

[70] Ibid., 245.
[71] Ibid., 238.
[72] Stein, 109.
[73] Bonnie Zimmerman. *The Safe Sea of Women: Lesbian Fiction 1969-1989.* (Boston: Beacon Press, 1990) 159.
[74] Joyce Cheney. *Lesbian Land.* (Minneapolis: Word Weavers, 1985), 95.

many womyn adopted vegetarian lifestyles.[75] The merging of socialist values with concepts developed by spiritual feminists, environmentalists, and animal rights activists gave womyn's culture a uniquely "earthy" and "holistic" feeling.

According to Lillian Faderman, a major concept of womyn's culture was self-sufficiency. "Their goal of self-sufficiency included all aspects of life, from food co-ops, such as the New York Lesbian Food Conspiracy where food was sold at cost, to women's credit unions, which were run by members for members."[76] Womyn's collectives also started publishing their own books and magazines, which they sometimes offered free of charge to poor womyn, or on sliding scales that allowed womyn to pay what they could. Collectives opened bookstores and coffee houses. They created health care centers, job-skills centers, and retirement homes for older lesbians. They formed artist communities and built a womyn's music industry. In 1973, ten separatists from Washington D.C. moved to the bay area of California to form the first womyn's recording company. Olivia Records became an institution in womyn's culture and provided the inspiration and training for womyn to start their own collectives, become independent sound and lighting engineers, stage managers, record distributors, and even producers of womyn's music festivals. These were the ideas and movements that inspired nineteen-year-old Lisa Vogel to form a collective to bring womyn's music to Michigan.

## Lisa Vogel's Narrative

In 1975 Lisa Vogel, her sister Kristie, and some of their friends attended two events that inspired Lisa to form a collective of women that would bring women's music to Michigan. The first was an outdoor festival in Missouri, with camping – but no music. The second was an indoor festival in Boston, with music – but no camping. The initial idea for the Festival came during the "stoned all night road trip" home from Boston. Lisa said they were "loaded, basically, and thinking what a bummer it was that everyone had to leave when the music was over, and drive fifteen hundred miles home."[77] That night, she started thinking about what it would take to produce a festival in Michigan. Lisa remembered, "It was just a bunch of radical lesbians being in the woods together. It was the first time that I'd actually lived in an environment with a couple hundred women, and it blew my mind. The desire to do the festival really did come out of being exposed to women's culture and wanting that to happen close to us."[78]

---

[75] For more information on lesbian land collectives, see *Lesbian Land*, Joyce Cheney, ed. This book contains information on over 20 lesbian land projects between 1969 and 1985.
[76] Faderman, 226.
[77] Lindsey Van Gelder and Pamela Robin Brandt. *The Girls Next Door: Into the Heart of Lesbian America*. (New York: Touchstone, 1996), 63.
[78] Sandstrom, 100 -104.

When they got home, Lisa, Kristie, and Mary Kindig approached Susan Alborell who ran a local food co-operative and record store.[79]  Together they formed the We Want the Music Collective, and immediately filed for status as a non-profit corporation, which they were denied.  Because of this denial, the Michigan Womyn's Music Festival has always been a "for profit" enterprise produced by its parent company, We Want the Music Corporation.[80]

Originally, the collective envisioned the Festival as a two-day event that would include men, but Ginny Berson of Olivia Records, who was Meg Christian's manager at the time, pushed for it to be a "women only" event because it was an outdoor festival, which meant that women would have to camp with men.  Some of the women in the collective were uncomfortable with the idea of excluding men because their male friends claimed to be feminists. However, Lisa, Kristie, and Mary eventually decided that "the festival would be identified as essentially an event for lesbians, and thus, an inappropriate environment for men, if women were camping outdoors.  This prompted some of the heterosexual women to leave the original group of festival organizers, leaving Lisa, Kristie Vogel, and Mary Kindig to co-produce the first festival."[81]

By 1976, the three women of the collective were making progress in their plans for the Festival.  In an interview with Boden Sandstrom, Lisa said, "Initially, funds were raised through bake sales and car washes."[82]  In another interview, Lisa told van Gelder and Brandt that, "The collective managed to cobble together their whole $22,000 budget from garage sales, keg parties, car washes, and the like."[83]  Lisa said, "We looked in the paper, and found a hundred-and-twenty acre site that this guy wanted to sell to urban Detroiters in 10 to 20 acre tracts.  I called him and said, 'We don't want to buy.  But we want to hold an event where there'll be a lot of them city people, and if you'll let us rent it for a week I bet we'll get you some interested buyers.'  We got a piano the same way, by telling this dude from a music store that we couldn't buy, but a lot of pianists would be at our event.  The dude brought a concert grand piano from a hundred miles away, to the middle of the woods, for fifty dollars."[84]

In 1976 the collective went to the second annual National Women's Music Festival, over Memorial Day weekend, to advertise their own upcoming Festival.  They passed out mimeographed fliers and gave a cold beer to anyone woman who agreed to take one-hundred Michigan fliers home and pass them around.  The collective also hustled performance bookings for their own festival from the artists who were there that weekend.[85]  Lisa said, "Because of that hippy egalitarian thing, we decided that the only way we could deal with pay was

---

[79] Ibid.
[80] Ibid., 103.
[81] Ibid., 105.
[82] Ibid., 106.
[83] Van Gelder and Brandt, 63.
[84] Ibid., 65.
[85] Sandstrom, 106.

to have a standardized performance fee, one for everybody. We still do that, though we could book more people from the mainstream if we'd pay famous people a lot more."[86]

The first Michigan Womyn's Music Festival was held in Mt. Pleasant on the 120 acres of land the collective rented for $400.[87] The ticket price for the three-day event was $20. Holly Near and Teresa Trull performed. Boo Price, who later became a significant figure in developing the Festival, attended that first year as Margie Adams' artistic representative. Lisa "hired Margot McFedries, from San Francisco, to do sound engineering. She originally hired a company in Ann Arbor to bring the sound equipment, but they refused at the last minute when they learned that no men were allowed into the Festival. Vogel then hired a company from Chicago, when they agreed to the policy."[88] The collective expected about one thousand womyn to attend, but were unprepared when two thousand womyn showed up at the gate.

In terms of the materials and equipment needed to produce the Festival, Lisa said "It was a dramatic thing that you go through when you're trying to do a woman-only show, I mean, learning how to deal with, how do you get that kind of equipment to your site without having guys there."[89] "We hadn't even thought about security, so we organized it at the last minute, by state. 'Ohio and Illinois, if there's an emergency, you're at the front gate.' We laugh about it now, but there was a lot of potential for trouble."[90]

According to Lisa, the first Festival was put together through grass roots scamming and "the stage was created by basically telling a fib." [91] The We Want the Music Collective "conned" the local lumberyard into renting them 2x10's if they agreed to only put two small holes in each end. They ran the electricity for the stage from a generator. After trying to locate water on the property, and having no luck, Lisa "conned" the Army National Guard.[92] "There was no plumbing in this big bare field, so we thought we'd truck water in. But we had no money. So who subsidized part of the festival – for years, actually – the U.S. Army. We were hippie, drug-dealer cons. I'd call up the Army and say I was a reserve person calling from some other post, and I was involved in a women's musical 'retreat' – which sounds respectable; it implies religion – and I'd bullshit. And I got a big water truck. The festival's opening, and this guy pulls up in this giant, like, fatigue truck . . . and freaks. I hadn't realized quite what the festival would look like on opening morning. We never had the Army *deliver* again. But I got a bunch of free cots and tents from them

---

[86] Van Gelder and Brandt, 64.
[87] Ibid..
[88] Sandstrom, 107.
[89] Ibid.
[90] Van Gelder and Brandt, 65.
[91] Sandstrom, 107.
[92] Ibid., 107-108.

too, and the big tents. We didn't rent tents for a couple years. I worked my way around maybe six reserve offices before they finally caught up with me."[93]

Since the first Festival was so successful, Lisa wanted to make it an annual event. The following year she became the central leader of the small collective. After raising a new budget of $46,000, she increased the length of the Festival to four days and rented property in Hesperia that became home to the Festival between 1977 and 1981.[94] In 1982, the collective lost the lease on the "old Land," and "after much fund-raising in order to meet the payment schedule for the new land [650 acres], which cost $332,000, the switch was made in time for the seventh Festival."[95]

Lisa talked openly about the ideas that influenced her thinking about the Festival. She said, "We were coming from a Leftist place and a working class political analysis. That's where politically we were coming from – collectivity and cooperative effort. It was the 1970s. If you were in the alternative community you were exposed to revolutionary, socialist, communist doctrines and you synthesized from that whatever worked for you. I don't think you could be a politically conscious person at that time and not have a left-leaning analysis or values about how the world could run – how things could happen. . . . So the food co-op movement, which was a whole movement unto itself in the 1970s that was powerful around collectively taking responsibility for eating healthy food and moving it out of the industrial food complex – that was where we were practicing our politics. . . . I think the whole basis of how the Festival operates comes completely out of that. . . . I always feel like one of the key factors in the festival being what it is, is our decision to not sell food but to provide it with the price of the ticket. The reason we did that was because of our value of people sharing food together. Again, that was completely out of that 1970s potluck, food co-op mentality."[96]

Lisa told Sandstrom, "Those were some of the influences in 1975. Seventy-six was really a crucial period of time of just the doors being blown off of lesbians feeling constricted, and you know we ended up having two thousand women come to that first festival, and yes we did some things right and we had a good booking. People were really interested, and for some reason these people would, one by one agree to play a show at a festival in Michigan with women who had never produced a coffee house before."[97] Lisa admits, "There's a lot we didn't know how to think about. But we were taken care of, one way or another. I mean the show was up, it was running. We had child-care, we had health care, we had very, very, very primitive food, but we fed

---

[93] Van Gelder and Brandt, 64.
[94] 2005 Michigan Womyn's Music Festival Program, p. 30.
[95] Sandstrom, 189.
[96] Ibid., 101-102.
[97] Ibid., 105.

people. And we had one stage, and we had a fabulous time. And we had two thousand women."[98]

Lisa's narrative reflects the socialist values of both the lesbian feminist and cultural feminist movements. However, other womyn's narratives included specific references to the ecological practices and the self-sufficient economic systems institutionalized at the Festival. In 1983, Susan Wiseheart, Alix Dobkin, Suzette Treesong, Mary Wisenski, and Jennifer Weston recorded a conversation they had in New York about the ecological aspects of the Festival, and how much it meant to them that womyn cared for the Land.

> It's real important for me that other women value the land. The way you can value it is to be on it, and smell it and look at the plants and look at the animals, and start to understand the ecology thru more than a textbook. Ecology consciousness. It became so obvious at orientation when we were setting it up, to remind people not to throw their cigarette butts down. They don't just disappear. You don't think about this until you're told. A real hands-on experience in what are we doing here. How are we living here? How fragile the ecology is? I love how concerned women have mulched the land afterwards with straw. That's built in to the program as much as getting the performers on stage. Remember the fall we went to the land after the festival was over? We couldn't tell that there had been a festival there.[99]

Other ecological practices institutionalized at the Festival included a massive recycling program, maintaining large "no-camping" areas to preserve "green space," using plastic or "reusable" plates rather than paper plates, leaving no structures standing after the Festival that could potentially interfere with the wildlife, and adopting an attitude of self-sufficiency on the Land. The only practice inconsistent with the ecological consciousness is the reliance on fossil-fueled vehicles to transport womyn across the land. Unfortunately, the transportation system requires a fleet of trucks, vans, and tractors to haul the massive weight of women's equipment, but many womyn choose to use their own energy to transport themselves and their equipment when possible. By institutionalizing these types of practices, lesbians saw themselves as womyn honoring Mother Earth, and building a "culture that would embody all the best values that were not male."[100] Womyn in the above conversation were also proud of the self-sufficient economic system that craftswomen institutionalized at the Festival. "There was all the visual culture brought there by the craftswomen, that whole shift of consciousness, making money flow. Keeping

---

[98] Ibid., 108.
[99] "Michigan," *Lesbian Land*, 96.
[100] Faderman, 216.

it in our community. Making ourselves more self-sufficient economically. If only we could live on pottery and jewelry."[101]

*The Kitchen Fire Pits – 2002*

But womyn could not live on pottery sales alone, especially after the Reagan/Bush administration ushered in a new conservative era. During the 1980s many women who had come out in the context of the lesbian feminist movement returned to heterosexual lifestyles after experiencing the homophobic backlash of the New Right. Faderman wrote of the Reagan years, "The liberalism that opened the way for the radicalism of movements such as lesbian-feminism had slowed to a shuffle. The temper of the times seemed to demand, if not retreat, at least moderation."[102] Even the collectives that became institutions in womyn's culture adapted to the new conservative climate by joining the ranks of capitalists. For instance, in order to survive the "recession" and "backlash" of the Regan/Bush era, collectives like Olivia Records found it necessary to go corporate. And furthermore, as the teens and twenty-somethings began growing older, many of them returned to the comforts of middle-class lifestyles and values. Because of this type of change in market demands, Olivia began offering luxury cruises for lesbians.

It is also important to remember that in 1982 the AIDS epidemic among gay men drew on the political, economic, and emotional resources of lesbians working to build womyn's culture. The AIDS epidemic "demanded soul-searching on the part of lesbians that not only led many to reconciliation with the men but also brought about a political and social unity on a scale much larger than ever before."[103] Lesbians began bringing gay men into their homes

---

[101] "Michigan," *Lesbian Land*, 98.
[102] Faderman, 272.
[103] Ibid., 293.

"so that they could die surrounded by peace and love."[104]  Lesbians were also among the first to raise money for AIDS research and care.  They were among the first to give blood and organize programs that delivered meals.  They cleaned homes, cared for pets, and did the shopping for gay men living with AIDS.  Both the conservative political climate of the 1980s and the raging AIDS epidemic worked to defuse lesbian feminism and dismantle womyn's culture before lesbians had a real chance to grow into their ideals.

Yet, these may be the very reasons that the Michigan Women's Music Festival has survived for as many decades as it has.  As lesbians watched previously heterosexual women return to heterosexual lifestyles, as they watched the conservative political backlash break-up collectives, and as they watched themselves giving their energy to gay men, many felt that Michigan was all they had left of themselves, and they claimed it as their homeland; the place where their values were centered and where they did not have to hide who they were.  Michigan was the place where they escaped the liminality of their everyday lives, the place where they saw their experiences reflected in the music, art, literature, and spiritual traditions of the culture.  Michigan was the place that "empowered" them to live as lesbians, in a community of lesbians.  From the beginning, the women I interviewed claimed that the Michigan Womyn's Music Festival was a place they felt whole, visible, and fully alive as participants in their own culture, even if the early Festivals were "very, very primitive."

## Womyn's Memories of the First Festival

Mary: "The first time I came to the Festival was during the time that the feminist movement was taking off down in Florida, and me and my white lover were trying to find the lesbian things that were happening around there.  It was different then, because you came in and parked your car over in the field and by the time you pulled into where you thought you were gonna camp, women were pullin' their shirts off, and that astonished ya.  And it was amazing because there were no structures.  Ya just came in and parked your car, and ran over this field and found a place to put up your tent.  It was very, very primitive.  And I remember it was cold.  The shower was cold.  But the energy, the energy was so spectacular I think I would have – I think I did – I slept on the ground.  It was cold.  I never took a shower.  But the energy was so spectacular."[105]

Ro: "When some friends asked me to come to this, you know, when there was going to be Holly Near and Meg Christen, and Ginni Clemmons – sure I'm up for that, you know.  So we all came, and it was so exciting – the music was.  But it was different because it was smaller, and so Holly Near was sitting at the blanket next to us listening to the other performers, with her friends.  And Ginny Clemmons led a campfire at night.  She was camped there next to us.  I don't even know if people know who she is, but she was right

---

[104] Ibid., 294.
[105] Mary Sims. Personal Interview. August, 2005.

there at the beginning. She was a wonderful folksinger, and wrote some women's songs, or changed some folk songs to fit women. She had a wonderful voice, and she was very charismatic. I'm sure she's still singing somewhere. I hope she is. She sang a lot of Malvina Reynolds songs.

"But, the festival was like, no one knew what to expect. It was the We Want the Music Collective – that was the name. So we wanted the music. And then when we got here, we had to plan for more than that. And it came out of the women who were here. Like there was no security, at all. Who thought you needed security. We got here and all these men started to try and come on the Land. And it was - how to deal with that. And I remember it was a big debate over who should be in charge – whether it was the women who were into martial arts – who wanted to fight – or the women who were pacifists. So I remember we all had to take turns. And I remember standing arm in arm – fifteen or twenty women across the road at night – when the men would come in their pick-up truck, and they would say things like, 'how can you have a party without any men, or any boys? We'll show you how to have a party. We'll show you right here on the road.' And we would just stand there across the road and not say anything, and not let them in. But around the edges of the Land – I don't think it was as isolated – there were places where there were breaks in the trees, and they would come and stand on the roofs of their pickup trucks and watch whatever they thought was interesting to watch. But that was kind of scary. And then at night we'd hear somebody say, 'There's men on the Land! There's men on the Land!' And they would push their car horns so everyone could watch out for each other.

"I was on the discussion forum [the Festival Bulletin Board] – online – this is like so incredible to have Michigan on-line now – and people were concerned about safety. So I wrote back and said that I think women will take care of each other, because we've been doing that since the beginning. Because no one wanted to let anyone be isolated if there was a chance that there was gonna be men comin' in. We're gonna take care of each other. Yeah, I felt physically threatened. I don't know about murder, but definitely rape. They said it right there, 'we'll show ya how to have a party, lay down on the road.' Yeah! Of course they had something to drink before they came, ya know. Some women saw guns in the racks of their trucks, because this is a rural area, a farming area. Yeah, it was a threat. So that's why everybody had to watch out for each other. But that whole thing of 'how can you do this without us,' that's still happening now. They are still trying to get in. In other ways, but they're still trying to get in. But we can do this without them. And it's wonderful when we do. It's just wonderful, and that's why I think, for this long, it's still happening, because to have women only space is just precious. It's just precious.

"But when we got here there was no plan. I mean there was a plan – they had food, they had a place, they had a stage and sound system. There was a big tank of water, a big tanker truck of water, because there was no –

anything. And there was a hose at the end of the tanker truck, and that was it. There was no shower. There was no way for anybody to, ya know – we all had to just use this big hose – the kitchen people, everybody. So of course there was big pile of mud at the end of the tank. So when I came back five years later to see pebbles and showers, it was amazing. But of course everyone learned from how it was. It was ruffin' it.

"But it was so exciting. And we didn't know there would be more than that first one. We just went for the music, and the music was exciting too. And it was very hot during the day, like it is now. And there was no health care – there was no Womb [medical tent] at the time. And suddenly women were getting heat stroke or really bad sunburns, so they'd announce from the stage, and they made a place. So the women who were there said, 'Ok, we have to do something.' They didn't just say, 'Who's gonna do something about this?' You know, 'Who's gonna do something about security? Who's gonna do something about women getting sick?' The women that were there did it – because we could do it. That's what I remember about it being so exciting and empowering."[106]

Kathy: "There were no facilities that first year. Nothing. Go dig a whole. There might have been a porta potty some place that was absolutely nauseating. There was nothing. There was nothing."

Lorraine: "And I don't know why they did this, but they put the water [tanker] up on this knoll, and the knoll was overlooking a main road, with another farmer's property on the other side of the road. And all the women were up there taking a shower, and all the town's people would be lining up on the road. And on Sundays, they would come after church. There'd be little ol' ladies and little ol' men just standing there lookin' at us."

Kathy: "And you're out there takin' a shower, so what they ended up doing was putting vans all the way around it. They encircled the shower. But the boys. The boys have always had an issue. In the beginning, they tried to get in. The town boys. And most of them were drunk at the time. So they tried to get in. The police have been pretty cooperative. They got them away before something happened. Because something surely would have happened. Because there were a lot of aggressive women, and the boys were pretty aggressive because they were drunk. And they were thinkin' that we just didn't know what was goin' on, because we hadn't been introduced to the right guy in our life. So they came along, and the town's folk would line up. And if they couldn't get in, they got in the trees. The boys were up in the trees with binoculars. So they could see over the top of the vans."

Lorraine: "It was really bad the first year because it was so disorganized. Nobody knew what to expect. I remember them having at least two gates, the main gate where everyone came in and the back gate. So they had certain women as a security force, and what they realized was that eight women, or

---

[106] Ro Rasmussen. Personal Interview. August, 2002.

even ten, weren't enough to keep these drunk boys out, because they'd be driving up and down the road, drag racing, and yelling epitaphs at the women. So there'd be a mass of women out there. One woman had attack dogs. She had two dogs that she was patrolling the perimeter of the Land with. And there was also a rumor that one of the participants had a gun – so we knew we had some kind of protection. But then they were worried about shootouts and everything like that. But that was kinda scary, because we were out in the woods all by ourselves – you know, with just women."

*Porta Janes - 2002*

Kathy: "That was also at the beginning of our relationship. We were like four years into it, and we weren't 'out' to anybody either. So here we were, coming to a town where nobody knew us, where we're supposed to be nice and safe. But we felt threatened by these guys."

Lorraine: "I can remember – like now they have the parking separate – then it was just like this big field. They made roads, or maybe we made the roads, I'm not really sure, but the cars were with us. There were cars all over the place, ya know."

Kathy: "Getting' stuck in the mud and everything. We had to get tow trucks to come and get 'em out. It was as haphazard a thing as it could possibly be."

Lorraine: "I think they were just goin' by the seat of their pants. And you know, people loved it! So they said, 'let's have another one.' I think they had Holly Near that first year, and Chris Williamson. I can remember they had this wooden stage, and it was just maybe a foot off the ground. It wasn't like a really tall one. And they had this gas generator right behind it, roaring! So it was really hard to hear the music over the roar of the generator."

Kathy: "And it failed. And then it rained. I mean it was just - everything went wrong. The speakers blew out. Everything, everything went

31

wrong!"

Lorraine: "But it was great fun because it was the first one – it was still dykes out in the woods. It was so rural and just basic camping. I just loved it. It was really great, because we had a need back then for lesbian community. Because there wasn't any. It was just the bars. And we came out in 1971, which was two years after Stonewall in New York, and before that it was just the bars. But then the women's movement became, and so they had women centers, and they had a lot of lesbian events around those areas."

Kathy: "And I can remember when I didn't agree with lesbian separatists, thinking that you had to incorporate gay men. But as I see it now, it's not such a bad idea – separatism – in the sense that it allows us to define our community, who we are, and what's important to us, because we are different. Just as women are different from men. And when you get into groups that involve men, it's different. It's just different. Maybe separatism wasn't such a

*Festival Showers - 2001*

bad thing."[107]

Ro: "The music meant so much, and it was more than just the music! That's why we started coming to Michigan. We were hungry for the music. And then once we got here, it was more than the music. And I think that's why it's continued for this long. It's a community. In fact, the music has changed as different women come in, but back in the old days there wasn't a lot of places to go hear the music, and there weren't that many records to buy, but we were hungry for it. And it was part of what was happening in the women's movement, with a lot of women coming out. It was just so important. At the time, I think women's music helped women come out. I mean I came out to 'Lavender Jane Loves Women.' I played it over and over and over again, so that

---

[107] Lorraine Alexis and Kathy Davis. Personal Interview. August, 2002.

the words didn't hurt, and they became something else. I came out to that music! It's just amazing. And I'm sure lots of other women did too! And that's what I meant about the music being so important. Now it's good, the music's good. But I think it's the larger context of Michigan that helps it endure."[108]

## Amazon Culture

Over the years, I have asked myself many times what Michigan is and why it means so much to the womyn who attend. As I sat there in that dark women's studies classroom so long ago, pride swelled in my chest as I watched naked women lift heavy sledgehammers high above their heads and swing them down, crashing onto giant tent stakes in the ground. I was humbled when I saw them dig trenches and stretch out yards and yards of drainpipe. I was inspired as I watched them heave 50-pound bags of onions and potatoes onto their shoulders, and then carry them down the steps of a refrigerated trailer. I felt empowered as I watched them throw 4x4 posts down an assembly line of women that stretched out in a zigzag pattern toward the stage they were building. Hearing Rhiannon sing "Amazon," and then seeing bare breasted Amazons drum their way across the Land sent a surge of emotion through me that was overwhelming. But what was even more powerful was when the stage announcer shouted "Welcome home women! Welcome home." Those words fed something in me that had always felt insatiable – home. What those words communicated was that there were womyn like me out there, that they had built a rich culture with strong traditions, and that they would welcome me home.

*Just Camping in the Woods Together – 2006*

But what I learned is that this rich culture with strong traditions was not built overnight. Lisa was right when she said that in the early years, "there were a lot of things we didn't know how to think about." Yet Michigan became the place where womyn thought about everything; about politics and spirituality, about home and family, about peace and safety, and about honoring their difference. At times, Michigan also became a battlefield where womyn fought both

---

[108] Ro Rasmussen. Personal Interview. August, 2002.

personal and political battles because they refused to sweep their differences under the proverbial carpet of womyn's unity. Today, most womyn come knowing that diversity may cause controversies, but they also remain committed to being uncomfortable for as long as it takes to deal effectively with those controversies.

According to Alix Dobkin, "Part of being at festivals is being angry and frustrated and miserable because our ideals are being tested."[109]  Bonnie Morris echoed this sentiment when she wrote, "Uncomfortable festival politics are not a planned obsolescence."[110]  When lesbians place themselves at the center of a culture, they begin feeling the full range of their emotional and physical selves, and according to Lisa Vogel, this means, "It is not only inevitable that this event would provide a cauldron of womyn's issues, it is a critical opportunity to meld, measure, and hone our evolving politics and culture."[111]

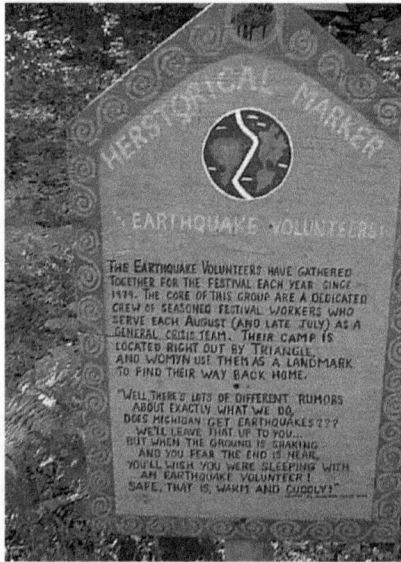

*Earthquake Volunteer Sign - 2001*

Occasionally the Festival is criticized for its uncomfortable politics and for creating a "cauldron of womyn's issues," and as Bonnie Morris has conceded, "Evidence of misunderstandings and hostilities can detract from the utopia festiegoers expect to experience."[112]  Over the years lesbians like Laurel, from Rockville, Maryland have written letters to *Lesbian Connection* that express open hostility toward the Festival.  Laurel's letter is representative of the women who come to Michigan for the first time, but fail to experience the ecstasy of living in an Amazon utopia.

---

[109] Morris, 10.
[110] Ibid.
[111] Sandstrom, 26.
[112] Morris, 10.

This year was my first Michigan Womyn's Music Festival and I went with high hopes. But from the moment I entered the festival grounds, my expectations began dropping. I was not warmly welcomed and I didn't immediately see throngs of smiling women. Because I was a "festie virgin," I was greeted with hoot and holler; I was ushered through orientation; I was told to select work shifts. Then I was left alone. I was to discover a world of unwritten rules, an inexplicable and incomprehensible form of organization. I struggled to make sense of the experience. I wanted to be open minded. What I saw were half-naked women, shaved heads, blue hair, body paint, nipple (and other) piercing, and communal showers. There was a mixing of children and nudity. There was ugliness. I had difficulty getting past the shock factor to see them as women, not as freaks. Their "in-your-face" activism assaulted me and offended my sensibilities. The public nudity crashed through my personal boundaries and I became more guarded and intolerant, not less.

For the first time in my life, I understood with alarming clarity how a straight person can feel repulsed by homosexuals. I arrived at the festival midweek, and paid $265 to camp in a tent, eat slop, attend workshops where speakers arrived late or didn't show. And they expected me to work? What a rip-off. Women got what they individually put into the festival. This "do-it-yourself" attitude didn't fit the high price tag. Although there were powerful speakers, talented musicians and performers, and friendly workers, I did not feel any sense of unity.

The festival depended largely on the volunteer labor of the attendees. We were expected to work one or two four-hour shifts doing kitchen, traffic, security or other duties. But there was little to no direction for the volunteers and many of them were clueless. There were also few signs indicating such simple things as where the lunch lines began, where to wash one's hands when exiting the port-a-janes, and where to find forks, knives, napkins and chairs if you were one of the unfortunate ones who didn't know you were supposed to bring your own. The accumulating trash on the site was disgusting, and I didn't trust that the food was prepared in a safe manner. I gathered from talking to others that the festival was supposed to be about empowerment, but there was no clear message from the organizers as to why we were there and what we were doing. One woman told me the event was promoted as a music festival so as not to attract the attention of subversives. I tried to make the best of the experience, getting into the spirit of it and attending workshops. But I didn't feel empowered. When I expressed my feelings of discomfort, I was told it takes at least a couple of days to assimilate to the festival; that many women were cranky because of all the rain; that the primitive facilities were designed to emulate those of the third world nations; that I must have internalized issues about body image; and that maybe for me the festival was about learning to express repressed anger. At $45-80 a day, why should it take several days to assimilate? And why weren't there decent provisions for rain?

Instead of being flooded out and frozen, women should have been forewarned of the rains and given advice about setting up tarps. Workers could have stood out at check posts, making sure women had batteries in their flashlights, helping them when they got lost, directing them to the store to buy additional provisions and just plain offering support. If I had wanted to discover how the third world lives, I would have used my ticket money towards plane fare. And any internalized body issues I had only became stronger at the festival as I grew sick of seeing everyone's business in my face. I am a feminist. I do support change toward a more equitable world for people of all races, nationalities and abilities. But we do not need women espousing radical ideas and methodologies that scare the wits out of our allies and enemies alike. It is time for my "repressed anger" to be expressed. I was taken and abused. I am enraged that the same festival that is supposed to empower women is royally screwing them over. We, as women, deserve better - Laurel[113]

Other women feel free to express outrage even though they have never been to the Festival. In 1995, Gladstone, from Missouri, wrote a response to a woman who felt violated at the Festival, but her letter suggests that the values womyn at the Festival hold dear are actually threatening to the middle-class values of other lesbians.

Too bad you and your partner live so far away, because me and my uptight-middle-class-suburban-based, Christian, country-lovin', deer-huntin' wo-man would probably love hanging out with you. If a bunch of psychodramatic aspiring victims want to spend their vacations walking around flop-chested and then screaming 'I feel so violated' every time someone looks cross-

---

[113] Laurel. *Lesbian Connection.* Jan/Feb, Vol. 20 Issue 4, 1998, 6-7.

eyed at them, then let 'em do it – but I'll pass. Those women who expect all of us to feel sorry for and indulge them forever because they are "of color," or "of size," or "a survivor" of one thing or another, had better grow up and realize that this is a cold, hard world. This particular lesbian is getting sick of hearing about "issues" and why they supposedly excuse a person from being a responsible adult – Gladstone.[114]

Clearly, not all lesbians define themselves as "womyn," nor do they define themselves as belonging to "womyn's culture." However, part of what makes Michigan work for the womyn who return year after year is that they know they are not expected to leave their "baggage" at home. Rather, they bring it with them and unpack it in the *safe*, nurturing Amazon culture they create.

For womyn who return year after year, the Festival is the "petri dish" of lesbian culture, where womyn's multiple identities converge, clash, stir up controversy, and transform themselves over and over again.[115] Boden Sandstrom argued that the Michigan Womyn's Music Festival created "…an environment and a space that has allowed a new culture to emerge in the 'belly of the monster.' Lesbians should not be essentialized, but nevertheless, there is a lesbian culture in the making in this space."[116] This "new culture" is what I call "Amazon culture," because it is not a generic "lesbian sub-culture" or generic "lesbian community." "Amazon culture" is a unique culture that unique womyn create at the Michigan Womyn's Music Festival. It is a culture created by womyn who live liminal lives in the "middle-class-suburban-based, Christian, country-lovin', deer-hunting" culture of contemporary America. It is a culture that nurtures and shelters "Amazons" (a term I use to signify the womyn who call Michigan their homeland). It is a culture that heals their wounds and helps them survive in a world that is hostile to their very existence. And even though Amazons represent a diverse group of womyn, coming from every background imaginable, as Kip's narrative suggests, the culture created at Michigan unites womyn across their own lines of difference.

Kip: "You know it's absolutely a culture of its own. It's absolutely the embodiment of lesbian culture. This place brings everybody. You've got leather dykes. You've got radical ecofeminists. You've got people over here grillin' hamburgers, and you've got people over there saying 'you're animal killers.' You've got every kind of representation. You know, you've got women in Birkenstocks, and women in L.L. Bean shorts, and women naked, and women in sarongs - there's everything here. And so the coming together and blending of that is really the embodiment, I think, of the worldwide lesbian

---

[114] Gladstone. *Lesbian Connection*. May/June, Vol 17, Issue 6, 1995, 42.
[115] Sandstrom, 118-119.
[116] Ibid., 151.

culture. It really is. This is when it all comes together in a fishbowl - so we can look at it. And that's what I love about this place."[117]

[117] Kip Parker. Personal Interview. August, 2003.

# ⚔ 2 ⚔

# On the Land

As soon as we pulled off the freeway in Hart, Bobbie and I knew we were in the right place. The parking lots of every convenience store, restaurant, hotel, and gas station were full of cars, pickup trucks, and R.V.'s loaded with womyn and their camping gear. Several of the vehicles had brightly colored homemade signs in their windows that read "Michigan or bust," "Festival bound," or "going home." Bobbie and I smiled at each other as we pointed to specific cars that had passed us on the road. She grinned at me and said, "I don't think we're in Kansas anymore, Toto." I laughed and said, "Welcome to lesbian land."

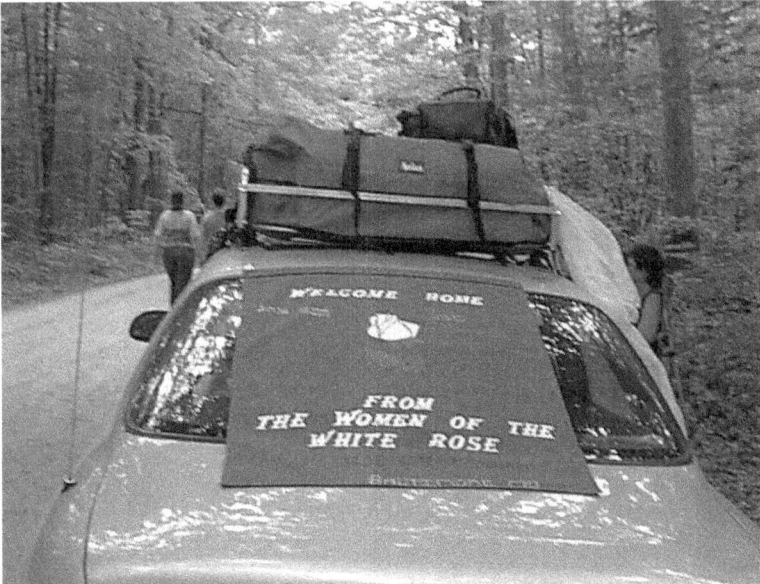

*Homemade banner offering the greeting of Welcome Home – 2002 - Kendall*[118]

There were womyn everywhere, and most did not hide the fact that they were lesbians. In this public place, lesbian couples boldly walked with their arms

---

[118] With the exception of the Womyn of Color Sanctuary pictures, all photographs were taken by Laurie J. Kendall.

around each other and greeted other womyn with warm embraces. Other than at Gay Pride parades, I had never seen so many lesbians being themselves in public. Everywhere we looked womyn were carrying ice, cases of beer, and bags of hamburgers to their cars. Like our sisters, Bobbie and I decided to make one last stop for a meal that included meat. At that time the only thing we knew for sure about the Festival was that, although quite nutritious, all of the meals served on the Land were vegetarian. For carnivores, Hart represented the last chance to sink our teeth into a juicy hunk of beef.

With thousands of womyn converging on Hart, the lines at Subway and McDonalds were quite long. But the mood was festive and even though we did not know any of the womyn in line, sharing friendly chit-chat made us feel like old friends. As individual womyn picked up their orders, they waived and said "See you on the Land." We returned their waves and replied, "See you on the Land." But with thousands of womyn attending the Festival, I wondered if we would really see each of them again. Still, that did not seem to matter. Making individual womyn feel welcome, and creating a feeling of comradery and familiarity seemed more important than actually seeing each of them again. As Bobbie and I picked up our order, I began to realize that this must be one of the ways that womyn make the Michigan Womyn's Music Festival so meaningful.

## The Rural Road

Finding the Festival grounds might have been difficult that first time had it not been for the one sure sign we were on the right road. It was about two o'clock on Monday afternoon when we came up over a little hill and saw the long line of brake lights ahead of us. Although we expected there to be a line, we never expected it to stretch down the three-mile rural dirt road and spill out onto the highway for a half-mile.

*The three- mile line of vehicles parked on the rural dirt road – 2001*

Honestly, when I first saw the line and realized that it was not moving, I groaned. We had experienced several mechanical problems along the way (two alternators, one fan belt, and an A/C clutch), and the last thing I wanted was to be stuck in line, melting in the heat, with nothing to do but watch the car in front of us and hope the van would start each time we needed to move forward.

Yet our travel experience was nothing compared to the Canadian womyn who tried to attend the 1979 Festival. That year, officers of the U.S. Immigration and Naturalization Service at Port Huron stopped Canadian womyn from entering the U.S. to attend the Festival. On August 14, 1979, the Associated Press reported:

> The women turned back at the border claimed they were improperly questioned about their sexual activities. A 1952 law forbids persons with a 'sexual deviation or a mental defect' from entering the United States. On Aug. 14, however, the immigration service issued an order to all border officials not to reject suspected homosexuals until a dispute over whether homosexuality will continue to be considered a sexual deviation under the law is resolved. McKinnon [head of U.S. Immigration and Naturalization Service] said the order was transmitted to all five border points in Michigan but for some unknown reason did not reach Port Huron. He said he did not know until Aug. 24 that the new order was being violated at Port Huron. Several of the women who were denied entrance last week said they were asked intimate questions about their sexual behavior by border officials. They said the officials asked whether they enjoyed sex more with women than with men and how often they had sex with men. The women also claimed they were asked for intimate details of supposed lesbian encounters.[119]

Several of the womyn who were stopped by U.S. Immigration officers simply turned around and drove to other places where they could cross the border peacefully to join the six thousand womyn that attended the Festival that year. Their experience generated "workshops, speak-outs, and calls to the Senate and Congress that landed the topic on the floor of the U.S. Legislature," after which all harassment of womyn at the U.S. and Canadian boarder stopped.[120]

Although I was initially aggravated by the fact that the line was not moving, my irritation quickly transformed into intrigue when I realized that waiting in line was a ritualized part of the Michigan experience. Long before dawn, on the day the Festival opens, womyn begin lining up on the shoulder of the rural road that marks the western border of the Land. Early in the morning they set up camp stoves to make coffee and invite other womyn to join them for breakfast. After the sun comes up they begin walking up and down the line counting cars, and stopping to share the stories of their lives with strangers they

---

[119] Associated Press, Aug. 30, 1979, PM cycle. [online]. researchport.umd.edu.
[120] 2005 Michigan Womyn's Music Festival Program, p. 30.

call "sisters." Later in the morning, womyn turn on their car stereos and dance to "women's music" while others pull out musical instruments and serenade womyn walking by.

*Playing a Board Game on the Line – 2003*

*Greeting of Friends on the Line - 2007*

Some womyn play board games, or challenge each other to answer gay trivia questions. Others just sit and offer bottles of water to womyn walking the line. Occasionally those who accept water, gratefully accept rolls of toilet paper farther up the line, and trek out into the woods for a private moment.

Around one o'clock the womyn working the *front gate* start singing Alix Dobkin's "If it Wasn't For the Womyn," which signals the gates are about to open.

> If it wasn't for the womyn, womyn – We would not be living, living.
> We would not be joyful, singing – Loved and beloved, womyn.
> If it wasn't for the Womyn, what would we do?
> We wouldn't have health or strength or beauty, (art, crafts, music)
> We wouldn't have a home (love) – And we wouldn't have food (truth)
> If it wasn't for the work of womyn![121]

Although very few womyn are close enough to hear the song, their cheers rise up and reverberate down the line signaling that the gates are opening. Once the cheer rolls past them, womyn on the road quickly pack up their folding chairs and camp stoves. Then they jump in their vehicles and wait for the roar of distant engines to reverberate down the line; a signal that the line is going to move. But the movement forward is slow, about ten car lengths at a time. So, as it rubber-bands its way along, womyn have time to jumped out and resume their conversations or start new ones.

As soon as Bobbie and I pulled onto the shoulder of the road that first year, we felt like this huge tailgate party was a planned "event" the Festival organizers wanted us to enjoy. However, it was not long before we were reminded of the politics that surrounds the Festival. As we got closer to the

---

[121] Planetearthgirrl. "15 yrs + at FEST" thread. *Michigan Womyn's Music Festival Discussion Forum.* 10-4-01. [Online]. http://www.michfest.com/ubb/Forum7/HTML.

*front gate*, we saw a camper parked off to the side of the road that had a bunch of posters taped to its side. A young woman was sitting on a blanket near the camper, but she did not look like any of the other women gathered around her. At first I did not understand what was going on, but after looking back and forth several times I began to understand that the young woman was a male to female transsexual.

## Camp Trans

Before the first Festival, Lisa Vogel and the other members of the collective debated the issue of including men at the Festival, and decided then to create it as a "womyn only" event. In 1979 the collective instituted the "women-born-women policy" to answer the growing question of whether or not men and male to female transgender individuals would be included at the Festival. The policy made it clear that the intention of the organizers was to reserve the Festival as a space for women who had experienced growing up as girls in a patriarchal culture, and all that entailed for womyn in their adult lives. However, according to Sandstrom, in 1991 the issue of transgender inclusion began boiling to the surface when "Nancy Burkholder, a transsexual who came in with a ticket to the Festival, was asked to leave the Festival because she was an MTF [male to female] transsexual, and therefore according to policy, should not have been admitted."[122] Over the next three years transgender activists challenged the Festival in publications like *Lesbian Connection*, and in 1994 Leslie Feinberg helped establish Camp Trans as a protest to the Festival's "women-born- women" policy. Womyn on both sides of the debate were outraged. For instance, Janis wrote a sarcastic response to Pat's support of the policy.

> To Pat, who would like to keep transsexual women out of the festival – right on! I think we should also keep out women who sing base, because their voices might be mistaken for male voices. And there should be work shifts for people like Pat who can unfailingly perceive traces of 'male energy'- they could do us all a service by standing at the front gate and scanning everyone who enters (sort of a psychic panty check!).[123]

Even though most womyn supported the Festival's policy and wanted to ignore the transgender activists in Camp Trans, the issue boiled over in 1999 when a pre-operative transgender individual snuck into the Festival from Camp Trans and exposed his penis while taking a shower in the R.V area. That night womyn in the dinner line exploded over issues of gender identity and the Festival's women-born-women policy, causing womyn on both sides of the debate to riot.

As a way to defuse the tension, the following year workshops on transgender issues were included in the Festival program. These workshops provided analyses of the transgender experience and encouraged womyn to

---

[122] Sandstrom, 129.
[123] Janis. *Lesbian Connection.* May/June, Vol 16, Issue 6, 1994, 9.

debate transgender inclusion openly. These debates also continued in womyn's letters to *Lesbian Connection*. Kristina's letter demonstrates the way individual womyn debated the issue in their own minds.

> I am most thankful this year for Charlotte Croson's workshop on her Radical Feminist analysis of certain politics in the Transgender movement. This came at the right time for me. I found it enlightening and convincing, and it helped me sort out my feelings around the question of Transwomyn at Michigan. In the past, I was unsure how I felt about the festival's womyn-born-womyn-only policy, but I was sure that many of the defenses of it that I had heard felt alarmingly ridiculous and Transphobic to me. I am now in support of the festival's policy. I can see that my regard for my lovely MTF friend had prevented me from hearing other arguments that today I consider well-reasoned. Blessings on the Michigan Womyn's Music Festival for providing me over the years with Radical Feminist spaces; the literal ground on which I can question, feel challenged, find answers, change my mind, change it again…[124]

As willing as most womyn were to discuss the "issue," their discussions did not signal any kind of concession. Most were quite tenacious about enforcing the policy, especially because the issue had caused physical violence, as Wendy's letter demonstrates:

> Every year my girlfriend and I look forward to the Michigan Womyn's Music Festival (she's been to all 27). This year, after leaving a pro-transgender poetry reading at the August Night Café, my girlfriend was punched in the face for vocalizing that she did not want transgenders at the Festival. She spent the night in the Womb and is OK. We will continue to go to Festival every year we can as long as Lisa Vogel keeps inviting us women-born-women.[125]

Before this incident, Lisa Vogel told reporters that although she would continue to enforce the policy, she would not become a gender cop. She said, "It's a complex issue, really hard. Everyone's exhausted around it. We could chase a cat's tail around gender questions forever. But I don't want to be a curator of that. Transsexuals are not going to be our focus. We are pretty *over* spending a lot of our time and energy having an event of seven thousand womyn be focused on three or four guys – and that's what these three or four guys are asking us to do, and that is such a guy energy thing! Men feel like they get to be

---

[124] Kristina. *Lesbian Connection*. Nov/Dec, Vol 24, Issue 3, 2001, 10.
[125] Wendy. *Lesbian Connection*. Jan/Feb, Vol 25, Issue 4, 2003, 28.

whatever they want, even if it's a lesbian."[126]

However, after the 1999 shower incident and the explosion in the dinner line, Vogel wrote her own letter to *Lesbian Connection*, where she stated her position quite clearly:

> We support deconstruction of gender roles, but we cannot sit by while the definition of woman becomes blurred to the point of denying the reality of our existence. . . . As we enter the 21st century, it's up to each of us who value an alternative to patriarchal culture to get clear on our priorities and to rally against this latest challenge to our autonomy and sovereignty.[127]

Most womyn agree with Lisa's statement and feel that the power dynamics of transgender activism are the same as those they experience in the dominant male culture. Ultimately they feel that once again, those who were born and socialized with male privilege are placing demands on womyn, and telling womyn what they must do to accommodate everyone else.

The womyn I interviewed are becoming angry and frustrated with the patriarchal assumptions embedded in transgender activism, and they are worried that Camp Trans is keeping women away from the Festival. They also feel violated by transsexuals, who assume they know what it is like to be a woman and demand entrance into the *safe* world womyn have created to transform the effects of patriarchal oppression.

Cindy: "I think they should be able to celebrate who they are, but not here! Because in my heart, I think it would change the festival. It wouldn't be women's space anymore. I think it would become more like the world out there. We'd have to shelter who we are. And for the few who are over in Trans Camp, that's not fair to the thousands of women who are in here."[128]

Kathy: "There are things that can tear things apart, and not to bring up a bad subject, but it's like this transgender crap! It's bringin' things down. It's makin' an issue. Because as it was stated in the beginning, it's women-born-women. But these people who are trapped in this body, and they go and change it, I understand all that, and I can empathize, but when you're talking about a genetic issue, you can't change that! So leave us alone. But they're forcing an issue, which to me is a patriarchal type thing. This is one week! So just stay out! Leave it alone. But that's not what happens. It inevitably comes up. Inevitably, it's in your face. Because there's always an issue. If it's not the trans issue, it's the S & M thing, or something else. Those things seemed to have resolved themselves, but this thing isn't going away. This is my space, my *home*, where I recover. This is the space to recover for the rest of the year. Why do I have to be confronted with an issue like that, which is so difficult to try and

---

[126] Van Gelder and Brandt, 77.
[127] Lisa Vogel. *Lesbian Connection.* Nov/Dec, 1999, 5-7.
[128] Cindy Avery. Personal Interview. August, 2002.

define? But when you look at the basic end of it, to simplify the whole damn thing, it's a genetic issue. If you got it, you got it. If you don't, you don't. That makes it cut and dry. You don't have to consider anything else."[129]

Susi: "Michigan is a women's world, and personally, I'm happy to see that it's women-born-women going up to Michigan. I love women's space, and women's energy. And I think if you introduce male energy into that, it totally changes everything. I don't have too much trouble with female to male transsexuals, because I think they had the same experiences we did growing up in a patriarchal world. But transsexuals who were born men, I don't think they can understand. And when they try to force themselves into a space, then it shows they have quite a lot of work to do on themselves. And if men try to force their way in, then go right ahead, but that's not where I want to be. I think women need at least one week to get away and chant, and be with the Goddesses, and be with each other, and just feel free to take their clothes off. I think that's really, really important. But the trans issue is an interesting one. I wonder what it will be in another ten years. Is it a fad? I mean, things become very trendy in the world. It became very trendy to be a lesbian. I know trans people who have transed, and then transed back."[130]

While womyn are actively redefining what it means to be a woman, the new definitions do not always challenge all the essentialized notions of womanhood. But transgender activism also presents other problems for the Festival. Even though Camp Trans has been reconstructed every year since 1994, it has remained extremely small and relatively disorganized compared to Michigan. It has not always provided food and basic care items for its campers, and on occasion young women who support transgender inclusion have stolen food and other items to smuggle out to Camp Trans. Unfortunately this type of action hurts the very institution these womyn claim to love. As some womyn argue, "Trans people have demonstrated over in Camp Trans that they can't even take care of themselves, even in their own small camp. It's no wonder they want in here! Like most men, they want to take advantage of real womyn's labor and our caregiving skills; they want us to take care of them all over again."

Also what some transgender individuals fail to remember is that the Festival is not a money mill with corporate sponsorship like Gay Pride. As Bonnie Morris wrote, "The festival is certainly not some well-financed behemoth like the IMF or Wal-Mart. Whatever one's view on the transgender issue, Michigan ain't 'the Establishment.' The performers are risk-taking, mostly lesbian artists whose stand on race, sex, and class limit their ability to get mainstream bookings and to have financial security. Then there are the longtime workers like me, usually 600 of us, who hammer and nail and schlep and mediate and cleanup after campers and performers, just because we dig being part of the story. . . . Wherever Michigan's meaning is being debated –

---

[129] Kathy Davis. Personal Interview. August, 2002.
[130] Susi St. Julian. Personal Interview. August, 2005.

Ph.D. dissertations, in music zines, at trans venues, poetry slams, and LGBT centers – the message needs to be passed along that ripping off the festival's music, melons, and massage care doesn't equal 'fighting the power' in corporate America."[131]

Well after this formal study was concluded, the issue of transgender inclusion continued. In 2011, demonstrations by trans-women and their supporters were clearly evident as they wore t-shirts with TWBH (trans-women belong here) printed on the front. That year there were several workshops on the issue. The first was called *"Allies in Understanding: Womyn-Only Space, the Shifting Concepts of Gender and Trans-Inclusion."* In the Festival program, this workshop was described as:

> This gathering is intended to foster open-hearted, respectful communication, rooted in feminist principals. Womyn-only space, gender expression and trans identities continue to be part of our Festival community discussion. Our focus will be to step back from the divisive rhetoric that can consume this discussion, moving to a place where we hear one another, heal, and live together as our most authentic selves. In order to create a safe space for this dialogue, we commit to honor each individual experience and voice as worthy of attention and respect.[132]

The workshop began with supporters of the women-born-women policy and supporters of trans-inclusion matching up in small groups of four to have personal discussion in hopes that they could find common ground. I attended this workshop, and found myself with three very lovely young women who were each as committed to their cause as I was. Our discussion was congenial as we talked openly with each other, sharing our stories and the reasons we supported one side of the issue over the other. My personal feelings were, and still are, that ALL people should be treated with dignity and respect, and I acknowledged that trans-people are very often the victims of violence and discrimination. I supported, and have fought for, Human Rights most of my adult life.

I also believe that though women-born-women and trans-women experience some of the same oppressions and violence, womyn who were born female have unique oppressions based on their reproductive systems, experience, and rights. Moreover, women-born-women who were socialized as females have traveled a very different road to becoming womyn, than the unique road trans-women have traveled. Each group deserves their own time and space, based on their unique biological, social, and spiritual realities. Just because I support the Festival as a women-born-women space does not mean that I would not support trans-rights in every other context (political, economic,

---

[131] Bonnie J. Morris. "At the Michigan Womyn's Music Fest." *The Gay & Lesbian Review*. Sept.- Oct.,18.
[132] 2011 Michigan Womyn's Music Festival Program, p. 29.

social).

In the workshop, I gave the analogy that I likened the situation to a European-American who "feels" like, and presents themselves as a Native American, and then goes to a First Nation Reservation and expects that the Native people will allow him or her to move onto the Reservation. The young trans-activists were quick to point out the flaws in my argument; however I reminded them that land and cultural appropriations have always been practiced by the same colonizing and neocolonizing forces of patriarchal privilege to take what they want from whomever they want, whenever they want. In this case, it's just womyn's land and womyn's culture, and womyn's labor and womyn's care. Which makes them that much easier to bully or shame into compliance. But saying you "are" a "Native" or a "woman" does not mean it's Ok to take our land, our home, our labor, or our time together.

As the time allotted for our discussion drew to an end, one of the young trans-inclusion supporters gave her suggestion for reconciling our differences. With an ever so gentle smile, she suggested that, "Just like there is a women of color tent and a Jewish women's tent, we could have a women-born-women tent." Tears filled my eyes and I quietly asked, "Are you sending me to my room? Are you telling me that you are moving into my home uninvited, and then relegating me to one room in my own home; the home my mothers and grandmothers have built?" Talk about colonization in your own home!

Although I knew that, historically, women were just as complicit as men were with the structuring and maintaining of patriarchal power and privilege; training their daughters to ignore their own needs and becoming the perfectly accommodating and caregiving women patriarchy demanded of them (mother is the first up in the morning, the last to go to bed at night, and the last to sit down at the table and eat the meal she has cooked). At the time, I did not realize just how embedded the "patriarchal maintenance" instinct is for young women in the twenty-first century. This revelation not only made me mad, it deeply saddened me because even though we have fought so hard for so many years to free ourselves from patriarchal oppression, it was very clear that we had barely scratched the surface of our unconscious support of the patriarchy and its demands on the labor and the caregiving practices of womyn. Now, in 2013, for me this issue is not about who is or isn't a woman, or about sex, gender, or human rights. Now, it is a personal fight for my home and family, and for my Land. And my fight is with uninvited people in my home and on my Land.

But back in 2011, I had no idea how far things would escalate in the coming years. That year, five additional trans-inclusion workshops were held, and included *Transwomyn Ally Toolkit*, *Visioning Inclusive Fest*, *Trans Basics*, and *For Trans Allies*. Only one supported the women-born-women policy. This workshop was led by Nedra Johnson, and titled *Girlhood is Significant*. Its description was very simple and declarative, "*This is a workshop for womyn who support the boundaries of Festival. Let's talk about girlhood.*"[133] This workshop was very well attended, with supporters of the policy growing more and more vocal and active in defending the policy than they ever had been before. It provided the space and time for policy supporters to come together and begin planning and organizing a concerted effort to defend their Festival and its policy. The next year, 2012, these womyn came ready to visually demonstrate their support for the Festival policy. Their visual support included wearing red t-shirts, red arm bands, red head bands, and red WBW (women-born-women) patches, all of which effectively covered the Festival in a blanket of red.

But this action did not deter the trans-activists. Even before the Festival began in 2013, the issue of trans-inclusion began to threaten the Festival's economic and social stability. Early in the Spring, Red Durkin, of Brooklyn, N.Y., started a petition that called for Festival performers to boycott the Festival. It read as follows:

> The official stance of the Michigan Womyn's Music Festival indicates that the Festival is open only to cisgender women and that transgender women are not officially allowed on the grounds as volunteers or attendees. This is in accordance with a long-standing policy of exclusion that founder and producer Lisa Vogel confirmed as recently as 2006. Although in the past some of the staff has "looked the other way," the policy against trans women that is in place has cultivated a climate of transphobia at the Festival. This situation is unwelcoming and unsafe for transgender women and has become a divisive influence on feminist communities, both at Fest and around the US.

> The reality is that Michigan Womyn's Music Festival is not safe for any women until it is welcoming for all women. We are asking you, as a musician, and as a person who believes in the dignity and equality of all women, to stand in solidarity with transgender women and our allies and to not attend or perform at the Michigan Womyn's Music Festival until Lisa Vogel and the other organizers fully and openly welcome all self-identified women.

> Although there is a small, devoted group of individuals working from within to change the transphobic policies put into place and enforced by the organizers, we believe that real change can not happen until all women are welcome to attend the Festival. We are asking you to respect the boycott of the Michigan Womyn's Music Festival until real, substantive

---

[133] Ibid. p. 37.

change has taken place. We believe that the markers of substantive change are three simple things:

1) The organizers must amend the festival policy to explicitly welcome all self-identified women to the annual MWMF.

2) The organizers must recognize the destructive impact that 20+ years of transphobic policies have had on our feminist and queer communities and issue a formal statement acknowledging and apologizing for this injustice.

3) The organizers must program at least one performer who is a transgender woman to perform at the Festival. This will show that transgender women are truly welcome and that they have a legitimate place and voice in the MWMF community.

Until these three demands are met, we call on you to not attend or perform at the Michigan Womyn's Music Festival. You are implored to respect the call to boycott this event because the organizers have maintained destructive and transphobic policies that are unwelcoming and unsafe for all women in our communities. This petition calls upon all attendees and performers of the 2013 Michigan Womyn's Music Festival to boycott the Festival until substantive change is achieved.[134]

After this petition went out on the internet, Red posted that two booked performers canceled their performances at the 2013 Festival. In addition, the Indigo Girls made an announcement on their website that they would honor the boycott by making 2013 the last year they would play the Festival, and that they would dedicate their earnings from the Festival to trans-activists.[135]

In response to the call for a boycott, many longstanding and intimately involved Festival performers wrote public statements and letters to support the Festival. For instance, Vicki Randle wrote:

As a person who on a daily basis perceives and endures sexism, racism, homophobia, and outright class-based snobbery, I really do understand what it feels like to be standing on the outside of the place where power resides.

Women born and raised as women in America have been inculcated in thousands of ways to believe they are not powerful. It's no surprise that women stand outside of the center of power in this country. Women grow up in this culture with an experience that at best is suffocating, condescending, intimidating, patronizing, demeaning, advantage taking and dream-crushing and at it's worst

---

[134] Red Durkin. http://www.change.org/petitions/indigo-girls-and-other-michfest-2013-performers-boycott-mwmf-until-the-organizers-fully-include-trans-women. 2013.
[135] http://www.indigogirls.com/correspondence_2006.htm. 2013.

terrifying, abusive, physically and sexually violent. The desire to create space that is safe, protected, nurturing and encouraging, drove the women in 1976 to create the one week once a year celebration that is Michfest. Now in its 37th year, it has literally raised generations of young women to adulthood, with the knowledge and support that the traditional and ubiquitous sexism that attempts every day to stifle their aspirations and hope is not true and will not win.

What is obvious is the ongoing need for a space for us as women-born-and-raised women. Our particular experience is valid and the desire to keep that time and space exclusive does not, by it's existence, imply that other equally valid struggles are less important or don't deserve a space of their own.

This year has seen much discussion, quarreling and some acrimony regarding the festival policy asking MTF transwomen not to attend the festival, equating this to discrimination. I reject that assertion as false equivalence, in the same way that women of color creating an exclusive space inside the festival as the People of Color Tent does not "discriminate" against white people.

There has always been controversy over attendance at the festival. In years past, the issue of straight women, male children and male allies have been lightening rods for divisiveness, name-calling, bad feelings all around. Somehow, eventually those issues were resolved in ways that the majority of the festival goers felt relatively comfortable with.

Trans women and men simply have a different experience and struggle, no less valid and equally important to gather together in solidarity to build, grow, encourage and celebrate. Like WBW, they stand outside the center of power in this country and I fervently hope we can learn to support and love each other and work together in this ongoing fight. As inclusionary as Michfest is, I do not believe that it can be all things to all people. I strongly support the festival's mission and hope that we can all, eventually, come to the understanding that when we give each other the space and encouragement to commune, we will be stronger allies in the ultimate struggle for human rights and dignity.[136]

---

[136] Vicki Randle. http://www.epochalips.com/?p=870. 2013.

Like Randle, Ubaka Hill (musician & workshop teacher) has fought for many causes, and still recognizes the need for a space like the Michigan Womyn's Music Festival. She wrote:

> As an adult-child of the Civil Rights Movement, Women's Rights Movement, Anti-War Movement, Anti-Apartheid Movement, Native People's Rights Movement, Gender Equality Movement, Student Rights Movement, Environmental Protection Movement, Animal Rights Movement, Worker Rights Movement, my response to your courageous request that I cancel my Drumsong Workshop and the Drumsong Performance by participating in a strategy of a boycott against my own employment, my fans, my students, my peers, my musical, spiritual and cultural community of womyn and against the collective MWMF community, this is not the method of change that I want to participate in.[137]

Another well known Michigan performer and director of "Chixlix," Alyson Palmer, also wrote a letter responding to the trans-activists call for a boycott of the Festival:

> Anyone who truly understands the suffering of sexual harassment and abuse; the constant small violations and dark steady threat of even larger ones; the savage horror of rape or any of the sick tortures that the penis-proud wield so easily against women and girls of every age, would rise up and DEMAND that WBW have earned the right to a place in which to cling to one another and heal. To parade the dangling tool of the oppressor in the face of a woman who has been debased  - as a transperson did in the showers at MichFest - is unconscionable. The insensitivity of trying to force the victimized to get over it already so someone else can party woot woot is an insulting layer of fresh misogyny. It is selfish, it reeks of entitlement and it is cruel.[138]

Clearly, bodies and bodily experience matter to many womyn at the Festival, and the "shower incident" that was mention earlier, and the one Alyson mentions in her letter, are not singular events. There have been many shower incidents where women and young girls were confronted with penises in the open showers at the Festival. In 2011, a grand mother took her young granddaughter to the showers early in the morning. While they were naked and exposed, two trans women disrobed and walked into the showers next to them. When the grandmother asked what they thought they were doing there, the trans women told her to "get over it." Again, in 2011, in my capacity as a

---

[137] Ubaka Hill. http://www.afterellen.com/2013/04/fight-about-mich-fest. 2013.
[138] Alyson Palmer. Personal letter in response to trans-activists call for boycotting the Festival. 2013.

worker in the Womyn of Color Patio, a womyn came to me to ask for help. She had brought a friend who had recently been raped. She told her friend that if she came to Michigan she would heal. This young womyn did start her healing process at the Festival, enough so that she attended a "self love" workshop. During this workshop, another woman shared that she enjoyed "self-love" by placing a "cock-ring" over her penis and "jacking off." The young rape victim was so traumatized by the statement and to find that she was sitting next to a person with a penis that she ran to her tent and stayed there for two days. Of course we reported the incident to Oasis, and counselors sat by her tent until the young womyn was ready to come out and begin her healing process all over again.

These types of bodily experience happen every year, and are not just singular, isolated, and exaggerated "shower incidents" as the trans activists argue. Rather, they are male-centered power-play "incidents" perpetrated by trans women for their shock value and violation of womyn's spaces and women-born-women bodies. Bodies matter, and trans-women, like men, continue to feel their penis has the right to strike fear in the hearts of girls and womyn. In essence though, what trans-women are saying is that gender is a choice and not a bodily matter. But when bodies do matter, they clearly feel their penis' are more important than the wombs of women-born-women.

Finally, Dianic High Priestess and longtime Festival performer, Ruth Barrett wrote a letter in response to the call for boycott. In it she pointed out the significance of female born bodies, and explained how over the last few years she and Falcon have received threats to their safety, home, and livelihood because of their defense of womyn only spaces. She also pleads for the trans-activists to understand the needs of womyn-born-womyn.

> Dear Community Sisters and Performers of the Michigan Womyn's Music Festival, …
>
> In sisterhood and solidarity, I am writing to add my voice in support of Lisa Vogel and the women who honor and respect the Festival's women-born-women (WBW) intention.
>
> My friend Kathy, who has attended the Michigan Festival for well over 30 years, said to me last night, "How is it that 'women' with penises are given more rights and compassion than female-born women? Why is my right to self determination being challenged by others, who at the same time ask me to accept their self determination?" I echo her questions.
>
> For 51 weeks a year I have unlimited opportunities to engage with male-born men and trans-people. For one week out of the year I want to be with my female-born sisters, girls and women. I come to Festival to help create, contribute and experience an embodied female reality. . . . My need, and the

need of other WBW, to spend time solely with WBW is not trans-phobic. We are not AGAINST trans-women. This accusation of trans-phobia is a distraction from what we are actually saying and asking for. I have great difficulty with those trans-women and their allies who refuse to honor the intention of Fest as a healing space for WBW and the boundaries we have set. I am heart sick and exhausted by their bullying tactics, their threats to my personal safety, my wife's safety, the safety of our home and our livelihood. Over the past years we have ignored death threats as we choose to stand for sacred space for WBW and girls. Trans-women and their allies can't seem to accept being told "no" by women. Why can you not respect our need to gather with our own kind to heal, to rest, to nurture and restore ourselves? What possible threat are we to you?

Two of my very close friends, one who is a survivor of multiple sexual assaults, were traumatized when they individually encountered fully naked adult males in the shower at Fest. When my friends asked in stunned voices, "What are you doing here?" They were told by the trans-women, that they were "women" and had a right to shower there, penis and all. I and other womyn like me stand for the original intention of the Michigan Womyn's Music Festival. We need and deserve a week set apart for female-born women and girls to celebrate our mysteries, our creativity, ourselves, without fear.

The boycott demand of MWMF performers is patriarchal in its bullying tactics, and only demonstrates further a power-over mind set by trans-activists who would destroy the Michigan Festival rather than respectfully help to protect and preserve the now rare female spaces left to us WBW. We need the respite of Michfest for our healing, to create and celebrate the swirling cauldron of music, arts, dance, theatre, ritual, and comedy that enriches us and empowers us to return to the patriarchal, penis-ruled world where female WBW continue to be defiled en masse, worldwide.

The self-centered actions of those who seek to bully their way into the Festival, threaten the performers, and plan to create a drama-filled Festival, clearly demonstrate their utter disrespect for the needs of female-born women. Their actions also clearly demonstrate their unexamined, undiagnosed and unchallenged misogyny.

I speak directly to all trans activists, Female-born sisters are not your enemy, and never have been. The feminist vision, intention, and work of creating Michfest solely for female born WBW simply does not include you because the festival was not created to address, and is not intended to serve your needs.

As a Priestess and elder of Women's Mysteries for over 35 years, I understand and value the importance of female-only space. This kind of sacred space has literally saved women's lives, and continues to do so. The Michigan Festival has provided this sacred space for female born WBW for decades, because our life experiences matter. This is why so many of us have been planning our lives around Michfest for decades, travel great distances, spend hard earned money, and make sacrifices too numerous to mention, in order to participate.

I choose to give my goddess-given energy to female-born women and girls. I will continue to defend the right of females to gather, the right to define ourselves as female-born girls and women, and will not be bullied into submission by anyone. I seek no war with anyone. I stand in my truth and for whom I love. I love women and our children.

May we, and the Festival survive to tell our stories of Festival to our great grandchildren. Should the Festival intention change, or the Festival be destroyed (as is clearly an acceptable intention/option of some trans-inclusion supporters), I and many Festival performers and elders will not return. To trans activists I say, the Festival that you have forcibly inserted yourself into will no longer exist, there will be no Michigan Festival left as we have known it. Trans-women and their supporters may stand on what was once our sacred space, now become a battleground, and insert their flag into the ground.

The taste of victory will turn bitter as wars on women and girls always are. Will their victory be that there be no place left for us to celebrate ourselves as female beings in all of our diversity, power, and beauty? The thought of this sickens me in my gut and heart. I feel sadness, anger and frustration. To trans-women who choose to violate the intention of the Festival, and the women who support their inclusion I say, "Stop. Stop. Stop!" May you learn respect for the needs of women and girls to have our time together. Stop making women who support the Festival your perpetrators and oppressors. We are not your oppressors. You are not our victims.

If you really love and respect women, let yourself feel the needs we have. May you come to understand our need to have our time together once a year, on women's sacred land. May those who have made the Festival their battleground, wake up. May they learn to respect the needs of women and girls that the festival has provided for 38 years. It has been a sacred honor to contribute my own gifts to the miraculous vision of the Michigan Festival for the past 29 years. I stand for the festival's intention with my body, my heart and spirit. It is my hope and prayer that I may contribute for many years to come.

Blessed be![139]

What most performers and womyn who attend the Festival argue, is that having one women-born-women space (one week a year) is not inherently trans-phobic, nor does it mean that trans-rights are not important. What it does mean is that womyn who were born and raised as girls have unique needs, which are different than the needs of women who were born and raised as boys, and made medical transition in their adult years. By continuing their fight for inclusion, and potentially winning that fight, trans-women and their allies are advocating for changing the very thing that makes the Festival unique.

As with most women's studies programs around the country, as well as all other women's festivals, trans-women are not only included, but their issues have become the focus. And just as post-modern theory has deconstructed identity to the point of invisibility (in terms of race, class, gender, and sexual orientation), so the trans-movement is working to make invisible women who were born female. When and if this happens, the Land, the culture, and the Amazons who create the Festival will suffer. As Lisa Vogel wrote in her response to the petition by Red:

> There is no doubt that complex political debate is healthy and necessary within our communities; however, a boycott, within this context, fails to advance resolution and only seeks to exact damage.[140]

While attempting to transform the meanings associated with gender and womanhood, most womyn still remain steadfast in their belief that one is *born a woman*, and one is born a lesbian. The transgender activists' fight has made many womyn more essentialist, more militant, and certainly more steadfast in their defense of their home. What is more, many feel that trans-women are uninvited people in their home, and would relegate women-born-women to one room in the home that their mothers and grandmothers gave their blood, sweat, and tears to build. Finally, in patriarchal fashion, trans-women demand that women-born-women apologize for not welcoming them into their home and appeasing them by placing their needs above those of women-born-women.

---

[139]Ruth Barrett. Personal letter in response to trans-activists call for boycotting the Festival. 2013.
[140] Lisa Vogel. http://www.afterellen.com/2013/04/fight-about-mich-fest. 2013.

Trans-women demand that their social, emotional, spiritual, physical, and political needs are met through the work of others, instead of investing in and working toward meeting their own needs, just as the womyn of the Amazon culture have.

Back in 2001, as Bobbie and I passed the young trans-woman on the road we did not understand that she was actually protesting Camp Trans, nor did we fully understand the complexity of the issue. At that time, transgender politics was the last thing on my minds. We were just about to enter the Festival and the excitement of that experience made me forget all about the politics that weaves its way into the very fabric of the Festival. However, now as we draw nearer to the 40ᵗʰ anniversary of the Festival, the issue of transgender inclusion is still clearly a raging controversy that is not only draining the financial resources and emotional energy of the Festival and its womyn, but it is an issue that few womyn of the Amazon culture are willing to negotiate on. The only question left for us to ask ourselves is, "Where will we go if our Land, labor, and culture is colonized by the trans-activist movement?"

**The Front Gate**

Driving through the *front gate* of the Michigan Womyn's Music Festival is like no other experience on Earth. Several womyn gathered around the van as we passed through the gate, where the huge multi-colored sign read, "*Welcome.*" One womyn talked to Bobbie through the passenger window while another spoke with me through the driver's window. "Welcome Home!" they shouted over the roar of so many engines. "Have you been here before?"

"No," we replied. Immediately they started clapping and cheering, and shouting to the other womyn milling around the *front gate.* "Festie virgins! We have two festie virgins here."

The one hundred or so womyn working around the *front gate* stopped what they were doing, looked our way, and began clapping and cheering for us in unison. "Welcome home! Welcome home!" they called. Suddenly I remembered the video that I had seen in my women's studies class. I remembered hearing the stage announcer shout, "Welcome Home, Women. Welcome Home." There at the gate, I realized that the words must be a traditional greeting for new womyn arriving on the Land.

After taking our tickets the womyn got right down to business. Working on both sides of the van, they reached in through the windows to clamp plastic lavender bands around our wrists. These, they told us, were our passes on the Land. Without them we would not be served meals. They also told us that we needed to go through orientation where we would see a short film about the services the Festival offered, sign up for our work shifts, and receive our Festival programs. "And remember," they said "we haven't had any rain here in the last five weeks, so the Land is really dry. Please be very careful. There are no campfires outside the designated fire pits, and be sure to field strip your smoking materials." Then they smiled and waived us into the unloading

57

zone where we would store our camping gear while we went through orientation.

*Front Gate – 2001*

**Orientation**

Orientation takes place in a huge yellow and white striped tent, which is the center of activity on opening day. A womyn wearing a bright yellow mud-print dress greeted Bobbie and I at the door. She asked if we were allergic to bee stings, and explained that because of the lack of rain in the area the bees were getting their water from the same sources we were; namely the water fountains and showers. If we had been allergic to bee stings, she would have marked a black dot on our wristbands to inform the medical staff of this fact in case we were stung. From there, because we were "festie virgins," she ushered us into a side section of the tent where another womyn explained to "virgins" how to get around on the Land, what to expect, and how important it was to choose work shifts and show up for them. Then she ushered us into a larger section of the tent where we watched a video that ran in a continuous loop. The video was well produced and gave valuable information about various services on the Land.

In the next phase of orientation, we signed up for our work shifts. This section of the tent was packed with womyn who were nudging and pushing (gently of course) their way around the room reading job description signs and waiting in line to sign up for the shifts they wanted. This was a confusing process for the uninitiated. Each womyn attending the Festival is asked to work two four-hour work shifts sometime during the week. The need for workers is tremendous at a Festival the size of Michigan. With so many services offered, Festival organizers and workers could never provide them all without the help of festiegoers. These services require hundreds of "womyn-hours" each day and skills that range from highly technical to relatively simple. However, because feeding six to ten thousand womyn and children three times a day is the largest job that goes on all day long, every day, most womyn work at least one of their shifts in the Kitchen. The other shift can be anything from greeting at the *front gate* to childcare or garbage recycling. That first year, Bobbie and I chose a shift in the Kitchen and one in the R.V. tent, where we would greet incoming R.V.ers and help them get situated. After orientation we headed back to load our gear onto one of the shuttles that would take us into the heart of the Land, but we stopped and smiled at each other when we heard another round of cheers rise up at the *front gate*. "Welcome Home," the womyn shouted, "Welcome Home."

## Feeling of Connection and Safety

In that moment an unexpected feeling came over me. It was a feeling that, in retrospect, is hard to articulate. It was as if I were suddenly aware that I was walking on sacred ancestral land and that every womyn was related to me through some ancient bond of understanding. At first, I chalked the feeling up to fatigue, but it was not the last time I would experience it. Later, I learned that the experience is not unique. Every womyn I talked with expressed some form of the feeling. Boden Sandstrom suggested that, "just as the footpaths establish well-worn, familiar pathways that orient festiegoers each year; the overall schema, or Festival map, establishes the channels along which a collective memory has taken shape over the Festival's history."[141] Part of the collective memory is that the Land belongs to womyn, and on it they are *safe*. Several of the womyn I interviewed talked about their feelings of *safety* and their feelings of connection to the womyn on the Land.

Joslyn: "This is my first year, and oh, I love it so far. I don't worry about people stealing anything. I don't worry about people grabbing me. I don't worry about anything. I don't know, it's just very different than walking out on the street in regular American society. I'm always holding my purse very close to me, and watching everything around me. And here, I don't even worry about it because it is so different. It's just the atmosphere or trust that's so wonderful, on such a large scale."[142]

Susi: "You do have to defend yourself out there, because it is a man's world. You have to learn to operate within that. And so there's a barrier that you have to put up. I mean, back home, I have my farm, and that's women's land. So there I'm a bit defended from that. I have had that for the last 20 years because I knew I need that. Because there is no way I could operate out there in the world all the time, and still be an open caring human being. And so – Michigan – I mean just flying to America, and two hours getting through customs, and being photographed. And then, getting into Michigan we could just relax because it's *safe*. You know that no man is going to come out of the

---

[141] Sandstrom, 276.
[142] Joslyn. Personal Interview. August, 2005.

woods with a gun. I don't know. It just had this amazing feeling about it."[143]

The feeling of connection womyn experience at Michigan, and the closeness they feel for each other helps generate the feeling of safety. This feeling is so precious and taken so seriously that some women volunteer to do their work shifts on the security force that patrols the perimeter of the Land both day and night. Even when men must come onto the Land to make food deliveries or to clean the Porta Janes at night, they have a full contingent of security workers escorting them. The security workers keep men focused on their work, rather than catcalling or staring at the womyn. As Ro said in her interview, "women take care of each other! There's a different level of *safety* and comfort here. The Festival is a *safe* place, and it's not that way in everyday life."[144]

## General Camping Areas

After Bobbie and I set up camp, we decided to follow the Festival map and check out the lay of the Land. The only road on the Land is called *Lois Lane*, a "U" shaped road where the shuttles run, making their way around the Land. Beginning at the *front gate*, the shuttle stops first at the R.V. section; a fairly open and treeless area. Next it stops at *Tree Line* where the general camping areas begin, and where the terrain turns into a densely wooded area where wild ferns flourish. Along the way we watched as brightly colored tents began popping up all over the landscape, creating neighborhoods in this temporary city of womyn. Some womyn hung homemade signs or flags from trees to announce where they were from, or to send out greeting to womyn passing by. "Alaskan Dykes," "Greetings from Down Under," and "Welcome Home" were only three of the many we saw.

The first camping area we passed was *Solanas Ferns*, a general camping area on the right. Across the road was an unnamed "scent free" area where womyn sensitive to fragrances can camp. Farther up the road we found *Crone Heights* on the right, another general camping area, with *Amazon Acres* a quiet camping area directly across the road on the left.

Next we came to *Bush Gardens*, the largest general camping area, with *Bread & Roses*, a "chem-free" campground, across the road on the left. "Chem-free" is a designation that restricts the use of any "chemical" in that area; i.e. tobacco, alcohol, or drugs of any kind. The last general campground, *Jupiter Jumpoff*, was located next to *Bread & Roses*, just north of the *Triangle*. However, one campground was not visible from the road. We had passed the *Twilight*

---

[143] Susi St. Julian. Personal Interview. August, 2005.
[144] Ro Rasmussen. Personal Interview. August, 2002.

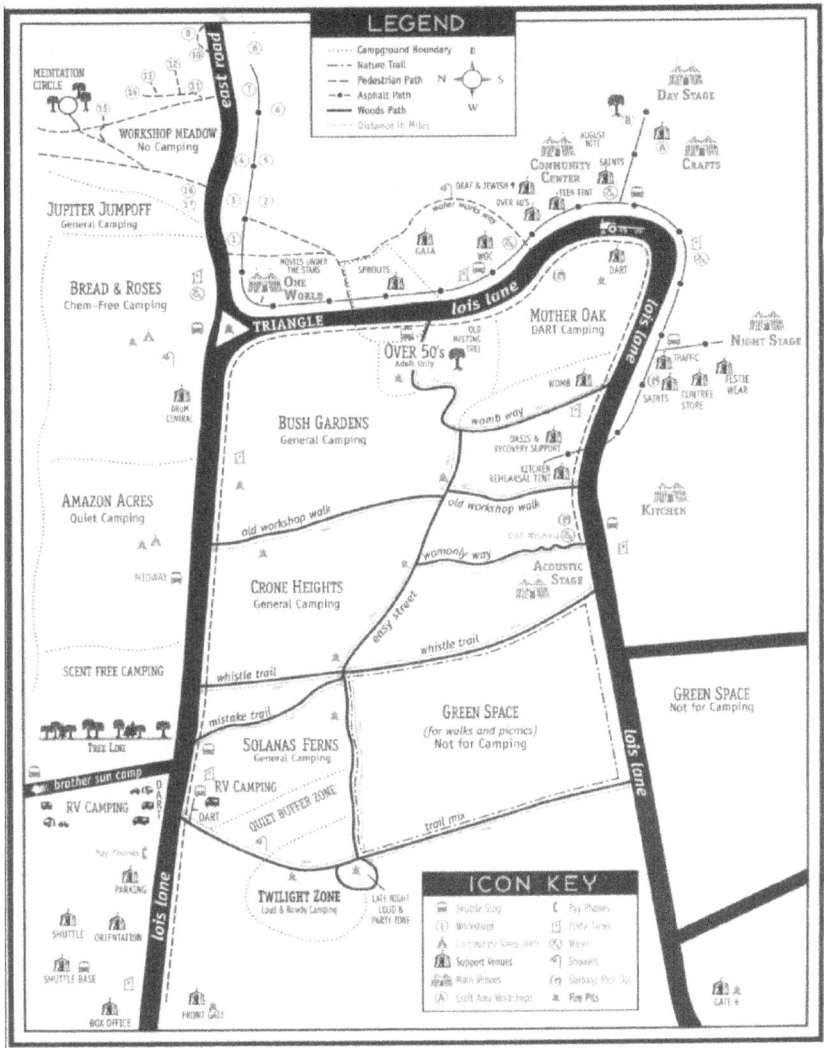

*2001 Festival Map*[145]

*Zone* before we ever made it to the first shuttle stop. The *Twilight Zone* is secluded out on the western edge of the Land because it was originally designate as the "loud and rowdy" partiers camping area. But in the 1980s, lesbian sex wars erupted and young lesbians who challenged lesbian feminist constructions of "appropriate sexual behavior" claimed the *Twilight Zone* as their *home*. Although lesbian feminist of the 1970s rejected compulsory heterosexuality, according to Lillian Faderman, "most lesbians continued to idealize monogamy," and failed to challenge their puritanical concepts of love and

---

[145] 2001 Michigan Womyn's Music Festival Program, back cover.

sex.[146] Ironically, during the 1980s, as the gay male sexual revolution was grinding to a halt because of the AIDS epidemic, young lesbians started their own sexual revolution. They began exploring pornography, casual sex, sexual role playing, and sadomasochism, and they wanted to continue their exploration during the Festival.[147]

However, lesbian feminists believed that sadomasochistic practices and pornography were harmful to womyn because they perpetuated violence and brought patriarchal attitudes and behaviors into Amazon culture. These attitudes and behaviors, they argued, had been the very ones that men had historically used to dominate women. Yet some womyn argued that the use of pornography was stimulating and enhanced their sexual pleasure. Some even argued that S & M helped womyn heal both spiritually and sexually from abusive experiences.

The argument came to a head in 1984, when lesbian pornographers wanted to audition womyn for their magazine during the Festival. Intending to head off an "ugly confrontation" between publishers, potential models, and the womyn who had organized a protest, Festival producers headed for the *Triangle*. In an interview about the incident, Lisa Vogel told journalists the following story:

> Like, all these leatherdykes were showing up in collars and whips, because they were auditioning to model. You couldn't tell who was who. So Boo and I were just waiting, and watching the jocks having a predinner volleyball game. Suddenly, there's this roar coming down the road: the protesters. So you have the jocks playing volleyball, the leatherdykes waiting to be models, and the antiporn dykes marching toward Triangle with the signs and the chants. And what they're chanting is 'No more porn!' But what the jocks hear is, 'No more *corn*.' So they're beside themselves, too. It was a perfect festival moment."[148]

Needless to say, the audition turned ugly and resulted in Vogel instituting a policy against making sadomasochistic scenes and pornography visible on the Land. Still, over the next decade the issue remained hot, and in 1990 S&M activists rented a plane to fly over and drop flyers that protested the Festival's policy on S & M visibility.

But by 1994, there were signs that things were changing. That year, Lisa Vogel decided to let the radical thrash band Tribe 8 play the *Night Stage*. Though this decision brought protests from womyn who accused the band of eroticizing violence against women, Vogel's decision to let the band play effectively transformed the policy against S & M and pornography on the Land.

---

[146] Faderman, 254.
[147] Ibid.
[148] Van Gelder and Brandt, 69.

The womyn I interviewed had mixed opinions about the change in policy, but seemed to accept that the *Twilight Zone* was for womyn who wanted to party till dawn and explore new sexual practices.

Ro: "I think S & M has always been an area of controversy. I think it has ended some other festivals and women's spaces. That's a hard one. I went to a workshop - I didn't know it was going to be quite that – and that was enough. And seeing them walking around. But I don't want to talk about that."[149]

Cindy: "They belong here too. I think everybody should be able to celebrate who they are. It doesn't matter."[150]

Susi: "It was interesting because we went out to the Twilight Zone, and we'd been told that it was quite a wild place, so we thought we should go out there. But it wasn't near as wild as people make out. But it seems like they are a little bit alienated from the rest of the women – I mean there's a space for you, but stay there. And I think that's probably not quite fair, because they are women, and they are there for a reason. They love it. When we were out there for the burlesque show, there was one woman who was a sex educator, and she had quite a lot of interesting things to say, actually. I can imagine that her workshops could be very useful to a lot of people, just as the Babes in Toyland workshops were very useful, especially to a lot of older lesbians. Because maintaining your sexuality through long term relationships is not an easy thing. And I think a lot of young women have a lot to say about that stuff, and we could learn a lot from them. There are a lot of intimacy issues that could be addressed, and they are really up front about that stuff. Because it's not easy to be up front about that stuff. And there is a lot to learn from some of those young women. And I think that would help them to listen to us about other things. I mean, penetration, in the 70s, that was a vile thing. I think we repressed a lot of things to fit in. I just wish I had the energy that they have, but that's the other thing – they do energize you."[151]

Although most womyn do not venture into the *Twilight Zone* because that scene is "not their cup of tea," most seem happy that womyn can express themselves safely at the Festival. Some are even curious about what "really goes on there." Most womyn feel grateful they can partake of any pleasure on the Land, but because the rest of the Festival is open to children, most womyn respect the fact that space has been set aside for certain kinds of pleasure.

## The Triangle

Finally the "rural shuttle" rattled to a stop at the *Triangle*, the only major intersection on the Land. There, arriving passengers disembark and wait for the "cross-town shuttle" to take them to downtown destinations. But walking

---

[149] Ro Rasmussen. Personal Interview. August, 2002.
[150] Cindy Avery. Personal Interview. August, 2002.
[151] Susi St. Julian. Personal Interview. August, 2005.

downtown may be preferable because the shuttles are often very crowded and hard to manage, particularly for womyn juggling luggage, shopping bags, or children.

*The Triangle – 2001*

*The Cross-town Tractor & Surry – 2001*

On the other hand, many new friendships are made on the shuttles precisely for this reason. Because womyn have to squeeze closer together at each stop, traveling the length of the Land can become an animated physical experience. Jennie Ruby, a reporter for *Off Our Backs*, wrote about a particularly enjoyable shuttle ride she experience at the 2001 Festival:

> On the shuttle bus one evening, four women wearing brightly colored cone-head wigs and evening gowns entertained the other riders with a hand-puppet beaver.[152]

While riding on the shuttles womyn often strike up conversations, spontaneously break into songs like "Downtown," or pursue an accidental touch. One might even meet a Hollywood celebrity and share her peanuts, as Bobbie and I did one afternoon with a womyn who acted in the film, *A League of Their Own.*

Because the *Triangle* is the only intersection on the Land, it is often the *home* for traffic workers. Their job is to manage the flow of the shuttles. In 1990 the Festival's motor pool increased dramatically when the open-air school bus and the two canopied surreys joined the Festival's fleet. Currently the fleet includes a long bus (Bo), two surreys (rural and cross-town), two short buses (Doris and Deming), and a flat bed trailer. The Festival also rents several panel vans that are used mostly on opening and closing days. During her interview I learned that Kip was a long time traffic worker when she shared the meaning of the shuttle driver's wave with me.

Kip: "There are many legends, just like in any other society. There's lots of these funny legends, grandmother's legends about why we have certain customs. You know, like the shuttle drivers' wave. That started out with the traffic people and the shuttle people butting heads. The shuttle people always want to get their vehicle through – their job is to move the people – and it's

---

[152] Jennie Ruby. "Michigan Values." *Off Our Backs: The Feminist Newsjournal.* Oct. 2001, vol xxxi, number 9.

traffic's job to make sure that happens safely. So, certain unnamed traffic workers have been know to stand in front of a tractor – in the middle of the road – going 'I don't care if you own the vehicle, this is my road, and if you want to drive your vehicle on my road, you'll do what I tell ya.' And so in the early days, before we had a lot of kids around, and had to be careful about the way we talked to each other, there was a lot of $&#!#$&, 'stupid damn shuttle drivers,' *&$%#!. And you know it wasn't contentious – angry contentious – it was contentious 'I love you, but you're a pain in my ass" contentious. And so that kinda got outlawed. There was this policy that happened – there was this discussion that happened about – 'You know, you have to talk nicer to people in front of the festies, because that's just not polite. And so you have to be nice and wave at each other.' So, the shuttle drivers made up this wave that means 'fuck you.' It's like flippin' us the bird. And so whenever you see somebody go like this to a shuttle driver [a type of wave common to royalty], they're not sayin' 'Hi, I love you.' They are, but their not – you know. They're sayin,' 'bag it Gladys,' is what they're sayin'. And it's just that friendly rivalry that happens between the crews. There's all these little things that happen here that I take for granted, because I've been comin' for so many years, that people who are new come and they go, 'why are ya doin' that.' And I tell 'em, 'well, we're doin' this because blah, blah, blah – once upon a time, somebody was drivin' a shuttle and the wheel fell off, and so this happened and now we do this.'"[153]

Before we made our way downtown, Bobbie and I decided to check out the facilities around the *Triangle*. Across the road to the east, is the volleyball court, and just north of the court is the *One World* and *Movies Under the Stars* complex. These tents offer a variety of services, from literature exchange tables to video viewing, and movies on a large outdoor screen at night. The Festival program says, "We have a rich tradition of oral history in the womyn's community and it is continued here through the extensive workshop and media program."[154] Up the path from the media complex is *Workshop Meadow*, where eighteen spaces are marked out to form the "natural" classrooms for daily workshops. Each morning during the Festival, 18 workshops happen every hour, on the hour. In 1986, when the Festival became a five-day event, "intensive workshops" were added to the schedule. These workshops are several hours long and run concurrently for two or more days.

Most workshops revolve around cultural, legal, spiritual, or health issues, and include titles like "Deaf Culture," "Demystifying PMS/Menopause," and "Filipino Stick Fighting." But on that first day, no one was in the meadow so Bobbie and I reversed our course and headed back to the *Triangle* where we caught the downtown shuttle. Along the way, we passed *Sprouts Family Camp*, *Gaia Girls*, the *Womyn of Color Tent*, *Over 50s* camping, and the *Over 40s Tent* before we arrived at the *Community Center*.

---

[153] Kip Parker. Personal Interview. August, 2003.
[154] 2001 Michigan Womyn's Music Festival Program, 26.

*Movie & Media Tent – 2001*

*One World Tent – 2001*

## Sprouts Family Camp, Bother Sun, and Gaia Girls

*Sprouts Family Camp* was established in the interior of the Festival. It is reserved for womyn with infants and toddlers of both sexes. "Located in a shady grove, *Sprouts* provides care for girl and boy toddlers through the age of four. There, toddlers have play spaces, special activities, a quiet nap tent, simple snacks and lots of attention."[155] This camp provides womyn with a large tent that houses cribs and playpens, and babysitting services so mothers can go out and enjoy all the Festival has to offer.

*Sprouts – 2002*

Later in the week, I overheard a conversation between two womyn who had just finished their work shift at *Sprouts Family Camp*. They were discussing the recent "baby boom" in the lesbian community. It seemed that a record number of infants were attending the Festival that year; 70 in all. When lesbian couples started having babies together, Festival organizers responded to their needs by establishing *Sprouts Family Camp*, *Gaia Girls Camp*, and *Brother Sun Camp*. Here, it is important to explain the difference between the "family camps" available for womyn with children. *Gaia Girls* is a "day camp" where young female children enjoy special crafts and activities designed for their specific age groups. *Brother Sun* provides the same "day camp" experience for boys, but it is located out on the Northwestern side of the Land. Boys over four are not permitted into the interior of the Festival.

---

[155] 2002 Michigan Womyn's Music Festival Program, 6.

Since the first Festival, womyn have brought both their male and female children because few could afford the high cost of childcare for a week. So in 1978, trying to accommodate mothers with sons, while at the same time maintaining the "womyn only space," Festival producers established a separate campground away from the main Festival, for womyn with male children. However, this separate space did not "gel" until the Festival was moved permanently to its own Land in 1982. Today, "Brother Sun is a self-contained camp where boys ages 5-10 enjoy camping, activities and special field trips to explore rural Michigan's summer fun. Field trips may include trips to the lake or waterslide, bowling, putt-putt golf and spontaneous fun."[156]

While understanding the financial burden *Brother Sun* alleviated, many womyn remained critical of male children on the Land. They objected because "male energy" changes the atmosphere of the Festival. In the early years, when womyn saw the way boys demanded the attention of girls, and saw womyn focusing their energy on male children, they challenged the wisdom of allowing male children on the Land. Several of the womyn I interviewed remembered the issue as one of the first political challenges the Festival community faced.

Lorraine: "It used to be that they didn't want boy children at all, and then they realized how hard it was on women who had children. That's when they started Brother Sun Camp where they allowed boy children up to ten, and then they allowed male infants on the Land, up to four. But at one time, they didn't want to see any boy children. I feel most comfortable with that. I still don't feel that comfortable having boy children around. So I guess in that way, I am a separatist. But for one week out of the year, I'd like to not see boys or men. I'd like it to just be women. Let us evolve into whatever we're going to evolve into. Let it be women only space."[157]

Ro: "The whole point is to have women only space - that there are some places that boys and men can't go. And that's really hard for women, for mothers, not to have their sons with them! But it does make a difference in the energy! Because I've been in other women only spaces where there were boys, and it does change things. I know a lot of women are not happy with how it is arranged now. In fact, I came with a new friend who's a mother, and some of her friends didn't want to come because they were gonna have to camp at the other end of the Land. They couldn't be on the Land with everyone else. Well, that's the way it worked out, and I think I'm comfortable with that. Some women wouldn't even want male babies here at all, but I think that's pretty unreasonable. But like I said, there is a difference in the energy."[158]

Mary: "Hey, I have two sons, and six grandsons. And you know, I never brought my sons. I started when they could have gone to Brother Sun, but this wasn't the place for them. It was a place for me and my daughter. And

---

[156] 2002 Michigan Womyn's Music Festival Program, 6.
[157] Lorraine Alexis. Personal Interview. August, 2002.
[158] Ro Rasmussen. Personal Interview. August, 2002.

that's the way I felt. There are women in my community who don't even know I have sons, because I didn't push them out front when the lesbian separatist movement was goin' on. But my daughter was the mascot. And it has made a difference for her, because my granddaughter be runnin' around talkin' about Girl Power! And sayin' to all of her brothers, 'this is for girls only!' She gets real uppity about her girl power. And it's not that we raised lesbians, cause there's some women we know whose daughters have been heterosexual. You know, we wish. But we want grandchildren, so it's ok. But we can only hope for the next generation [laughs out loud]."[159]

At times, the issue of male children on the Land has turned ugly, causing some womyn to feel hurt by other womyn's rejection of their sons. Some were so angry they left the Festival, vowing never to return. Still, the Festival producers have tried to accommodate womyn with children, while at the same time maintaining the integrity of the womyn only space. Balancing the needs of womyn with male children and those of womyn who need womyn-only space was challenging. It required compromise on both sides. Brother Sun is a compromise that allows mothers to bring their sons to the Festival, but more than this, it provides a nurturing space where boys enjoy fun activities while learning how to respect the privacy, autonomy, and strength of womyn, which is a lesson that even the adults are still struggling to learn.

### Womyn of Color Tent

In the early years of the Festival, very few womyn of color attended. Even today, womyn of color are a small minority in the predominantly white Festival population. Arlene Stein argued that lesbians of color seem missing in women's culture because "dominant visual codes in lesbian/gay communities, which determined 'what a lesbian looked like,' often assumed whiteness and marked women of color as heterosexual. The identity work required of women of color was therefore doubly demanding, requiring the skillful manipulation of white-defined visual codes."[160] Indeed, in the early years of the Festival, the culture being created did not redefine race in any meaningful way. And there were other problems as well. First, white womyn were more likely to discuss "lesbian" identities openly, and they were more likely to be in the social locations where "lesbian" events were advertised. Second, white womyn were often more familiar with camping than urban dwelling womyn of color, and they were more likely to conceptualize the camping experience as pleasurable. Third, more white womyn had paid vacation time and could afford the ticket price. The womyn of color interviewed for this project discussed several of these issues, as well as their personal Festival experiences.

Akosua: "Mary was saying the other night, when she first came, there were only twelve Black women that came. That must have been very hard.

---

[159] Mary Sims. Personal Interview. August, 2005.
[160] Stein, 82.

Particularly if there was no commonality between her and the other eleven. Can you imagine what that must have been like?"[161]

Mary: "The first time I came was in 1978. I came with my white lover. But a lot of women of color say, 'I ain't sleepin' on the ground.' But it frees you up, cause you're not playin' to the world. But a lot of women say, 'I'm not sleepin' on no ground.' But it ain't about that. It's about the energy. Girl, once you get in here, you can be soakin' wet, freezin' your ass off, and you don't even care. You find that fire space, and you there. And I'll tell ya, that air-mattress I blew up sure felt better than that mattress in the hotel room I stayed in on Sunday. My shoulder hurt when I got outta' that bed. But I'll tell ya, this air-mattress has been wonderful for me. Pump it up – pump it up, and it was good to go."[162]

Van: "The first time I came I didn't like it at all. I didn't like the showers – I didn't like the food. I've never been a camper. I didn't like the whole camping thing. And I never came back after that first time. But then I got together with my current partner [a white womyn]. Now I come because of her. I'm still not a camper. I don't think she will ever make me a camper person. I'm a high maintenance lesbian. But the important thing is that we are together, and being able to reach out and touch her, and not worry – that's what this is about. Although I think there are some parts of this philosophy that are very Eurocentric, in my mind. In my mind, camping is a Eurocentric philosophy. I have never thought it was exciting to live out in the sticks, in the woods. Fuck no. That makes no sense to me. I think they could have a bed and breakfast out there [laughs out loud]. But that's just me."[163]

Lauren: "This is my first time camping and I thought I was too high maintenance to come, but I got in here and set up shop. I pitched a tent. And if I can do it – I mean, I've never gone so long without looking in a mirror, or checking my hair. But in here you don't even think about it. It's nice to get out of that box that society puts you in. And we have so many luxuries in my camp. Like, I'm sleeping on an air-mattress. Shoot, I'm getting better sleep out here than I ever have."[164]

But womyn of color have had to fight to make a place for themselves at the Festival. In 1980, womyn of color held a spontaneous meeting to discuss the lack of diversity on the Land. During that meeting, womyn of color drew up a list of demands and presented them to the Festival producers. Some of the demands included hiring more womyn of color performers and having womyn of color space. Over the next three years, Festival producers made an effort to increase the number of womyn of color on stage, and by 1986, 15 percent of the Michigan performers were womyn of color.[165] In an interview with Dee

---

[161] Akosua. Personal Interview. August, 2005.
[162] Mary Sims. Personal Interview. August, 2005.
[163] Van. Personal Interview. August, 2005.
[164] Lauren. Personal Interview, 2005.
[165] Sandstrom, 174-175.

Mosbacher, Lisa Vogel said, "The significance of the women of color performers was that they came in and they just didn't do a gig. They came in and they laid ownership."[166] Performances by jazz, funk, and Latin jazz artists forced the Michigan audience to grow aesthetically, but initially "there was actually resistance among the majority white audience members, because they were much more used to pop and folk."[167]

The producers also tried to meet the demands for space at the Festival by womyn of color. In 1981, Festival producers designated a small space in the *Community Center Tent* as a "political space," where discussion on diversity continued. Womyn of color flocked to this space as word spread, and soon there was standing room only. The following year the space in the back of the *Community Center* was again designated as a political discussion space, but that year so many womyn of color showed up that they overflowed the space and had to open up the walls to accommodate all the womyn wanting to meet other womyn of color. In 1983, womyn of color negotiated for their own space, and that year the Festival producers erected a tent behind the *Community Center* and designated it the *Political Tent*. The *Political Tent* was split between womyn of color and womyn wanting to discuss other political issues. Over the next few years the number of womyn of color increased to the point that they overflowed their half of the *Political Tent*, and finally the Festival producers recognized that womyn of color needed a larger tent of their own. In 1986 the *Womyn of Color Tent* was inaugurated, and the Festival producers developed a travel fund for womyn of color. For womyn of color, the *Womyn of Color Tent* is often the most meaningful and important place on the Land.

Akosua: "What's brought me back every year is the women. Particularly the women of color space. It's really important for me. I'm 49 years old, and so the space was already here when I came the first time, but I understand the fight and the legacy that went into creating this space. So for me, it's real important to honor this space. And the women whose names are on the altar in there – those women had to fight to get it – and I appreciate that.

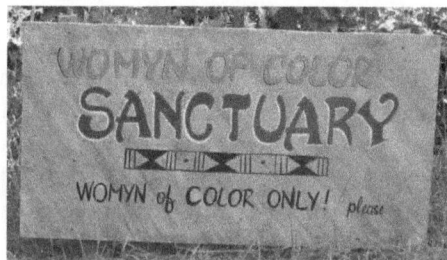

*Womyn of Color Tent & Sanctuary – 2005 - Thom*[168]

---

[166] Ibid.
[167] Ibid.
[168] Pictures of the Womyn of Color Sanctuary provided by Kate Thom, 2005.

And even though the original creators of the space were white, there's still a real sense of *community* amongst women of color, and that's real important to me. It feeds me in a way that I can't be fed in other places. So for me, coming from upstate New York, it's real important for me to be in a space with Black lesbians. Particularly, political Black lesbians."[169]

Colette: "The first time I came, I was surprised by the number of women in general, but particularly by the Womyn of Color Tent. Because that gave me a place where I felt like I found my *community* here at the Festival. It just gives me the opportunity to relax, and pull myself away from all those stresses in my life, back in Oakland, California. I just love being around all these supportive women, these beautiful women, these smart, intelligent women."[170]

Chelly: "I can honestly say that if it wasn't for the Womyn of Color Tent, I probably wouldn't be here. I mean, last year, I guess because I had the safety net of my friends and my wife, I had people around me who loved me. They were all women of color. So I didn't see any of the things that I noticed this year. Now that I am by myself, I have to realize that just because they're women doesn't mean that they like me. That, to me, has been an eye opener. But it's fine. I mean, it's not going to shy me away. It just makes me more aware. I mean, last year when I first heard about the Womyn of Color Tent, I was just like, 'why do we have to have a separate tent?' Why can't we just join in with everyone else? Why can't we do what everybody else does? It's like that just separates us that much more. I felt that much more segregated. But when you get here, and you see it, it's definitely a mandatory thing. Just to have our own events. We need that, you know. And it's a great thing. And just knowing some of the sisters here from Chicago, and everywhere, I can sit down and talk to them. Cause I don't do that at home, outside the Festival, just to bond."[171]

During the years of this study, Bobbie and I worked our work shifts in the *Womyn of Color Patio*, a space where white womyn hold anti-racist workshops and discussions about why women of color need the *Womyn of Color Tent*. We continued this work after the formal conclusion of this study, by becoming the *Womyn of Color Patio* coordinators. Often, we are asked by other white womyn if we think racism is still a real problem on the Land. I usually respond with a lecture about how we all bring racist assumptions to the Festival because we are all raised in a culture where racism is structured into the social matrix. However, overt or hostile racism is rare. When racism does manifest, it usually takes the form of ignorance and blindness to white privilege. For instance at the 10th anniversary celebration of the *Womyn of Color Tent*, a white womyn entered the tent wanting to buy drugs, and assumed womyn of color could sell them to her. Most white womyn do not take the time to get to know womyn of

---

[169] Akosua. Personal Interview. August, 2005.
[170] Colette Winlock. Personal Interview. August, 2005.
[171] Chelly. Personal Interview. August, 2005.

color, nor do they understand why that constitutes an act of racism. Morris confirmed this idea when she wrote, "Many white festigoers have the luxury of seeing racism as a series of single incidents. . . . But racism is the ongoing story for women of color, on and off the land. And the disinterested white festiegoer has the luxury of believing that racism, like hurricanes and thunderstorms, is just some unexplainable phenomenon that 'hits' festivals now and then."[172] Although I have not seen hostile acts of overt racism during the Festival, what I have seen are the subtle forms of racism that white womyn do not recognize as racism. This is one reason the *Womyn of Color Patio* was constructed just outside the *Womyn of Color Tent*.

There, white womyn teach other white womyn about our own unrecognized racism, and how our white privilege keeps us from seeing how patriarchal constructions of race, as well as gender and sexuality, intersect in the lives of womyn of color and lock them into systems of inequality. But educating liberal white womyn about their own subtle forms of racism is a difficult and ongoing task. It also takes patience, particularly when white womyn claim the privilege of entering the *Womyn of Color Tent* because they believe they were "womyn of color" in previous lives, or their partner is a womyn of color, or the just "feel" like a womyn of color. These types of arguments have been made more than once, and they have been admonished in letters like the one Maryanne wrote to *Lesbian Connection* in 1995:

> Girls! Girls! Use your heads! How can you not get it that some women of color might want some space? If you are of unapparent color, but trace your spiritual life to your long ago African or American Indian or Asian heritage, well, good for you. But your personal spiritual beliefs do not give you automatic entrée into the community of women of color. We may all have one Mother, but women of color are subjected, daily, to both overt and subtle racism. I can well imagine needing relief from racism, just as the MWMF (largely succeeds in) giving all lesbians who attend relief from sexism and homophobia.[173]

Most womyn of color are passionate about their space, and say that their time there is a bonding experience that heals them. Most womyn in the tent are African American or Native American, although Latina, Asian, Middle-Eastern, and Polynesian womyn are also welcomed. Since 1986, womyn of color have been reclaiming and revisioning their cultural traditions in this space, and negotiating what it means for them to be womyn of color in the Festival community, as well as in the larger culture.

---

[172] Morris, 156.
[173] Maryann. *Lesbian Connection.* May/June, Vol. 17, Issue 6, 1995, 41.

*Womyn of Color Sanctuary – 2005*

## Over 40s, Mother Oak, Jewish Womyn, and Deaf Way

Along with womyn of color, other womyn negotiated community spaces around issues of difference. In 1986, the *Over 40s Tent* was inaugurated across the street from *Mother Oak Campground* (for campers over 50). Jewish womyn and deaf womyn began sharing a tent of their own in 1991. For Jewish womyn, the space becomes a community resource center where they can network, share their experiences, plan the Friday night Shabbat service, and attend workshops. For deaf womyn, the space is also a networking and social space. But beyond this, it is where deaf womyn can enlist the services of sign language interpreters.

The *Over 40s Tent* is open to all womyn, but most young womyn are usually too busy to spend a lot of time there. However, some drop in to work on the quilt. Womyn in the *Over 40s Tent* have made a quilt every year since 1986, and it is raffled off at *Night Stage* on Saturday. The theme for each year's quilt is chosen before festiegoers arrive, and during the week womyn of all ages are invited to drop by and put a stitch or two in the quilt, even if they have never used a needle and thread before. Legend has it that you cannot win the quilt unless you put in at least one stitch. These quilts are one-of-a-kind, and uniquely designed to represent images and themes from the Festival. They are

73

highly prized among festiegoers and workers, and womyn buy large quantities of raffle tickets hoping that they will be the one to win the coveted quilt. Another notable event that took place in the *Over 40s Tent* was the 100th birthday celebration of Ruth Ellis, the oldest known "out" African American lesbian.

*Festival Quilts*

## Downtown

Downtown is a series of huge yellow and red striped tents that house the *Community Center*, *Crafts Bazaar*, *Saints by Day* refreshment stand, and *August Night Cafe* complex. These are all busy hubs of activity throughout the days and nights of the Festival, and seeing them for the first time was an amazing experience indeed. The whole area is a spectacle of color, light, movement, smell, and sound, all designed to tantalize every sense.

Experiencing "downtown" is particularly delightful on a busy morning. The energy that flows in this area is truly mesmerizing and indescribable for the festie virgin and old timer alike. The *August Night Café* consists of several long folding tables and chairs set up in the open air beside a relatively large and colorfully decorated wooden stage. This stage offers an open-mic program where non-professional entertainers present their talents to crowds that gather spontaneously. Near the stage, a temporary wooden basketball court accommodates games between "shirts" and "skins." *Saints by Day* is a refreshment stand where festiegoers can buy a morning cup of coffee and then sit and watch womyn take Salsa dance lessons on the *August Night* stage. But refreshments were not always available. The first snack sold on the Land was in 1981. It was called "Mama-corn" (popcorn).[174]

Over in the *Crafts Bazaar* festiegoers can buy hand made drums, pottery, jewelry, clothing, and wide variety of other goods made by crafts

---

[174] Morris, 80.

womyn. They can even get a massage or hair cut. However, attention may be drawn immediately to the body painters under a huge oak tree, who create breathtaking landscapes, detailed super-heroine costumes, or any other design a womyn might want on her naked body.

*The Crafts Bazaar – 2001*

*The Community Center – 2001*

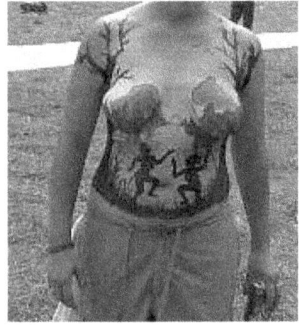

*Body-Painting – 2003 & 2005*

On the other hand, festiegoers might just as easily pass the time watching any one of the parades that go on during the week, including the "red head parade," the "femme parade," the "butch strut," the "*Gaia Girls* parade," the "Chocolate Womyn's streak" (nude womyn who have rolled in a kiddy pool filled with chocolate pudding), or the "Stiltwalkers" parade.

*Festival Parades*

75

Social services are coordinated through the *Community Center*. This is where arrangements for "other than English" interpretation are made and where festie virgins, as well as veterans, can find a wealth of information. In the past, the *Community Center* has housed displays of Festival historical memorabilia and other "cultural" exhibits. This is also where changes to workshop schedules are posted, and requests for various other services are made.

**DART, Womb, and Oasis**

DART (differently abled resource team) was established in 1979 to help womyn who are differently abled enjoy as much of the Festival as possible. It is centrally located next to the *Womb* (the medical facility on the Land) and *Oasis* (the mental health center), as well as the *Kitchen* and stages.

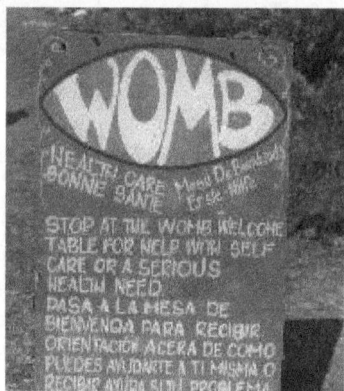

*The Womb: Medical Tent – 2001*

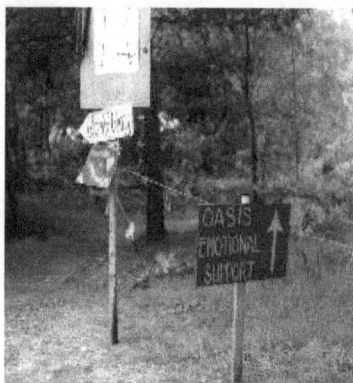

*The Oasis Emotional Support Tent – 2001*

*The Womb* and *Oasis* are designed to help womyn care for their own medical and psychological needs. They offer "over the counter" type medications such as Pepto-Bismol and Band-Aids, as well as herbal healing teas and peer-group counseling sessions. However, should a serious medical emergency arise, there are medical professionals available 24 hours a day in the acute care tent.

Unlike womyn of color, large numbers of womyn who are differently abled attended the Festival from the very beginning, and Festival producers tried to attend to as many of their needs as possible. During the earlier Festivals, snow fencing was put down to create "sidewalks" for womyn in wheelchairs, but today carpet is turned upside down and nailed to the ground with long spikes. In addition, the Festival obtained buses with lifts to make it easier to transport womyn in wheelchairs, and at the fifth Festival, sign language interpreters began interpreting from the stage for deaf womyn. Over the years, DART developed special campgrounds for womyn who are "differently abled" that included accessible showers, Porta Janes, dining services, and electrical systems to run personal medical equipment. Today, a paved sidewalk gives womyn on wheels access to a larger portion of the Land, where workshops and other activities take place every day. Womyn with every kind of challenge attend the Festival. Even womyn with unimaginable medical issues manage in this "rustic" environment. Several of the womyn I interviewed made their home in DART.

Kathy: "There was a woman here on an iron lung! Seriously! There was a woman on a respirator here. She was on a stretcher. She couldn't move. And there was a woman who just recently passed away, Connie, from New York, who came here every single year. The only thing she could move was her mouth. She was in a wheel chair, and there were people here who assisted her with her every need – emptying what ever bags needed to be emptied, cleaning, getting her into bed, feeding her, clothing her, washing her – everything."

Lorraine: "I think she brought a health aid with her, but then they also have people here to aid you. They'll set up your tent for you. They'll move your gear for you, in the DART area, which is the differently abled resource team."

Kathy: "But there's a whole *community* in here, and people are willing to do it. Just for a thank you, or maybe not even that. Because people are people, and sometimes they take advantage of you. But I think even that turns it around and people realize this is something different. Because it is something different! Think about a wheelchair. A wheelchair. Just a wheelchair. Before motorized wheelchairs, on this land – and this is even land. When we were in Hesperia, that was as bumpy and uneven as you could get. And just try pushing a wheel chair on unleveled ground. And now they've got blacktop areas. That's why this is located up here [DART camping], so it's close and centralized for people who are wheelchair bound, or walk on crutches, or whatever their disability is. Whether it is a visual one, or one you can't see, they're making compensations for it."[175]

Akosua: "One thing that I've appreciated – each year my mobility has gotten a little less - and there's always women willing to carry something for you, or help you get the scooter out of the sand, or to put it up on the tram for you, or whatever. So for me, I don't like to ask for help – so the other thing for me – that I've had to learn this week, is to accept help with gratitude and humility. And then I see other women out here with no mobility, and they manage to camp out here in the woods. And I find that so fascinating first of all, and second of all – amazing! They really do a good job making things accessible."[176] However, as reported in *Off Our Backs*:

> Despite the development of an accepting atmosphere within
> the Festival, womyn with disabilities still identify as a separate
> group with a need for their own boundaries. These women

---

[175] Lorraine Alexis and Kathy Davis. Personal Interview. August, 2002.
[176] Akosua. Personal Interview. August, 2005.

still feel some degree of distance from the non-disabled Festival participants.[177]

This feeling is understandable because as late as 2004, I was asked to sign a petition for paving the steep incline up to the *Acoustic Stage*, which is nearly impossible for womyn on wheels to climb by themselves. Most womyn who camp in the DART area have to access the Acoustic Stage from the back side, which means that their trek is an even longer one. However, "the Festival also provides an opportunity for womyn without identifiable disabilities to interact with disabled womyn in new and creative ways, thus creating growth opportunities for all Festival participants."[178] Some of these new and creative ways of interacting are both humorous and inspiring.

One day I was riding the DART bus because my feet were so blistered I could not manage the quarter mile walk back to our campsite (the nice thing about the political philosophy of disability operating at the Festival is that, "each womyn decides when and how she is disabled"). That day the driver needed to back up in order to turn the bus around, and she called out for someone to give her directions. A womyn outside yelled, "a little more to your left – that's good – now a little to your right - you got it." Suddenly the womyn on the right side of the bus burst out laughing because the womyn calling direction to the driver was blind. Interestingly enough, her directions were quite accurate from where I sat.

## The Kitchen

Across the road from DART, Bobbie and I came upon the three tents, fire pits, and two refrigerator trucks that make up the *Kitchen*. The *Kitchen* is extremely busy most of the time, offering three hot vegetarian meals each day to between two and ten thousand womyn and children at a time. From unloading the refrigerator trucks to cooking over pit fires, to serving the final meal and doing the pots and pans in a child's wading pools, it takes well over three hundred womyn a day to feed everyone. Needless to say, it is quite a job meeting this challenge while maintaining health standards. But health standard are strictly supervised by trained professionals, especially after the Shigella outbreak in 1988. Shigella is a bacterial infection that causes severe nausea, cramping, and diarrhea. That year, according to epidemiologists, the outbreak was caused by bacteria that was delivered to the Festival in the tofu:

> In August 1988, an estimated 3,175 women who attended a 5-day outdoor music festival in Michigan became ill with gastroenteritis caused by Shigella sonnei. Onset of illness peaked 2 days after the festival ended, and patients were spread throughout the United States by the time the outbreak was

[177] *Off Our Backs: The Feminist Newsjournal.* Vol.XXXII, 11 & 12, November-December, 2002.
[178] Ibid.

recognized. An uncooked tofu salad served on the last day was implicated as the outbreak vehicle. Over 2,000 volunteer food handlers prepared the communal meals served during the festival. This large foodborne outbreak had been heralded by a smaller outbreak of shigellosis among staff shortly before the festival began and by continued transmission of shigellosis from staff to attendees during the festival. . . . Limited access to soap and running water for hand washing was one of the few sanitary deficits noted at this gathering.[179]

*The Kitchen & Watermelon Tree – 2001*

Of this incident, Bonnie Morris wrote, "[The] county health inspectors praise[d] the festival for its quick response to the crisis," and later determined that the Shigella outbreak was not caused by careless or unsanitary conditions in the Festival's Kitchen.[180] Rather, they attributed the outbreak to a batch of infected tofu delivered to the Festival in its regular food order. The tofu was used in a recipe for uncooked tofu salad, which was served in previous years without incident.

---

[179] L. A. Lee, et all. "An Outbreak of Shigellosis at an Outdoor Music Festival. *American Journal of Epidemiology.* Mar 15,1991; 133 (6), 608-15.
[180] Morris, 151.

What is not generally known by festiegoers is that the reason the Festival gates do not open until one o'clock on Monday, is that county health inspectors are going over the food preparation tables, utensils, kettles, and refrigerator trucks with a fine tooth comb to make sure that everything meets health regulations. Having worked in the Kitchen, I can personally attest to the strict management of food preparation. Each shift is thoroughly supervised by womyn who have been specially trained. Before handling any food, each worker is required to wash her hands in a sanitizing solution, and each time a specific food is chopped, diced, or sliced, the preparation tables and knives are washed in their own sanitizing solution. One time, while I was chopping tomatoes, one of the womyn at my table accidentally cut her finger. While only a single drop of blood hit the table, our supervisor was there immediately, instructing us to push all of the tomatoes into a trashcan and to wash all of our knives and the table with the utensil sterilizer. With over two thousand womyn preparing food during the week, sanitation is a major concern and the Kitchen supervisors take their job very seriously.

So, what does it take to feed so many womyn and children? "A typical recipe of Mixed Vegetables for ten thousand – Michigan Style – combine 1,800 gallons of corn, 1,300 of diced carrots, 1,500 of chopped zucchini, and 300 gallons of parsley – add pepper to taste – about 50 pounds."[181] At early Festivals, dinners included spaghetti, sloppy Josephines, and fireside chili, but today no such fare is on the menu. Contemporary Michigan dinners include Nut Loaf, Moroccan Stew, and Penne Pasta Puttaneca. Of the meals, I will say only this – they are quite healthy. For the vegetarian, I am sure they are delightful and satisfying. However, as a carnivore my mouth watered every time I smelled ribs grilling, or bacon frying on a distant camp-stove. But whatever is on the menu, and regardless of weather conditions, the *Kitchen* produces up to 100,000 meals in a week. It took several years to learn how to cook for thousands of womyn, and several of the womyn I spoke with had terrible stories to tell about the food at the first Festival.

Ro: "I guess I been telling this story since the first time I came. They had some food, and they were gonna try to cook it outdoors. So I went to help. I washed the potatoes. And then somebody came and said, 'wrap all the potatoes up in aluminum foil,' so we all wrapped up the potatoes in aluminum foil. And then somebody else came along and said, 'don't wrap them up in aluminum foil – that's terrible,' so we unwrapped the potatoes from the aluminum foil. And then of course, you know, the first women came back and said something about 'why didn't you wrap the potatoes up in aluminum foil?' And at that point I left. I don't think I had any potatoes. Some friends said they were raw. But you know, everybody was learning what to do. There really

181 Westcot, Margaret, director. *Stolen Moments.* [Video Tape]. (New York: First Run/Icarus films, 1999).

wasn't a lot of food. But you know, I don't remember even being hungry, or what we ate. It wasn't really that important at the time."[182]

Lorraine: "Kathy is a wonderful cook, and so that year they said food would be provided, but we were used to camping on our own, so she brought stuffed artichoke hearts and all this food to eat. Which was a good thing!"

Kathy: "Because the potatoes weren't cooked and neither was the corn. And that's all they had, raw potatoes, raw corn, and watermelon."

Lorraine: "Well they made an attempt to cook it, but they were cooking in a big 55 gallon drum. You know, with a fire under it. But they were cooking for hundreds of women, and they weren't used to it. I remember they made coffee with the loose grinds in the water. I don't even think they strained it. I think they just threw eggshells in it, or cold water, or something. But it was great - it was fun, you know."

Kathy: "It was terrible! Nothing like it is now. Now it's almost gourmet vegetarian."[183]

For some womyn, becoming vegetarian is part of claiming a lesbian identity, which many conceptualize as both a spiritual and political act. The concept revolves around caring for animals, the planet, and the self. But some womyn joke about it. "Becoming vegetarian is just one of the things on the list in the back of lesbian handbook. It's like buying a pair of Birkenstocks, getting a dog, and cutting your hair short."[184] But the issues around food often break down along race and class lines. Morris argued, the issue of food "...also reflects the tension between those who grew up viewing meat as a luxury in the family stew pot and those who put down meat eaters as politically incorrect."[185] For working-class womyn, bringing home the bacon can mean working double shifts at two or more jobs. When these womyn can afford to eat meat, they do not want to be criticized for doing so.

For the vegetarian and non-vegetarian, food is a political issue, but each group is free to eat as much or as little of the Festival food as they want. For those wanting meat, they are free to bring and cook their own. However, these womyn have to prepare for two possibilities. The first is that they might have to endure insulting comments from vegetarians who pass by and smell meat cooking. The second is that they might run short on meat because they invite womyn to join them, who "just stop to smell."

## The Stages

Finally, Bobbie and I came to the *Acoustic Stage* at the end of *Lois Lane*. We had passed the other two professional stages, *Day Stage* (located next to the *Crafts Bazaar*) and the *Night Stage* (located next to the *Kitchen*). In 1979, the first

---

[182] Ro Rasmussen. Personal Interview. August, 2002.
[183] Lorraine Alexis and Kathy Davis. Personal Interview. August, 2002.
[184] Suzanne Westenhoefer. *Hilarith: The Best of Lesbian Humor*. Uproar Entertainment; Unabridged edition (October 1, 1999).
[185] Morris, 157.

*Day Stage* was set up near the *Kitchen*, but initially it was nothing more than a pallet and a small PA system. [186] However, by 1990 it had grown large enough to host its own comedy lineup, and by 2004 it accommodated Michigan's first circus performance.

*Day Stage*

*Night Stage*

*August Night Café Stage*

*Acoustic Stage*

In 1984, the *Acoustic Stage* was built at the bottom of a curving hillside that made it a natural amphitheater. Our first year at the Festival, Bobbie and I were lucky enough to see Cris Williamson's return to the Michigan stage after 15 years. I will never forget the *Acoustic Stage* audience rising to their feet when Cris began singing her landmark song, "The Changer and the Changed." Released in 1975, this song titled the first women's music album to sell 250,000 copies. To this day, "The Changer and the Changed" remains a legend in the women's music industry, and even though I was still unfamiliar with women's music, I felt very honored and privileged to have heard Cris perform.

Another performer we particularly enjoyed at the *Acoustic Stage* was Alix Olson, whose "slam poetry" style presented a radical feminist message that was both exciting and inspiring. We sat motionless, completely captivated by this young womyn's performance as she shouted out the defiant lyrics to her piece called "Daughter."

---

[186] Sandstrom, 109.

I'll teach my daughter to bang on anything that makes a beat.
She'll shake-a-boom, she'll quake a room.
She'll paint her cheeks warrior-style,
smile, beguile you.
Turn your inside out till your guts plead guilty,
She'll be built like a truck,
Built to work you down as she works herself up.
She'll make holes in the streets in her ten inch spikes,
In combat boots, stilts, on roller wheels.
She'll stroll through male pride – Amazon babes at her side.
She'll insist on apologies twice the size of his offense, and for
other Women she'll relinquish her privilege, observe, and be
wise.[187]

The defiance in Alix's slam poetry was quite new to Bobbie and I, and it excited us in a way no other poetry had done. Alix's rhythm and almost militant tone gave us a sense of pride in who we were, in being lesbians. For generations, lesbianism was narrated by patriarchal institutions as immoral and perverse, but in those few moments Alix Olson redefined all that and constructed a narrative of lesbian power, justice, and wisdom. Suddenly, the lesbian was a superhero Amazon warrior, standing strong against male pride and privilege, and using words like a sword to slay the oppressor. But as powerful as Alix's act was, it was just the warm up for the thrilling performance to come during the opening ceremony at the *Night Stage*.

The *Night Stage* is located in a meadow encircled by thick woods. It is the largest stage and audience arena on the Land. If they attend no other concert during the week, almost every womyn at the Festival will attend the opening ceremony on Wednesday night. According to Boden Sandstrom, the 10th anniversary celebration, in 1985, "marked the beginning of formalized opening ceremonies at Michigan. It was during this Festival that certain elements started coalescing as ritual components of the ceremony – singing the song *Amazon*, greetings to the Festival from women in their native languages representing different cultures, and a formal blessing of the Land and participants."[188]

Although each opening ceremony since the 10th anniversary has included these ritual elements, the themes and types of performances change each year. One year, skydivers parachuted into the *Night Stage* bowl. Another year, giant puppets floated over the audience. In other years, there have been fireworks, trapeze acts, fire eaters, and huge Maypole dances. In the 2001 opening ceremony, Elvira Kurt responded to the rumors that women from the American Family Association (a Christian Right organization) had infiltrated the Festival. From the *Night Stage*, she "gave a memorable comedy performance in

---

[187] www.alixolson.com/lyrics/BLT_daughter.html.
[188] Sandstrom, 193-194.

which she cited the 'Top Ten Ways to Spot an Infiltrator at Michigan.' Some ways included; "the infiltrators are the only women who have eaten festival food all week, and are still constipated. They are the only festiegoers who have a tarp made of gingham. And they are the only ones who think the sound of a 'super orgasm' coming from the woods is an animal noise."[189]

Although Kurt's "top ten" list was funny, Bonnie Morris argued that infiltrators are "regrettable" because not only do threats come from within radical factions of the lesbian, gay, bisexual, and transgender community, but from "right-wing religious groups. State family-values groups continue to probe the festival and its bulletin-board Internet communities for any proof of 'child welfare endangerment' (casual public sex or illegal drug use on the land), so today's festiegoers are warned not to create conditions under which conservative infiltrators – who do exist! – could move in swiftly and shut things down forever. This concern has placed limits on some of the more provocative workshops on sexuality, but it has also re-opened serious dialogue about what public behaviors are appropriate when so many children and adolescents are present with their moms."[190] Because of accusations made by the religious right, in 2002 the State's Attorney scheduled a tour during the Festival to see what children were being exposed to. What he saw convinced him that the charges brought by the American Family Association were unwarranted, and dropped them immediately.

As well as humorous commentary from the MC, the opening ceremony often becomes a platform where feminist opposition to current political events is demonstrated. Such was the case in 2002, after the beginning of the war in Iraq. During that ceremony, womyn clad in black and carrying giant black hands made of cardboard, rose from the audience. The words "No War" and "Peace" in several languages, including Arabic and Hebrew, were painted in white on the palms of the hands. From the stage, drummers and dancers pounded out a chant of "NO WAR!" During every set change that night, Bitch and Animal (a duo of popular Michigan performers), drummed out different verses of their song "The Revolution." From the stage they told the Michigan audience that "the revolution would not be televised," and that "Bush, Ashcroft, and Chaney, are not our big strong daddies, protecting us from terrorism while they terrorize the world."[191] Even the traditional lyrics of "Amazon" were changed that night to include a chorus of "No more war in my name!" That year, antiwar themes played on each of the three stages and their audiences responded with militant approval.

However, when Bobbie and I walked into the *Night Stage* bowl on our first tour of the Land, we had no idea what to expect in terms of politics or

[189] Karla Mantilla. "The Michigan Womyn's Music Festival: Another World." *Off Our Backs: The Feminist Newsjournal.* Oct. 2001, Vol XXXI, number 9, 41.
[190] Bonnie J. Morris. "At the Michigan Womyn's Music Fest." *The Gay & Lesbian Review.* Sept.- Oct., 2003.
[191] Bitch and Animal. "The Revolution." Quoted from their stage performance at the 2002 Michigan Womyn's Music Festival.

performance. Supposedly, the Michigan Womyn's Music Festival was about music. At least that was what I understood at the beginning of my research. Lesbian feminists had built the women's music industry in the 1970s because as Bonnie Morris claimed, "talented women discovered that few performance venues welcomed 'chicks' at all, particularly if their dress and political message called for female resistance to sexual objectification."[192] Lesbian feminists built the stages at Michigan so womyn like Alix Dobkin, Maxine Feldman, Holly Near, Cris Williamson, Meg Christian, and Sweet Honey in the Rock could sing the stories of womyn's lives and the political consciousness they were generating in the interstices of dominant culture. But most of all, womyn built these stages so they could "hear the sound of lesbian culture."[193] These stages became a place where womyn could stand together and say, "*This* is my tribe. And *this* is its music."[194]

But where was the music? So far, the only music Bobbie and I had heard was out on the road. As we stood there in the *Night Stage* bowl, there were no artists warming up on stage, no spotlights creating a carnival atmosphere, no "women's music" pulsing through the speakers. Why did the Festival open its gates on Monday if the "opening ceremony" was not until Wednesday night? If these stages were so important, where were the performers? If *music* was the reason some six thousand womyn had come to Michigan, where was it? Why couldn't we hear it?

Standing there in the empty *Night Stage* bowl so many years ago, I did not know how to interpret the Michigan Womyn's Music Festival. There was no one there to explain my strange feeling of connection; no one except the tree frogs and crickets, who started croaking and chirping as the sun dipped below the trees. Then suddenly, as Bobbie and I turned to leave, I saw something standing out against the tree line. It was a statue of some kind. As we walked over to take a closer look, we saw a web of yarn surrounding her; an Amazon goddess carved from a tree trunk. Mythic symbols covered her body, and on the ground before her feet, womyn had left offerings of candles, perfume, chocolate, feathers, beads, and small bits of change. She seemed to be standing guard over the Land and the womyn who had prayed at her feet.

It was then I began to suspect that Michigan involved more than women's music and feminist politics. There was obviously another consciousness at work on the Land, but what was it? How did it connect to lesbian feminists' political consciousness? What did it mean in the context of women's music? I had no answers at that time, but later during the opening ceremony I began to understand that an *Amazon consciousness* had shaped the landscape and culture of the Michigan Womyn's Music Festival.

---

[192] Morris, 3-4.
[193] Ibid., 1.
[194] Ibid.

*Goddess Carving at the Night Stage – 2001*

## (⚔) 3 (⚔)
# Embodying Amazon Consciousness

The myth of the Amazons has stirred the imaginations of writers since the ancient Greeks, but during the 1970s lesbians claimed the Amazons as their own, and looked to them as a symbolic source of female strength, courage, tenacity, self-sufficiency, and unity. Lesbians also claimed the mythology as historical precedent for creating their own contemporary womyn-only matriarchal culture. They looked to scholars like Helen Diner, Merlin Stone, and Marija Gimbutas for historical and archeological evidence to support their ideas.[195] For instance, in her book *Mothers and Amazons: The First Feminine History of Culture*, Diner told readers of "two foci of the Amazon system: Northwest Africa and the Black Sea region around the Thermodon River."[196]

Amazons of the Thermodon were "bestial" in battle, but when victorious, their "gentleness and foresight earned them the adoration of the vanquished."[197] Diner wrote, "The entire Ionian tradition refers to [Amazons] as the founders of cities and sanctuaries. Their tradition was maintained uninterruptedly by temples, graves, cities, and whole countries."[198] According to Diner, Amazons denied men "in order to unite the two fundamental forms of life in paradisiacal harmony," at a point in time when "the issue was which of the two forms of life [male or female] was to shape European civilization in its image."[199] Though vanquished by the Greeks, Diner claimed that "all of Hellas permitted itself to be impregnated by the spiritual image of the mannish Amazons. Every art was suddenly big in their nature. Their expulsion began their omnipresence."[200]

Lesbians also looked to feminist utopian fictions for contemporary images of Amazons and matriarchal cultures. As discussed earlier, feminist

---

[195] Each of these scholars either wrote specifically on Amazons or pre-patriarchal cultures. Donald Sobol. *The Amazons in Greek Society*. (London: Barns, 1972). Helen Diner. *Mothers and Amazons: The First Feminine History of Culture*. (New York: Anchor Books, 1973). Marija Gimbutas. *Goddesses and Gods of Old Europe, 6500-3500 BC.* (Berkeley: University of California Press, 1974). Merlin Stone. *When God Was a Woman.* (New York: Harvest Books, 1976).
[196] Helen Diner. *Mothers and Amazons: The First Feminine History of Culture.* (New York: Anchor Books, 1973), 97.
[197] Ibid., 99.
[198] Ibid., 99.
[199] Ibid., 101-105.
[200] Ibid., 105.

utopian fictions were highly influential during the 1970s, but none more so than the rediscovered works of Charlotte Perkins Gilman. Gilman wrote *Herland* in 1915, as a serial for her monthly magazine, *The Forerunner.* When it was rediscovered in the mid-1970s, *Herland* became a classic text in feminist utopian literature. However, had Gilman written it when it was finally published in book form (1979), the Michigan Womyn's Music Festival might have very well been her inspiration.

Gilman described the country of *Herland* as pristine woodland with manicured forests and orchards, inhabited by only women who "had eliminated not only certain masculine characteristics, …but so much of what we had always thought essentially feminine."[201] Yet the three men telling the story of Herland found that the women they encountered in this ideal world were much stronger, faster, and more intelligent than they were. After learning that they could self-procreate, the women of *Herland* developed a culture that revolved around motherhood and producing stronger, more intelligent, better children with each generation.

In *Herland* the women had no concept of private ownership of property or children. "To them the country was a unit – it was theirs. They themselves were a unit, a conscious group; they thought in terms of the community. As such, their time-sense was not limited to the hopes and ambitions of an individual life. Therefore, they habitually considered and carried out plans for improvement which might cover centuries."[202] Improvements for the women of *Herland* included the "deliberate replanting of an entire forest" with trees that produced fruit all year.[203] Herlanders also did away with raising cattle for food, which was not an environmentally sound practice. In addition, they adopted a female deity. "The religion they had to begin with was much like that of old Greece – a number of gods and goddesses; but they lost all interest in deities of war and plunder, and gradually centered on their Mother Goddess altogether."[204] While most utopians concerned themselves with creating new social worlds, Gilman was concerned with creating a new consciousness and how women, when in a separate physical world, would embody such a consciousness.

For lesbians in the 1970s, the Amazon became a symbolic way to embody their oppositional consciousness. They resurrected her image in lesbian art, music, and literature. Collectively, images of the Amazon in these forms reshaped and redefine how many lesbians conceptualized their own identities and the culture they were actively creating. At the Festival, the Amazon is memorialized in songs like "Amazon." Her images are scattered across the landscape in Festival arts and crafts, and womyn wear her symbols on

[201] Charlotte Perkins Gilman. *Herland.* (New York: Pantheon Books, 1979), 57.
[202] Gilman, 79.
[203] Ibid.
[204] Ibid., 59.

their bodies in the form of Amazon costumes, jewelry, and tattoos. Through symbol, myth, and ritual, womyn embody an Amazon consciousness because she represents all that the patriarchal world denies contemporary womyn. But nowhere is she more embodied than in the opening ceremony.

**The Opening Ceremony**

By the time Bobbie and I went to the opening ceremony on Wednesday night, the *Night Stage* bowl was nearly full. Thousands of womyn had already staked out their places by spreading out blankets and unfolding their chairs. We stopped to check the "Seating Etiquette" chart in the program before negotiating the walkways between the politically correct areas for smoking and no smoking, Chem ok and Chem free, DART and Deaf seating.

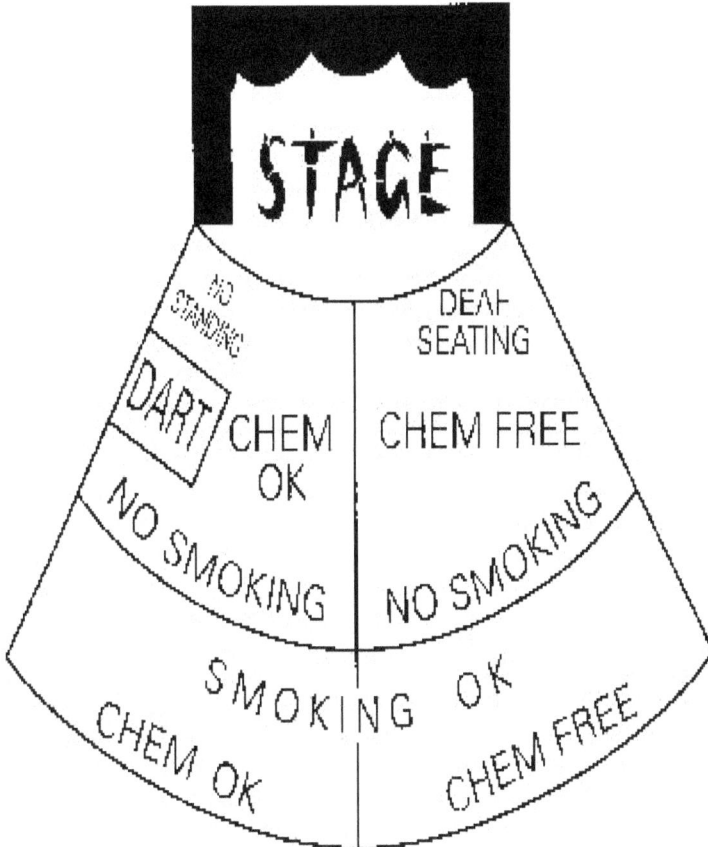

*Night Stage Seating Chart*[205]

---

[205] 2001 Michigan Womyn's Music Festival Program.

Across the field, next to the tree line, several womyn were tossing around Frisbees and gathering in circles to play hackie sack. Up near the stage, womyn sitting in low folding chairs tried to keep a giant beach ball in motion above their heads. It bounced from hand to hand across the bowl. We heard a bunch of them laugh when one womyn fell over backward after reaching too far back to bat the ball. At the back of the seating areas, a few womyn were playing catch with a softball, while others practiced Ti Chi. Bobbie and I unfolded our chairs and joined the vast majority who were just chatting with friends and people-watching. As we sat there surveying the crowd, it was the first time we were able to get a real sense of just how many womyn were on the Land. From the back of the bowl, we could see that there were thousands of them playing, laughing, chatting, and passing around bags of munchies and cans of beer.

*Opening Ceremony - 2001*

Then suddenly a sound like distant thunder rolled out from the stage. The opening ceremony was starting. Just a low, slow rumble at first. The vibration of the drums pulsed through the audience, causing everyone to settle down. Then the rhythm began to oscillate. Loud and fast, then soft and slow, up and down the beat of the drums coursed through the audience like a roller coaster that finally came to an abrupt stop with a crashing crescendo. The audience exploded with applause. A few seconds later, a womyn dressed in white walked to center stage and lifted her arms in greeting. "Hello," she said softly so the audience would quiet down. Then she gently continued:

> I'm here to remind you of other things, your ability to vision other things. So I'd like you to stand with me. And those of you who can't, just make sure your feet are flat on the ground. I'm also gonna ask you to take the hand of the person next to you and close your eyes. And I'm asking you to remember all the times you've been in this place, and what visions and

energy you have produced. Once you're there, I'm going to sing a prayer to you. [Womyn in the audience rose, and took each other's hands. They bowed their heads, closed their eyes, and after a few moments the woman on stage sang out in a low, soft voice]. I am listening to the Holy Spirit. Oh what a song, she is singing. And I listen all day long. As I listen, my faith is strong. Oh ya hey ah. Oh ya hey ah, hallelujah.[206]

After she concluded her blessing, the audience remained motionless for a few seconds. Then they erupted in another round of thunderous applauds. When they finished and took their seats again, womyn from several nations took the stage. Speaking in their mother tongues, they greeted the audience. "Welcome to the 26th annual Michigan Womyn's Music Festival" they shouted in Navajo, German, Japanese, French, Spanish, Russian, Italian, Hebrew, and American Sign Language. By the time all of them had offered their international greetings, the sun had sunk below the tree line at the back of the bowl.

Then, a group of musicians took the stage and began strumming out the first few cords of "Amazon."

Amazon Women Rise.
Amazon women weavin' rainbows in the sky.
Amazon women fly. Amazon women fly.
I am, and once was called Amazon.
Now I am called Lesbian.
I know the matriarchy ruled back then.
Sister, the matriarchy's gonna rule again.
I once knew you from a long, long time ago.
Aren't you the women who came knockin' on my door?
Aren't you the women who practice the craft of the wise?
Priestess and warriors step right on in, step right on in.
The Goddess has not forsaken me.
She's just reawakenin' in you and me.
Heal yourselves, practice your craft of the wise.
Amazon nation is about to rise.
Amazon witches have returned from the flame.
And we will dance; we will dance in our moon circles once again. We will dance because we've known each other and loved each other in our past. Amazon nation is rising at last.
Amazon Women Rise.
Amazon women weavin' rainbows in the sky.
Amazon women fly. Amazon women fly. [207]

---

[206] Akiba Onada-Sikwoia. Blessing at the Opening Ceremony of the Michigan Womyn's Music Festival.
[207] Maxine Feldman, "Amazon."

Instantly the womyn in the audience were back on their feet, lifting their hands in the air, and swaying to the rhythm. "Amazon women rise," they sang in unison. "Amazon women weavin' rainbows in the sky." Suddenly I flashed back to my women's studies class and felt the same surge of emotion that brought me to tears so long ago. Back then, I had only heard one verse of the song, but now I was hearing it in its entirety, and the tears were flowing again.

*Audience Dancing to "Amazon" 2007*

Like any symbol, the image of the Amazon has the power to communicate a meta-ideology. What I did not know before attending my first opening ceremony was that the song had become legendary, with a rich history dating back to the very first Festival. Each year since 1976, various artists have sung the song, but in 1985 "Amazon" became exclusively linked with the opening ceremony as a way to communicate the collective matriarchal values embedded in the culture created at Michigan. Boden Sandstrom wrote "the opening celebration creates an imagined world that for a brief moment engenders a feeling of one identity among the multiple identities that each woman brings with her to the Festival."[208]

The sense of unity in the opening ceremony is indeed powerful. Chela Sandoval theorized that events like it create an environment where participants "move through one layer of...relationship and into another, 'artificial,' or self-

---

[208] Sandstrom, 183.

consciously manufactured ideology and back again..."[209]  During the opening ceremony, the apparatus of love constructed three ritual elements (blessing, international greeting, and singing "Amazon").  These elements not only maintain the ceremony's continuity over time, but they move womyn's consciousness out of a system that separates them from each other and into a matrix of meaning that connects them.

As I wiped the tears from my face, the womyn sitting next to me noticed.  I made a little shrug, indicating my embarrassment.  She leaned over and gently touched my arm.  "It's ok," she said with a warm smile, "this is our heritage you know."  Wiping more tears, I nodded as if I understood what she meant.  But at the time I was not sure that I did, at least not on a conscious level.  Then she pointed to the tree line at the back of the bowl and said "Look."  I turned to see where she was pointing.  Suddenly, I felt like I had been transported into the mists of an ancient past.  There, along the tree line, living Amazons emerged from the woods.

Standing tall and proud, they seemed like sentinels guarding the audience.  Their bodies exuded strength and power, no matter their size or stature.  Dressed in leather, they appeared raw and feral, while at the same time their bare breasts gave them an aura of dignity and sovereignty.  A few wore Celtic symbols on their armbands, while others had feathers tied in their hair.  Most of them also wore labrys tattoos or necklaces.  Their commanding carriage and confident bearing immediately captured my imagination.  Were they part of the performance of the song?

Most of the womyn in the audience did not seem to notice the Amazons, or if they did, they did not give them any special attention.  They just kept on swaying back and forth as they sang "Amazon women rise.  Amazon women weavin' rainbows in the sky."  But I watched carefully, waiting with anticipation to see the Amazons take the stage.  After a few minutes though, as the last cords of the song reverberated over the trees and a thunderous applause rose from the audience, it was clear that they were not part of the performance.  One by one, the Amazons spotted friends in the audience and drifted off to sit with them.

So why had these womyn dressed like Amazons for the opening ceremony?  Did their costumes represent a personal performance, something like the gender performances Judith Butler theorized?[210]  If so, what did their performance signify?  What consciousness did the Amazon costume embody?

As argued earlier, part of the Festival's staying power was its ability to generate a new cultural matrix that nurtures and strengthens womyn inside the Festival, as well as sustain them on the outside from August to August.  Part of this cultural matrix evolved out of what I am calling an Amazon consciousness.  This type of consciousness develops in the interstices, when womyn realize their

---

[209] Sandoval, 111.
[210] Judith Butler. *Gender Trouble.* (New York: Routledge, 1999).

own subordination and oppression in the patriarchal culture, and then seek ways to both survive and resist its rigid ideologies and institutions. In the interstices, this consciousness generates new images and narratives to explain itself to itself. Gloria Anzaldua talked about her Mestiza consciousness, that evolved in the borderland where she was cultureless because she challenged the collective patriarchal beliefs of both Indo-Hispanics and Anglos.

*Amazons – 2005*

"Yet," Anzaldua wrote, "I am cultured because I am participating in the creation of yet another culture, a new story to explain the world and our participation in it, a new value system with images and symbols that connect us to each other and to the planet."[211] In a world that marginalizes womyn and their relationships, abuses their minds and their bodies, and trivializes their visions and dreams, womyn develop an oppositional consciousness in order to survive. But when they come to Michigan, their oppositional consciousness transforms into an Amazon consciousness that does more than survive – it thrives.

Barbara Myerhoff described this process as a "transformation of consciousness" that causes a "major and lasting change: in structure, appearance, character of function. One becomes something else, and since we are emphasizing consciousness, we must add, one has an altered state of consciousness, a new perception of oneself or one's socio/physical world, a conversion in awareness, belief, sentiment, knowledge, understanding; a revised

---

[211] Anzaldua, 102-103.

and enduring emergent state of mind and emotion."[212]   This process of transformation was described by Anzaldua when she wrote that the Mestiza "is willing to share, to make herself vulnerable to foreign ways of seeing and thinking.  She surrenders all notions of safety, of the familiar.  Deconstruct, construct.  She becomes a *nahual*, able to transform herself into a tree, a coyote, into another person."[213]   At the Festival, womyn transform into Amazons and their altered state of consciousness helps them believe they are connected to an ancient heritage and culture that gives their lives meaning and purpose.  And in order to manifest the "change in structure, appearance, and character of function," they use the tools of symbol, myth, and ritual to create a new matriarchal Amazon culture.

These contemporary Amazons used what Chela Sandoval called, "technologies necessary to [those] who are interested in renegotiating postmodern first world cultures, with what we might call a sense of their own power and integrity intact."[214]   The symbol of the Amazon re-narrates the integrity of womyn's lives and empowers them to use the tool of love to do the work of building a matriarchal culture.  As Sandoval describes it, this is "the work of (1) 'semiology' for reading the signs of power, concomitant with (2) the 'mythology' used to *deconstruct* those sign-systems, while (3) creating new, 'higher' levels of signification built onto the older, dominant forms of ideology in a radical process I call 'meta-ideologizing' are three emancipatory technologies capable of restoring consciousness to history.  This manipulation of one's own consciousness through stratified zones of form and meaning requires the desire and the ability to move through one layer of …relationship and into another, 'artificial,' or self-consciously manufactured ideology and back again, movement that is (4) differential.  Indeed, it is this differential movement . . . that allows consciousness to challenge its own perimeters from within ideology."[215]   The rest of this chapter explores how contemporary Amazons use the technologies of "semiology," "mythology," "meta-ideologizing," and "differential movement" to read and deconstruct dominant meanings, and more specifically how they use differential movement (ritual) to create a new image (symbol) and a meta-ideology (myth) that embodies their consciousness and sustains them in a matriarchal culture.

## Symbol

In her study of lesbian feminists, Arlene Stein argued that creating symbols was an important part of the "identity work" women do to "signal

---

[212] Barbara Myerhoff. "The Transformation of Consciousness in Ritual Performances: Some Thoughts and Questions." In *By Means of Performance: Intercultural Studies of Theatre and Ritual.* Richard Schechner and Willa Appel, eds. (New York: Cambridge University Press, 1997), 245.
[213] Anzaldua, 104.
[214] Sandoval, 177.
[215] Ibid., 110-111.

membership in the group to others."[216]  But the symbol of the Amazon does much more that signal group membership; it gives womyn a new identity and a new culture.  When talking with Ro, she told me that "being a womyn, being a lesbian, being an Amazon is a special thing.  And it can help you go places you wouldn't be able to otherwise."[217]  For womyn like Ro, claiming an Amazon identity counters the dominant narrative of shame and guilt associated with lesbianism, and provides a symbol of dignity and confidence they carry with them into their everyday lives outside the Festival.

Ro: "You know, after I came I was able to look men in the eye, in a way that I never had been able to before.  Things were clearer for me in some ways.  I grew up in New York City, and I was always on the subway.  And after I came here, I could look people in the eye.  Men especially.  I noticed that, that looking in the eye – I was able to do that in a different way – not in a challenging way.  Just as a person, not being so afraid."[218]

Even for womyn like Akosua, who do not dress like Amazons or see themselves as warrior priestesses, the symbol is empowering and one that gives her a remarkable sense of self-esteem.  In her interview, Akosua talked about the power of the song "Amazon" and what it meant to her.

Akosua: "It's really important for me to hear that song even though I don't necessarily identify as an Amazon.  For me, it means women rise.  You know we fought really hard battles, and really hard struggles.  So for me, it's just very moving and very empowering to hear that song.  It's really important!  It's really powerful for me to hear that song because it just solidifies your self-worth as a woman.  So I just have to hear that song once each Festival and I'm cool."[219]

For Akosua, the song "Amazon" commemorates womyn's struggles in a way that no other religious or patriotic symbol can.  Yet, for womyn like Kip, the symbol of the Amazon gives their lives a ritual purpose and meaning, and the myth grounds that purpose in history.  When I talked with her, Kip told me that the Amazon is a "shared meaning."

Kip: "Historically, we know from the Gimbutas' research that there were matriarchal tribes.  They were referred to as the Amazons.  Where they got the name, I don't know.  But they traditionally defended themselves.  They were self-sufficient.  And, depending on who ya ask, they either did or didn't visit with the men's tribes.  In my book, they visit.  And this symbol [the tattoo on her shoulder] is a labrys.  That's two labrys' actually, crossed.  The labrys is a short hand ax about that long [holds hands out about shoulder width].  And it has blades on both sides.  It came into use, I don't know the exact date, but about the time the men's tribes were using big broad axes.  And those big broad

---

[216] Stein, 68.
[217] Ro Rasmussen. Personal Interview.  August 2002.
[218] Ibid.
[219] Akosua. Personal Interview.  August, 2005.

axes, the heads were too heavy for most women to swing effectively. Women are better quick, inside fighters. So the hand ax came into being for women because they were lighter. You wore them on your belt – crossed – crossed in front of you so you could pull them when you needed to defend. So that's the symbol of defending the women. When you see a person with crossed axes like that [pointing to the crossed labrys on her shoulder], they're defenders of the women. They consider themselves warriors."[220]

*Labrys Necklace*

For Kip, the Amazon is more than a symbol. Kip is a student of archeology and mythology, and she believes the myth of the Amazon is more than a literary tale. Kip reads the myth as the history womyn share, and she believes contemporary lesbians embody the legacy left by the ancient Amazon.

Katherine Hagedorn observed this same type of phenomena in her study of Afro-Cuban's use of Santeria to construct a national identity, which meant that those wanting to be included in the religion had to redefine themselves and claim a "mythical African heritage."[221] Barbara Myerhoff also described this type of phenomenon as "a transformation of consciousness, in which small groups or communities have profound, subjunctive experiences, whereby a community propels itself into conviction about the truth of its invisible kingdom: an invented, recent culture that is an adaptation to contemporary circumstances. In that work, the persuasive, performative dimension of ritual is seen as highly significant in allowing individuals collectively to experience, perceive and portray their invented common, fictive

[220] Kip Parker. Personal Interview. August, 2003.
[221] Katherine J. Hagedorn. *Divine Utterances: The Performance of Afro-Cuban Santeria.* (Washington: Smithsonian Institution Press, 2001), 147.

reality, to themselves... Here, doing is believing."[222] Womyn at the Festival achieve this "fictive reality" by studying archeologists like Marija Gimbutas and poets like Judy Grahn, and writing their own mythical histories and creating their own symbols and rituals to sustain their meta-ideology.

## Myth

In contemporary patriarchal culture, myth is often conceptualized as something imagined and therefore not real. However, a more critical definition suggests that myths are "traditional stories" based on apparently historical events. These apparent historical events are preserved in myths as ways of communicating larger concepts, world-views, and even personal life-lessons and morals. Mythmaking was a prominent feature of womyn's culture in the 1970s and 1980s. Author and activist Elana Dykewomon recalled being told "what makes a people cohere, was a sense of common cultural origin, a creation myth."[223] She wrote that an early version of the Amazon myth went something like:

> Once the world was organized into matriarchal tribes that were more or less peaceful; the women controlled the means of reproduction and did most of the labor; men hunted and engaged each other in the testosterone-driven rites of passage. At some point, those rights of passage became battles for territory and rebellions against 'the mother'; Amazon tribes rose up to fight the patriarchal tide, but lost. If you go into the Metropolitan Museum in New York, one of the worlds' 'great' museums, at the top of the marble staircase stands a statue – the first piece of art a visitor would notice. The statue is Perseus holding the head of Gorgon – white male Greece in triumph over the African Amazon. The rest is *his*tory.[224]

Womyn who feel disconnected from patriarchal histories use the technology of myth making to narrate a different history; one which gives them a sense of belonging to both a people and a place. For instance, in the *The Planting Rite: Book 1 of the Rememberer's Tale*, Kip creates a shared history for womyn by weaving their life circumstances into a relationship with a Goddess worshiping Amazonian past:

> But these books are not intended to be the story of a writer. They are the story of a race. My race. Maybe yours, too. Only fragments of pottery and little fat female statues remain for our scholars, like Gimbutas and Monaghan, to try and piece

---

[222] Myerhoff, "The Transformation of Consciousness in Ritual Performance: Some Thoughts and Questions," 248.
[223] Elana Dykewomon. "Lesbian Quarters: On Building Space, Identity, Institutional Memory and Resources," *Journal of Lesbian Studies* 9, no. 1/2 (2005): 32.
[224] Ibid., 33.

together. But aside from the archaeological fragments, there are also fragments of memory. Memory that flirts with us in the dark at the Michigan night stage. Memory that make us all want to stand together and howl when the moon is round on rocky hills in Ireland or Germany. Memory that make us create theories about who and what we are channeling. Racial memory perhaps? Maybe. Maybe one day, with a few helpful hints, we will all remember. May the Great Bear Mother grant it.[225]

What Kip recognizes is that all histories are constructed, mutable myths. As an Amazon, Kip uses the same process of myth making that the Mestiza does. Gloria Anzaldua wrote that the Mestiza "…puts history through a sieve, winnows out the lies, looks at the forces that we as a race, as women, have been a part of. This step is a conscious rupture with all oppressive traditions of all cultures and religions. She communicates that rupture, documents the struggle. She reinterprets history and, using new symbols, she shapes new myths."[226] In Kip's mythology, a matriarchal Amazon culture will rise in the memories of modern womyn, who will embody the wholeness of the female archetype as they revive their ancient Goddess traditions.

In her discussion of the patriarchal co-optation of the feminine archetype, Janice Hocker Rushing argued that during the rise of the patriarchy, the female archetype was drawn and quartered into four parts; the pure virgin, the good mother, the harlot, and the devouring mother.[227] This quartering of the divine female served three purposes. First, it ensured women would lose their autonomy because these images of women were only meaningful in their relationship to male images. Second, three of the female images only served male pleasures. "Appearing as Mother, Virgin, and Mistress, the feminine is, thus, defined in relation to masculine needs and desires and also in terms of mutually exclusive roles…"[228] Finally, the images of the harlot and the devouring mother constructed a mechanism of social control, whereby women monitored their own behavior for fear of losing male patronage. "In order to be suitable and limited to continuing a patriarchal family lineage, a good woman had to be a good breeder and limit the use of her body to her lord whose property she was to be."[229] This fact reminded me of the young trans inclusion supporters, who seem afraid of appearing "transphobic" and losing their connections to trans-women, who by their very presentation uphold the dominate patriarchal image of what it is to be feminine (and in most cases, ultra feminine).

---

[225] Kip Parker. *The Planting Rite: Book 1 of the Rememberer's Tales.* (Philadelphia: Xlibris, 2002), 1.

[226] Anzaldua, 104.

[227] Rushing, "Evolution of 'The New Frontier' in *Alien* and *Aliens*: Patriarchal Co-optation of the Feminine Archetype," 98-99.

[228] Rushing, 96.

[229] Ibid., 99.

These female images, as Alison Futrell claims, form the foundation of gender constructed in contemporary American culture. "Popular wisdom tells us that it is among the ancients – their symbols, standards, and traditions – that we find the fundamental institutions of Western civilization." [230] Yet for many, these archetypes, as well as the patriarchal history that constructed them, fail to provide stable meanings in an ever-changing world. According Craig Detweiler and Barry Taylor, "Mythology has arisen as the crying need of a world in which the facts have lost their power."[231] This crying need is satisfied at the Michigan Womyn's Music Festival by narrating the myth and embodying the symbol of the Amazon. Her symbol gives these womyn a sense of self-worth and dignity that patriarchal myths and gender construction cannot.

In workshops at Michigan, writers and poets like Judy Grahn teach that Amazons were legendary city builders. In her book, *Another Mother Tongue*, Grahn described two tribes of Amazons, one Black and the other white:

> Historically, there were two distinct groups of Amazon people on the European and African continents. The oldest were Libyan, in Northwest Africa; some stories connect them to the continent of Atlantis, off the coast of Africa. They were known not only as warriors but as founders of cities. One well-known queen, Myrina, took her wandering army on a tremendous trek across North Africa, through Egypt, up through the islands of Greece and around the coast of Anatolia, establishing cities. Throughout the northern areas there were local monuments, called "Amazoneia," established by local people who hailed them as liberators and told legends about their adventures.[232]

Grahn's narrative is based on the work of scholar, Donald Sobol. Sobol suggested that the Amazons date to around 3000 B.C. and that the word "Amazon" was created "from a Phoenician word meaning 'Motherlord.'"[233] Grahn's narrative suggests that when the African Amazons reached the area around the Black Sea, they passed on their traditions to white women who later became mythologized in Greek legends. She wrote, "The Amazons characteristically ruled with a two-queen system; one queen was in charge of the army and battle campaigns, the other staying behind to administer the cities."[234] An imaginative interpretation of this system meant that Amazons based their

---

[230] Alison Futrell. "The Baby, the Mother, and the Empire: Xena as Ancient Hero." Frances Early and Kathleen Kennedy, eds. *Athena's Daughters: Television's New Women Warriors*. (Syracuse: Syracuse University Press, 2003), 13.

[231] Graig Detweiler and Barry Taylor, Barry. *A Matrix of Meaning: Finding God in Popular Culture*. (Grand Rapids: Baker Academic, 2003), 303-304.

[232] Judy Grahn. *Another Mother Tongue: Gay Worlds, Gay Words*. (Boston: Beacon Press, 1984), 170-171.

[233] Donald Sobol. *The Amazons in Greek Society*. (London: Barns, 1972), 161. Cited from Grahn, Another Mother Tongue: Gay Worlds, Gay Words, 171.

[234] Grahn, 171.

culture on the principle of "collective" rule. Although, at the time, it may not have been a conscious choice for women's culture to mimic the Amazon system, several women's institutions did in fact form collectives to govern their various projects. Some of these collectives included Olivia Records, *Lesbian Connection, Off Our Backs*, and finally the We Want the Music Collective, which gave birth to the Michigan Womyn's Music Festival.

Yet power sharing systems and women's building projects were not the only characteristics shared between modern womyn and ancient Amazons. Others were even more ideologically useful. For instance, the image of African Amazons as warriors, liberators, and builders of cities offered African-American womyn powerful counter images to those of slaves and mammies. These images also helped white womyn conceptualize a common heritage with Black womyn, and even to see them as mythological ancestors.

One of the favorite sources for authenticating the myth for womyn at the Festival is the archeological work of Marija Gimbutas. Gimbutas studied pottery and used the term "Old Europe" to distinguish the years between 6500 and 3500 B.C.E., which she argued were the years that a matriarchal culture "built magnificent tomb-shrines and temples, comfortable houses in moderately-sized villages, and created superb pottery and sculpture. This was a long-lasting period of remarkable creativity and stability, an age free of strife. Their culture was a culture of art."[235] Gimbutas claimed this culture was "matrifocal, sedentary, peaceful, art-loving, earth and sea-bound."[236]

Amazon type cultures have been documented in many places around the world. For instance, when reporting on the Tupinamba Indians of Brazil in the fourteenth century, Pedro de Magalhaes de Gandavo wrote, "there are some Indian women who determine to remain chaste: these have no commerce with men in any manner, nor would they consent to it even if refusal meant death. . . They wear their haircut in the same way as the men, and go to war with bows and arrows and pursue games, each has a woman to serve her, to whom she says she is married, and they treat each other and speak with each other as man and wife."[237]

Of this report, anthropologist Water L. Williams wrote, "Gandavo and other explorers like Orellana were evidently so impressed with this group of women that they named the river which flowed through that area the River of the Amazons after the ancient Greek legend of women warriors."[238] Williams, as well as other anthropologists like Evelyn Blackwood and Saskia E. Wieringa, have furnished several accounts of Amazonian type women among Native

---

[235] Marija Gimbutas. *The Language of the Goddess.* (San Francisco: Harper and Row, 1989), 321.

[236] Marija Gimbutas. "Women and Culture in Goddess-Oriented Old Europe." In *Weaving the Vision: New Patterns in Feminist Spirituality.* Judith Plaskow and Carol P. Christ, eds. (San Francisco: Harper and Row, 1989), 63.

[237] Pedro de Magalhaes De Gandavo, "History of the Province of Santa Cruz." In *Documents and Narratives Concerning the Discovery and Conquest of Latin America: The Histories of Brazil.* John Stetson, ed. 2(1922):89.

[238] Walter L. Williams. *The Spirit and the Flesh: Sexual Diversity in American Indian Cultures.* (Boston: Beacon Press, 1992), 233.

American and Malaysian, as well as African and European cultures.[239]  It would seem that several cultures around the world had their own versions of Amazon cultures, and the womyn at the Festival interpret all of these as lesbian cultures.

For most womyn at the Festival, the image of the Amazon is important because, as a myth, she is both mutable and immutable.  As womyn challenged dominant concepts of gender and sexuality, and demonstrated the mutability of both, a paradox emerged.  How could they build an identifiable "women's culture" on something as unreliable as gender or sexuality?  "To put the matter simply," as Colleen Lamos wrote, "lesbianism can be seen, nearly simultaneously, as the purest form of female identification and as the wholesale rejection of all that is feminine.  The lesbian may at once stand as the woman par excellence and as not a woman at all."[240]  If the definitions of "lesbian" or "woman" were so negotiable, how could either serve to fix a recognizable culture in space or time?  Sally Moore wrote about this same kind of paradox in her own work on symbol, myth, and ritual.  "Every explicit attempt to fix social relationships or social symbols is by implication recognition that they are mutable.  Yet at the same time such an attempt directly struggles against mutability, attempts to fix the moving thing, to make it hold.  Part of the process of trying to fix social reality involves representing it as stable or immutable, or at least controllable to this end, at least for a time.[241]  For women's culture, and particularly the Amazon culture at the Michigan Womyn's Music Festival, the fact that the Amazon was mythical meant that she could entertain and encompass the paradox, while at the same time providing a relatively stable identity for the culture.

In her work on identity construction, Arlene Stein wrote that those who have a "long-term investment in a particular self-conception" transform the "narrative templates" of their culture.[242]  In other words, like the trope of "womyn," the Amazon provided a new "narrative template."  She was both woman and lesbian, and at the same time, something else entirely.  And because the Amazon culture was mythic, womyn at the Festival could transform it to meet their own cultural needs.  Barbara Myerhoff found this type of creative culture building among the elderly Jewish immigrants she worked with.  She wrote that, "the culture they had invented to meet their present circumstances in old age was bricolage in the best sense – an assortment of symbols, customs, memories, and rituals blending in a highly ecumenical spirit.[243]  At the Festival, this "bricolage" of Amazon symbols, myths, and rituals is scattered across the landscape.  A campground bears her name and she is reflected in Festival art

[239] Evelyn Blackwood and Saskia E. Evelyn, eds.  *Female Desires: Same-Sex Relations and Transgender Practices Across Culture.* (New York: Columbia University Press, 1999).
[240] Colleen Lamos.  "Sexuality versus Gender: A Kind of Mistake?"  In *Cross-Purposes: Lesbians, Feminists, and the Limits of Alliance.*  Dana Heller, ed. (Bloomington: Indiana University Press, 1997) 45.
[241] Sally F. Moore.  *Secular Ritual.*  (Amsterdam: Van Gorcum, 1977), 41.
[242] Stein, 182.
[243] Myerhoff, "Life Not Death in Venice: Its Second Life," 264.

and campsite décor. Her symbol is inscribed on womyn's bodies in the form of costumes, tattoos, and jewelry. Historically, in women's culture, "ideas were shared and developed in 'Myth-Making Workshops' where womyn were encouraged to view their lives mythically, and thus see themselves as facets of a universal experience."[244]  At Michigan, the Amazon myth is taught in workshops like "Ancient Amazon Survival Skills I, II & III."[245]  But the universal experience of the Amazon begins at the opening ceremony, when she is made visceral as she is embodied in song and dress, and ritual performance.

**Ritual**

The tradition of singing "Amazon" started when its composer Maxine Feldman, one of the original artists in the women's music industry, performed it at the first Michigan Womyn's Music Festival.[246]  In an interview with historian, Bonnie Morris, Feldman said, "I opened the Michigan festival singing "Amazon" until 1989.  I had ruined my vocal cords doing drugs, although I got sober in October 1976, and I had to have polyps removed.  So Rhiannon began singing "Amazon" because I could no longer trust my voice; I was terrified.  But as long as "Amazon" is sung at Michigan, I'm there.  And I got to select the artist to give my baby to.  I talked to Rhiannon, we cried, I wrote the lyrics down for her, and she took off.  Yeah, I cried for another 24 hours without stopping.  But once Rhiannon opened that first note, I felt a burden lift."[247]

In an interview with Boden Sandstrom, Feldman said that she gave the Festival ownership rights to the song at the 10th anniversary celebration because she had no other gift to give except her music.  "I wanted to say that Michigan had meant a lot to me – a lot."[248]  Several of the womyn I spoke with expressed gratitude to Feldman for giving the song to the Festival.  They also talked about how important the song was in their lives, and how it helped them see themselves in a positive way.

Lorraine: "So, 'Amazon Women Rise,' I'd like to give credit to Maxine Feldman because she's the woman who wrote it.  She's just a really dynamic person, and I don't ever know what happened to her, but I'd like to personally thank her because it's a phenomenally strong song!  You know, it has evolved here.  And I know that she had dedicated it, and given it to the festival for its use."[249]

Ro: "Now see, last night they sang Maxine Feldman's 'Amazon Women Rise.'  Maxine singing that song is one of my favorite memories.  It was so great to hear them do it last night.  It's hard to articulate.  Ya see, at the beginning

[244] Jane R. Dickie, Anna Cook, Rachel Gazda, Bethany Martin, Elizabeth Sturrus. "The Heirs of Aradia, Daughters of Diana: Community in the Second and Third Wave," Journal of Lesbian Studies 9, no. 1/2 (2005): 101-102.
[245] 2004 Michigan Womyn's Music Festival Program, 30.
[246] Sandstrom, 193.
[247] Morris, 91.
[248] Sandstrom, 195.
[249] Lorraine Alexis.  Personal Interview.  August, 2002.

there were hardly any songs about loving ourselves, loving another woman, at least not in a positive way. So that's what I meant that women were hungry for that. And I didn't appreciate whoever came up after that and was makin' fun of it. [Reference to stage comic Elvira Kurt's performance of 'Amazon']. Amazon women flyyyyyyy [squeaky voice]. No, don't mess with Maxine with me."[250]

Over the years various artists have interpreted and performed the song differently, but from the beginning of the Festival, artists and audiences both recognized that "Amazon" provided a narrative template for the culture womyn wanted to build. It provided an explanation for what womyn felt they knew on an instinctual level, that they were connected to each other through ancient lineages and traditions, and that their lives had a special meaning. The song satiated womyn's hunger for words to describe their feelings, words that made conscious what was subconscious before, words that helped heal their spirits, words that gave them a vision of how things could be in a matriarchal culture. "Amazon" fed womyn in ways no other song ever had, and they were not willing to let it drift off into oblivion as a golden oldie.

According to Lisa Vogel, ritual specialists Z Budapest, Kay Gardner, and Rhiannon pushed her to recognize womyn's need for ritual in the opening ceremony.[251] Originally, Vogel was worried about all the Goddess imagery that Budapest, Gardner, and Rhiannon were bringing into the ceremony. She was afraid it would offend Jewish and Christian womyn, and she asked them to tone down all the ritualism. Vogel suggested changing the lyrics of "Amazon" that referenced "Amazon witch's return from the flames." In her version, womyn would "see" rainbows in the sky, rather than "weave" them, and the reference to witches would be left out entirely. Furthermore, she wanted to do away with the reference to the "matriarchy," and argued that the line "we ruled back then" would carry the same meaning.[252] The performers fought the changes Vogel wanted to make, by arguing that "changing a belief in a 'matriarchy' to a more generic 'we ruled back then,' made less of a distinction between present day reality and the past."[253] Rhiannon "expressed the importance of singing 'Amazon' with its original lyrics so that women [would] not forget their history." [254] But Vogel was the Festival producer, so the changes were made. However, the changes were so devastating to the womyn in the audience that they rebelled and demanded that the song be sung the way Maxine Feldman wrote it.

Lorraine: "One year they didn't play it right – I guess they were trying something new. But there was a big out roar! It was like, "where's Amazon Women Rise? We want that song!" So now, every year since then, it's been played, but it's open to interpretation, whoever is singing it. But nobody can

[250] Ro Rasmussen. Personal Interview. August, 2002.
[251] Sandstrom, 193.
[252] Ibid., 196.
[253] Ibid., 246.
[254] Ibid.

sing it like Maxine. She was powerful."[255]

In the end, Rhiannon and the other ritual performers won the argument when the audience began chanting the original lyrics. Vogel failed to understand just how important the song had become to the womyn, but ultimately she recognized that an "...entire cosmological system" had been communicated through the song, and that many womyn had already constructed their identity and sense of history around it.[256] Barbara Myerhoff suggested that "one of the most persistent but elusive ways that people make sense of themselves is to show themselves to themselves, through multiple forms: by telling themselves stories; by dramatizing claims in ritual and other collective enactments; by rendering visible actual and desired truths about themselves and the significance of their existence in imaginative and performative productions."[257] For the Michigan audience, singing "Amazon" in a ritual performance is a collective enactment of story telling. The song has become a sacred text of sorts; one that names the significance of womyn's existence. It is a text that helps womyn "make sense of themselves." It narrates the community's cultural heritage in a mythical past, where womyn built their own cities and ruled according to their own traditions and values systems. But more importantly, it dramatizes the "desired truths" womyn want to believe about themselves and their relationships.

Julianne: "Well see, that's 'herstory' again. There's a herstory of the Amazon women. They were strong women. They know who they are! They are in touch with who they are, and they don't care what other people think. And they're proud of who they are. And all those feelings, all those words combined together equal Amazon. And that's why at the beginning of every festival we sing that song with pride, because we created this wonderful place. We are Amazon women! And that's why we sing it. Just the feeling of singing that song sends chills and energy through my body. It makes me want to conquer the world. It makes me want to stand up and just yell with joy for who I am. To be able to turn around and conquer any fear that I have, and to know that I'm not alone, that there's many women out there. It's an energy that flows! It's like a current, and it reminds me of waves, like the ocean. And it just builds and builds, and the drums and the voices. The Amazon builds and builds, and takes over your whole body, and it just keeps going, and it takes energy from you and goes on to the next person and the next person and the next person, and by the time it reaches everybody, it's an energy that could reach this whole world. It's so wonderful! There's nothing like it. Experiencing that song explains what it means! Because it's so powerful! [Julianne began to cry]. It just makes me tear up, like I am right now. Because it wakes your soul, it tells you you're alive. And it kinda shocks ya, cause it's so

---

[255] Lorraine Alexis. Personal Interview. August, 2002.
[256] Stokes, 2.
[257] Myerhoff, "Life Not Death in Venice: Its Second Life," 261.

powerful that it's the only thing it can do. It shakes you and makes you realize. So that's what it means to me. I'll probably never put a tattoo on my body, but I don't need one. It's right here [patting her chest]. It's all right here. I don't need a tattoo to tell me I'm a lesbian, cause it's on me, it's everywhere around me. It's already there. We are Amazons!"[258]

For artist and audience alike, the lyrics of "Amazon" have the power to move body, soul, imagination, and memory. The song draws the minds eye to a mythical world where womyn are strong and independent, and where a divine feminine energy guides the culture. Over the years, the womyn have memorized the lyrics of "Amazon" and they rise to their feet the moment they hear it. Lifting their arms in unison, they sway back and forth to the rich rhythm, imagining that they really are "weaving rainbows in the sky." During my first experience of the song at the opening ceremony, the scene reminded me of a charismatic worship service, where those "filled with the spirit" sing and pray in ecstasy. This analogy may not be far off the mark, for just as "spirit filled music" draws the mind of the Christian believer to the spiritual realm of God, so "Amazon" draws the mind of the Michigan audience to the mythical world of strong warriors and powerful priestesses.

On the Land, womyn ritualize the Amazon in several ways. For instance, Kip leads workshops where womyn are encouraged to "call forth their memories of ancient times." Falcon leads workshops that teach womyn "Ancient Amazon Survival Skills." There was even a workshop for "Amazons on Horseback."[259] But the most consistent rituals are those performed by drummers. According to Bonnie Morris, "drumming rhythms and compositions tell or accompany ritual stories and rites of indigenous peoples all over the planet. . . . Particular types of drums and drumming styles, once used by men only, have been revived and popularized by women in diaspora communities as a means of continuing traditions and beliefs threatened by encroaching Westernization or racism. Drumming is thus a significant aspect of women's [culture] because of its oral storyline, [and] its configuration as a medium of ritual ..."[260]

Crafts womyn in the bazaar supply womyn with the ritual elements they need to embody the Amazon. Several crafts womyn make drums and teach basic rhythms to their customers. Others make labrys jewelry, necklaces, earrings, and charms. Some sell portraits of Amazon warriors and priestesses. Some make beautifully carved walking sticks, bows, and other wood products decorated with Amazon symbols. But there is only one womyn who makes the Amazon costumes, and her booth is always filled with eager womyn wanting to experience the "primal" feeling of identification that the leather provides.

Regardless of whether womyn are students of archaeology, or have read

---

[258] Julianne Meyerle. Personal Interview. August, 2001.
[259] 2004 Michigan Womyn's Music Festival Program.
[260] Morris, 161.

the myth, or even believe that Amazons existed is irrelevant to the meaning they give her at the Festival. Knowing that the myth exists allows womyn to manipulate their own consciousness, as Sandoval might argue, "through stratified zones of form and meaning [giving them] the ability to move through one layer of relationship and into another, 'artificial,' or self-consciously manufactured ideology and back again.[261] Through self-determined manipulation of their consciousness's, womyn at the Festival weave Amazon symbols, myths, and rituals into a cultural tapestry, a meta-ideology, a new narrative template that moves them beyond patriarchal structures and into a female centered world where *love* is the ideological framework that structures matriarchal culture. For womyn like Kip, the symbol of the Amazon and the matriarchal culture she represents is a source of power.

Kip: "How that relates to Michigan is, it RESONATES! I mean, these women resonate with that! They all think they are defenders of the women. And they are! They go out there and live in the world, and get oppressed and beaten up, and killed, and just beaten down out there, day after day after day, because they won't not be who they are. They will obstinately go out there and be who they are, no matter what you do to them. Those are defenders of the women. And that's why that symbol resonates with us, because it's a time in ancient history when we know we were strong, and we know we had the ability to defend ourselves."[262]

The womyn I spoke with used this narrative template in a number of ways. Some used it to strengthen and justify their opposition to the dominant culture. Others used it as a moral compass. A few used the narrative template to link lesbians in a common cultural heritage. Others used it to construct a positive self-image and lesbian identity. Each of their narratives was slightly different, but what became clear was that symbols, myths, and rituals created a matrix of meaning that helped womyn explain themselves to themselves, and to transform their oppression into liberation.

**An Amazon Matrix of Meaning**

Kip was right when she said womyn are oppressed in the dominant culture. At work, womyn experience the wage gap and the glass ceiling. Despite their recent gains in education and employment, Marie Richmond-Abbott wrote, "Women still earn on the average approximately 76 percent of what men earn," and that while on the job they experience "differentials in fringe benefits, the lack of a chance to train for better jobs, increasing pay differentials as men were promoted, sexual harassment on the job, inadequate child care facilities, the stress of the multiple roles of wife-worker-mother, and

[261] Sandoval, 111.
[262] Kip Parker. Personal Interview. August, 2003.

extremely limited leisure time."[263]   Women often have to work twice as hard and twice as long to meet the average male standard, and on top of this, they also work what Arlie Hochschild called "The Second Shift."  Hochschild's study showed that "women worked roughly fifteen hours longer each week than men. Over a year, they worked an extra month of twenty-four-hour days a year. Over a dozen years, it was an extra year of twenty-four-hour days. . . . Just as there is a wage gap between men and women in the workplace, there is a 'leisure gap' between them at home."[264]  In a world where women service men, exhaustion is a daily reality and it leaves little time to fight oppression.

Being oppressed, as Marilyn Frye defined it, means being "caught between or among forces and barriers which are so related to each other that jointly they restrain, restrict or prevent motion or mobility."[265]   American culture demands that women make themselves beautiful for men, but then calls them vein when they spend too much time in front of the mirror.  It demands that women remain virginal, but then calls them frigid bitches when they refuse men's advances.  American culture demands that women service men sexually, but then calls them whores if they enjoy sex.  It demands that women submit to men's authority, but then calls them weak willed or demure when they submit. Our culture demands that women care for children, but then calls them unfit when they work outside the home to put food on the table.  For womyn, these related forces are a kind of terrorism, one that Carol Sheffield suggests "so pervades our culture that we have learned to live with it as though it were the natural order of things.  It targets females – of all ages, races, and classes.  It is the common characteristic of rape, wife battery, incest, pornography, harassment, and all forms of sexual violence.  I call it *sexual terrorism* because it is a system by which males frighten and, by frightening, control and dominate females."[266]

While lesbians experience all of these forms of terrorism, they also experience added layers because of their perceived resistance to patriarchal demands.  As second-class citizens, lesbians risk much when they come out. They can lose their jobs.  They can lose their homes.  They can have their children taken from them because they are seen as unfit mothers.  They can lose the love and support of their friends and families.   They can be excommunicated from their churches.  They can even lose contact with their partners, as Sharon Kowalski did when her father petitioned a Minnesota court for her custody after she was permanently disabled in a car accident.  "Within twenty-four hours after being named sole guardian, the father cut off all contact

[263] Marie Richmond-Abbott. "Women Wage Earners." In *Feminist Philosophies.* Janet A. Kourany, James P. Sterba, and Rosemarie Tong, eds. (Upper Saddle River: Prentice Hall Inc, 1999), 164.
[264] Arlie Hockschild. "The Second Shift: Working Parents and the Revolution at Home." In *Feminist Frontier IV.* Laurel Richardson, Verta Taylor, and Nancy Whittier, eds. (New York: McGraw-Hill, 1997), 264.
[265] Marilyn Frye. "Opprssion." In *Feminist Frontier IV.* Laurel Richardson, Verta Taylor, and Nancy Whittier, eds. (New York: McGraw-Hill, 1997), 7.
[266] Carole J. Sheffield. "Sexual Terrorism." In *Feminist Philosophies.* Janet A. Kourany, James P. Sterba, and Rosemarie Tong, eds. (Upper Saddle River: Prentice Hall Inc, 1999), 45-46.

between Thompson [Sharon's lover] and Kowalski, including mail."[267]  All of the institutions that are supposed to provide aid and assistance to people in crisis can become the most frightening and oppressive institutions in the world for lesbians.  But living in the closet is also a form of terrorism.  It means avoiding social situations (drinks after work), relationships (with coworkers), personal comforts (a picture of a lover on a desk), and personal expression (mannerisms and attire) that others take for granted because these might risk being discovered.  It means constantly lying about yourself, about what you did on the weekend, about who you are dating, about who you love.  And it also means keeping track of your lies, and living with the fear that at any moment your lies can be uncovered.

On an individual level, most womyn develop a survival consciousness and coping mechanisms to help them survive the terrors of their everyday lives.  They become invisible.  They do not smile or acknowledge each other in public spaces.  They isolate themselves, and they take up as little time and space as possible in hopes that the patriarchy will terrorize them less.

But on a collective level, when they come to Michigan, womyn rebel against the strategies that oppress them.  They rebel against the coping mechanisms that keep them from liberating themselves in the patriarchal world.  They rebel by making themselves visible, by claiming time and space for themselves, and by smiling at each other as they gather together in unity.  When womyn come to Michigan and ritually perform the Amazon, it helps them, as Boden Sandstrom wrote, "perform themselves as whole and equal instead of as second-class citizens within society. . . . Therefore being in a women-only space, safe from men, created an environment in which women could perform their health, vulnerability, strength, and personal narratives in corpora (in the body)."[268]

The environment created in the opening ceremony is so powerful and so liberating that even my young research team, all of whom had never been to the Festival before, was able to perform themselves "in corpora" the first time they heard the song "Amazon."  Until that moment, they had been very conscious of their differences; Jewish, Muslim, Christian, Wiccan, Black, white, wealthy, and poor.  They were brought together to live in a tent without really knowing each other.  But suddenly, when they heard the song, they jumped up and started swaying back and forth, and then formed a circle to dance with each other.  I sat there watching them in amazement, wondering what the song could possibly mean to these young heterosexual college women.  But the song seemed to break down all their differences, and when it ended they were laughing and crying, and hugging each other like they were long lost sisters.  In

---

[267] Nan D. Hunter.  "Sexual Dissent and the Family: The Sharon Kowalski Case." *The Social Construction of Inequality and Difference*. Tracy E. Ore, ed. (New York: McGraw-Hill, 2003.
[268] Sandstrom, 125.

other words, the song became an "apparatus of love" between them.[269] "Oh my God," one of them said as she tried to catch her breath, "I never felt anything like that before. That was amazing! Did you see us?"[270] Dumbfounded, I just smiled and nodded my head. Suddenly, they were Amazons, unified as womyn across lines of difference and creating a shared consciousness that they "will never be able to explain to their friends back at school."[271]

*Research Team – 2005*

Being in a womyn only community is transformative even for a "research team," and what these young women experienced was no different than what another young team of undergraduate researchers experienced when they studied the lesbian community of Aradia in Missouri. This team wrote of their experience, "Understanding women's communities on paper is a lot different from the actuality. The more we studied the women of Aradia, the more our own research team became a feminist community. We were becoming the community we studied. . . It became an all-encompassing consciousness that filtered into every activity we did."[272] For my team, this "all-encompassing consciousness" began in the opening ceremony.

Boden Sandstrom suggested that "the opening ceremony gathers the community and creates a psychic space for a collective consciousness-raising

---

[269] Sandoval.
[270] Maryam Gbadamosi. Personal Statement at the 2005 Opening Ceremony.
[271] Lauren Wethers. Personal Statement at the 2005 Opening Ceremony.
[272] Dickie, "The Heirs of Aradia, Daughters of Diana: Community in the Second and Third Wave," 9.

with regard to the ideals and values of the Festival."[273]  Ritually performing Amazon in the opening ceremony helps womyn name their rebellion and embody the strength of the Amazon in order to build their own matriarchal culture.  The opening ceremony is the type of ceremony Barbara Myerhoff called "definitional."  "Definitional ceremonies are likely to develop when within a group there is a crisis of invisibility and disdain by a more powerful outside society."[274]  In this case, the ceremony openly rejects the patriarchal disdain of womyn, and uses symbol, myth, and ritual performance to unify womyn in an Amazon matrix of meaning.

For Julianne, the Amazon matrix includes strength, courage, and unity. In her interview, she told me that "the Amazon women were a tribe of just women, and they had to conquer many things – men, invaders.  So they had the people that were the warriors, and there were the mothers, but they all had strength, and they all banded together to fight off their enemies.  I believe the reason why she's the symbol is because of the strength – and the reason that some people have the battle ax tattoo or jewelry is cause it's just kind of a reminder of the strength, that we are strong women.  And we band together to conquer our fears, our hurts.  Everything we have to deal with, we deal with it together.  And it's just a reminder of that, of the strength of a woman."[275] While strength is a dominant meaning, the Amazon matrix also includes territorial and spiritual meanings.

Susi: "Yeah, I kind of grew up with the Amazons, in my young lesbian years.  We had two or three women's lands in Australia, and one of them was Amazon Acres.  And there were a lot of women in my twenties, who operated on that level.  And still, because we're in the country, we get a lot of feral women who dress like that.  I think the revival of the Amazon tradition at Michigan draws us together, in a country space, where it's ok to wear very little clothes, and be earthy, and practice whatever you want to practice.  I don't think that in the world, we can do that.  It threatens the patriarchy to be strong, and Goddesses.  It's threatening.  It's totally threatening to the patriarchy.  I mean, you're not going to be able to wear your pagan whatevers, and practice witchcraft, especially in America.  I mean, women were burned at the stake. Women are still burned at the stake!  I mean, I believe that's how it would be here in America."[276]

For Susi, Amazons are strong "earthy" womyn who rebel against the authority of patriarchal religion by claiming and serving a goddess rather than a god.  She also connects the symbol to "womyn's land" and living in the country, which she associates with womyn's political and economic rebellion.  Thus, the

---

[273] Sandstrom, 181.
[274] Myerhoff, "Life Not Death in Venice: Its Second Life," 261.
[275] Julianne Meyerle.  Personal Interview.  August, 2001.
[276] Susi St. Julian.  Personal Interview.  August, 2005.

Amazon matrix of meaning expands to encompass personal strength, the unity of womyn, goddess religion, and womyn's political and economic autonomy.

What makes the symbol of the Amazon so powerful is that it does not have to conform to only one meaning. Because she is a matrix of meaning, the Amazon does not have to sacrifice individual meanings for the sake of the whole. She can encompass many meanings and connect them in the larger matrix of what Clifford Geertz called "webs of significance" or "culture."[277] In his discussion of culture, Geertz wrote that symbols were important to explore because "they are tangible formulations of notions, abstractions from experience fixed in perceptible forms, concrete embodiments of ideas, attitudes, judgments, longings, or beliefs."[278] But he also warned against staying in the heady concept of consciousness. "To undertake the study of cultural activity – activity in which symbolism forms a positive content – is thus not to abandon social analysis for a Platonic cave of shadows, to enter into a mentalistic world of introspective psychology or, worse, speculative philosophy, and wander there forever in a haze of 'Cognitions,' 'Affections,' 'Conations,' and other elusive entities. Cultural acts, the construction, apprehension, and utilization of symbolic forms, are social events like any other; they are as public as marriage and as observable as agriculture."[279] What Geertz was after was an exploration of the cultural activities that symbols, myths, and rituals inspire. In other words, the question becomes, what do womyn *do* once they have named and embodied an Amazon consciousness at the Festival?

One way to answer this question is to look at the Amazon as a "female cultural hero." In her study, Alison Futrell wrote that the female cultural hero's "mission tends toward the defense of domestic, female-centered institutions and goals, the home and the community – spheres where women traditionally played a prominent role. By representing the family and the home as essential to the concept of 'good' and as jeopardized by androcentric ancient social, political, and ethical structures, [the Amazon] celebrates the traditional feminine sphere, giving voice to those conspicuously silenced in the ancient texts."[280] Therefore, the Amazon matrix of meaning expands to encompass the domestic sphere of *family*, *home*, and *sacred* traditions.

In her study of "Old Europe," Marija Gimbutas argued that there is strong evidence of matrilineal systems. "The Goddess-centered art, with its striking absence of images of warfare and male domination, reflects a social order in which women, as heads of clans or queen-priestesses played a central part."[281] The concept of Amazon clans has given some womyn at the Festival the idea that they are genetically linked to each other through these ancient lineages. Boden Sandstrom confirmed this when she argued, "the lyric, 'I am

---

[277] Geertz, *The Interpretation of Cultures*, 5.
[278] Ibid., 91.
[279] Ibid.
[280] Futrell, "The Baby, the Mother, and the Empire: Xena as Ancient Hero," 14.
[281] Gimbutas, *The Language of the Goddess*, 325.

and once was called Amazon' connotes what could be considered a genetic identity – an invocation of ancestors' power and practice."[282]  In essence, some women believe that lesbians share a genetic connection that dates back to ancient Amazon clans.  While I am not prepared to argue for a genetic connection between lesbians, I do argue that the idea fosters family building practices at the Festival.  The *idea* of a familial connection and lineage is both comforting and healing for womyn who have, in many cases, been rejected or disowned by their biological families.  In the following chapters, I want to move away from abstract concepts like consciousness and embodiment, and explore the material reality of what womyn *do* at the Festival.  And what they *do* is build *families*, *homes*, *sacred traditions*, and *communities* that sustain them throughout the year and sometimes over the course of a lifetime.

---

[282] Sandstrom, 212.

# ⚒ 4 ⚒
# We Are Family

In many ways womyn on the Land conceptualize "family" the way that women in *Herland* did. In Herland, families were not structured on the patriarchal model. In *Herland*, lovers and children were not conceptualized as private property. Rather, the whole community was thought of as "family," and children were raised in a community of mothers who were not necessarily linked biologically to the children. For womyn at the Festival, who think communally, families are not closed units housed in private homes. Rather, families are made by people who choose to love and care for each other, whether they are biologically related or not. On the Land, even biologically related families have permeable boundaries. In this type of environment, familial relationships are not contingent upon biology, nor are the roles granted to family members based on age, gender expression, sexuality, race, or income.

Queer scholars like Valerie Lehr argue that the traditional concept of "family" is founded on the oppressive patriarchal model of marriage, an institution that excludes people on the basis of race, gender, social class, and sexuality. "The 'family' problems that gays and lesbians face in the United States," Lehr argues "are much more extensive than what marriage rights can address"[283] Lehr suggested that fighting to enter an oppressive system like marriage limits the truly revolutionary potential of the queer movement. She argued for a radical discourse in which family care is discussed as a function of community, one in which the democratization of family could "keep alive a movement that addresses family and private life even if liberal demands begin to be met."[284]

Likewise, Mary Bernstein and Renate Reimann argue that the conservative lesbian and gay movement seeking marriage rights wants acceptance for their "normal" families rather than redefining the entire concept of family itself, which they suggest is a relatively recent and "short-lived phenomenon" that has not worked for many Americans. The lesbian and gay movement, they argue, marginalizes those queer (working-class, racial, and transgendered) families who might negatively affect the otherwise "normal"

---

[283] Valerie Lehr. *Queer Family Values: Debunking the Myth of the Nuclear Family.* (Philadelphia: Temple University Press, 1999), 10.
[284] Ibid.

image of conservative lesbian and gay families. They maintain that the entire concept of the "traditional family" needs to be redefined, and that "queer families present new challenges to the privatized-nuclear family, contradicting the sexual dimorphism upon which the ideal family is based."[285]

The issues these scholars raise are important because they demonstrate the tensions between "acceptance" and "transformation" of the traditional nuclear family model. While not dismissing either "acceptance" or "transformation," this chapter explores the "apparatus of love" womyn use to negotiate both at the Festival.[286] It focuses on womyn's relationships with their families of origin and what they *do* to build *families* at the Festival. It asks what womyn mean when they use the word "family" to describe their experience, and what they *do* to make their experience of family meaningful. Is "family" simply a metaphor for friendship networks? What are the types of family relationships womyn build, and how do these differ from the relationships they have with their families of origin? How is "family" being redefined, or is it? And what do these families mean outside the Festival? Are they maintained across space and time, and how do they function in everyday life?

The womyn I spoke with used the word "family" to signify multiple meanings. Womyn who use the word as a metaphor for "community" seemed to maintain close loving relationships with their families of origin. Others used it specifically to signify membership in the lesbian community. Womyn with children tended to use the term in the traditional sense of the nuclear family, with the only difference being that the two principle adults are womyn. Others conceptualized traditional mother, daughter, granddaughter, and sister relationships between womyn, but did not base these relationships on biological connections. Rather they based their relationships on Kath Weston's concept of "families we choose." However, a few womyn believed in a genetic connection between lesbians, and suggested that these connections dated back to ancient Amazon lineages.

At the Festival, the term "family" has a complex set of meanings, and how womyn choose to construct and make those relationships visible at the Festival often depends on the degree of marginalization they feel within their family of origin and the larger American culture. Interestingly, as Kath Weston noted, people "taking on a new, ostensibly sexual, identity find themselves talking as much about kinship as sexuality."[287]

After coming out, some lesbians are accepted and supported in their families of origin, as well as their social, political, spiritual, and economic networks. For them, life is relatively stable and secure, and whom they call "family" changes very little. However, other womyn are not so lucky. For

---

[285] Mary Bernstein and Renate Reimann, eds. *Queer Families, Queer Politics: Challenging Culture and State.* (New York: Columbia University Press, 2001) 3-4.
[286] Sandoval.
[287] Kath Weston. *Families We Choose: Lesbians, Gays, Kinship.* (New York: Columbia University Press, 1991).

these womyn, coming out as a lesbian has meant being rejected by their families of origin, loosing custody of children, being fired from jobs, being excommunicated from churches, and even being forced out of their homes. Loosing any one of these familial, economic, or spiritual relationships can have devastating consequences for womyn who are already marginalized in American culture because of their race, social class, and gender. For these womyn, Michigan gives them the opportunity to make emotional investments in relationships that replace those of the traditional family. Quite literally, the types of relationships womyn build at the Festival can mean the difference between life and death, particularly as they age or become ill. Ultimately though, what womyn mean when they say "family" is *love.* This type of love and familial relationship is what Chela Sandoval described as a "complex kind of love in the postmodern world, where love is understood as affinity – alliance and affection across lines of difference that intersect both in and out of the body."[288]

This chapter begins with the experiences womyn have in their families of origin after they come out. Often these experiences shape how womyn conceptualize family, and whom they include in their Festival experience. It then moves to explore the types of familial relationships womyn build at the Festival and how those relationships are structured and made visible. Finally, the chapter concludes with a discussion of what these family relationships mean outside the Festival and how they are maintained across time and space. Although the chapter is situated in the larger discourse of acceptance and transformation with regard to the meaning and function of family, it stays close to womyn's narratives, paying particular attention to what they say about family, and what they *do* to create family at the Festival.

**Families of Origin**

Womyn who find themselves loved and supported by the women in their families of origin often bring their family members with them. During our first year, Bobbie and I did a work shift in the kitchen, chopping tomatoes for that evening's burritos. Around the table, we worked with five generations of women from the same family. The woman working next to me carried her baby daughter in a "snuggy" on her chest. To her right stood her mother, her grandmother, and her great-grandmother. Her great-grandmother had flown over from Germany to attend their "family reunion" at the Festival. I remember how surprised I was by this family, and commented that they were a tribute to the true meaning of motherhood. But mothers and daughters are quite common, and as Bonnie Morris wrote, tributes to mothers are plentiful on the Land. "Festival culture is, after all, the matriarchy, and *everyone* is some woman's daughter. Many, many festiegoers long to bring their own mothers to

---

[288] Sandoval, 170.

the annual women's music celebrations we call home."[289]  And many, many do. Several womyn interviewed for this project brought their mothers, daughters, grand-daughters, aunts, and nieces to the Festival.

Akosua: "The other thing that's been good for me, you know, is that I brought my mother and my daughter.  And I was dreading bringing my mother because I thought I would have to be this caretaker, and I wouldn't have a chance to enjoy myself.  But the women on the Land have embraced her.  So I have been able to let some of that go.  In fact, I've been able to let a lot of that go.  And that's been good for her too.  She's become sort of a celebrity."[290]

Veronica: "You know my mother comes.  I brought her the second year I came.  So to have her here, and being with all these other womyn of color, that really is home."[291]

Womyn, who remain close to their biological mothers and bring them to the Festival, enjoy relationships that many womyn can only dream of sharing. Having one's mother at the Festival means that the daughter is not forced to make sharp divisions between her family of origin and her Festival family.  She does not have to hide her relationships with other womyn and therefore retains much of the security and emotional support that other womyn lose when they come out.

But other womyn are not so lucky, as Margaret Vandenburg notes. "Like everyone else, lesbians are born into perfectly respectable homes and showered with a particularly American brand of parental love that immediately dries up when they find out we're gay.  How, our parents ask themselves, did my daughter manage to slip through the cracks of the divine scheme of heterosexual propagation?  Even mothers, whose love is renowned for its constancy, turn their backs on us.  The expression, 'that is a face only a mother could love,' does not apply to us."[292]  For womyn who experience their own mother's rejection, the wound is sometimes unbearable, but especially so at the Festival.   As Bonnie Morris noted, "The music, workshops, theatrical performances, and woman-made crafts…intentionally draw attention to our foremothers, our female bloodlines, our mother-daughter rites of passage (no matter how stormy), our visions and heritage as kinswomen from ethnic traditions.  And yet within this very harvest of mother-naming, many women are in pain because their actual mothers do not condone or understand feminist politics or a lesbian lifestyle."[293]

I am one such womyn, and I can say with heartfelt grief that when a mother rejects her lesbian daughter it cuts a wound that never stops bleeding. But on the Land mothers who attend the Festival are often adopted by womyn

---

[289] Morris, 141.
[290] Akosua. Personal Interview. August, 2005.
[291] Veronica Jones. Personal Interview. August 2005.
[292] Margaret Vandenburg. "Home-phobia." In *Chasing the American Dyke Dream: Homestretch*. Susan Fox Rogers, ed. (San Francisco: Cleis, 1998), 53.
[293] Morris, 142.

like me, and their love does provide a measure of healing. Likewise, adopting other womyn's children provides a measure of healing for mothers who have lost custody of, or been rejected by their own children. Healing also comes when womyn adopt each other as sisters and begin building large extended Festival families networks.

### Festival Families

The first year Bobbie and I attended, we camped alone because we did not know anyone at the Festival. However, after meeting Cindy and Marnie we established a "sisterly" relationship with them. We kept in touch throughout that year and as the following summer rolled around, of course we began making plans to camp together. But after setting up our home on the Land, our Festival family began growing immediately.

On the first morning, as we sat around our dining room table drinking coffee and waking up, we noticed a womyn across the road. She had come in by herself during the night and tried to set up her tent in the dark. Needless to say, it was a bit lopsided. When we saw her struggling with it, we all got up and went over to see if we could help her out. She told us her name was Beth and that she had never been camping before, which meant that she was a festie virgin. In less than two minutes we had her tent erected properly and she was so grateful that she lit up a cigarette and offered us a six-pack of beer to thank us.

*Laurie & Bobbie's Festival Family – 2004*

"Oops," Bobbie said, "do you know that you are set up in the Bread & Roses campground?" Beth did not have a clue what Bobbie was talking about. "Bread & Roses is a 'chem-free' campground," Bobbie explained, "No smoking. No alcohol. No nothing." Beth was horrified that she was breaking two rules at once, but loathed the idea of moving her equipment to the other side of the road. "I just got set up," she groaned.

"No problem," I said. "Everybody take a corner of the tent and lift." Bobbie, Cindy, Marnie, and I each grabbed a corner, heaved up the stakes, walked the erect tent across the road and plunked it down next to us. Within five minutes Beth's tent was re-staked and she was sitting in our dining room drinking coffee and smoking away. That day our Festival family grew as Beth became a sister to all of us, and that relationship became even more concrete as we all stayed in contact with each other and then camped together in the years that followed.

Festival families are created through fictive adoptions. They are what Kath Weston called "chosen families."[294] Festival families form when womyn choose to love and support each other across great distances and differences. Chela Sandoval argued that these types of families are "analogous to that called for in contemporary indigenous writings in which tribes or lineages are identified out of those who share, not bloodlines, but rather lines of affinity. Such lines of affinity occur through attraction, combination, and relations carved out of and in spite of difference."[295] Festival families also employ Donna Haraway's notion of "joint kinship" as they intersect and accommodate families of origin, creating even more complex relationships and networks of love and support.[296] These complex relationships span all ages, races, social classes, and sexualities, and often revolve around children. Relationships between mothers and their children expand as "community mothers" care for both.

According to Lisa Vogel there were very few children at the early Festivals, but by the mid '80s the lesbian "baby boom" vastly increased the numbers of children attending the Festival. Boden Sandstrom reported that at the 2002 Festival, "there were approximately 150 girls in GAIA, 90 in SPROUTS, 30 in worker and intern day care, and 27 in Brother Sun."[297] While the vast majority of womyn do not have children of their own, most become "community mothers" to other womyn's children. Nearly all the womyn I spoke with talked about the joy that the Festival children bring into their lives and how they believe these children benefit from growing up in a community of womyn.

[294] Weston.
[295] Sandoval, 169-170.
[296] Donna Haraway. "A Cyborg Manifesto: Science, Technology, and Socialist-Feminism in the Late Twentieth Century." In *Feminist Theory: A Reader.* Wendy Kolmar and Frances Bartkowski, eds. (Mountain View: Mayfield Publishing, 2000),364.
[297] Sandstrom, 157.

Kip: "Early on, when I first started coming, there were no children. You'd see one or two, tops, in the whole year. I mean if somebody had a baby it was a big to-do. People would gather around them and go, 'Look, a baby! Oh cool, where'd ya get it?' And there were a few straight women that came, and there are still a few straight women who come, and we'd honor them. And they would bring their kids, and we would bend over backwards to be good to them. And there wasn't Gaia Girls yet, and there wasn't Brother Sun yet, and all that wasn't happening early on. And then the lesbian baby boom happened out in the world, and you see what happened. My kid is eleven and she's been here nine times. I know kids who are twenty and twenty-five who have been here twenty and twenty-five times. They grew up here. This is their *home*. And they were raised by these women, by this *community*. And their whole sensibility in the world, their whole way of being in the world is different than the one's who don't come here. They have a different sense of what's diversity, of what's Ok, and of where *safe* is, then kids that I know who don't come here. And it's amazing."[298]

Lorraine: "What I find incredibly exciting is that there were young children who grew up here, for twenty-seven years, and I think that's so miraculous. They are definitely going to have a different outlook."[299]

Over the years the Festival producers have taken great care to ensure that children's needs are met and that their mothers receive the "adult time" they need to enjoy the Festival. The three childcare facilities are equipped with everything from cribs to bottles, and boxes stuffed with arts and crafts supplies and snacks. They are also staffed with womyn like Cindy who look forward to doing their work shifts in these playful centers.

Cindy: "*Sprouts* is the day camp for the children. I helped out with the preschoolers. They are some very mature preschoolers. Some very loved children. You can tell that they feel *safe* and secure when they're dropped off at *Sprouts*, they don't know any of us, but they're just happy to be there to play. They know they're *safe*. It's all fenced in. Basically, up and away from the rest of the festival. It's their own little private space. There are preschoolers, toddlers, and infants. They have cribs for the little ones to sleep in. They have their little snackies, and sand boxes, and swings, and all the things little kids love to do. They dress-up and have imagination play. I had lizards in my ears [she laughs]. This little girl was playing doctor, and checking my ears, and I had lizards in my ears. It's very nice to see them being so young and feeling so *safe*. They feel *safe* in here. They know they're not going to be harmed here. If Mommy were to drop them off at a drop-in daycare, I'm sure those children would be crying. They wouldn't be sure of that situation. But they are here. From infants on up."[300]

---

[298] Kip Parker. Personal Interview. August, 2003.
[299] Lorraine Alexis. Personal Interview. August, 2002.
[300] Cindy Avery. Personal Interview. August, 2002.

Several womyn remarked about the safety that children feel at the Festival. Children are told that they can turn to any womyn on the Land for help, and they do. More than once I observed womyn drop whatever they were doing and run to the aid of a crying child.

Chelly: "And the children! At first, I really had to take a step back when I saw little girls naked. It really threw me because I've been through molestation, and I grew up in a very strict household where you didn't walk around without your clothes on. Very sheltered and coveted. And to see these babies walkin' around and able to be free and comfortable in their bodies, and *safe*. I mean, to me, it just warms my heart to see them running and playing and just able to be happy and free. Because our children have so much to go through. So, to be so free, that's a beautiful thing to me."[301]

Veronica: "Seein' kids runnin' around naked, or they're playin' in the mud. And their completely free, cause they know they have a *community* of mothers to take care of them. You know. You'll see them goin' down here and it's ok. They know that they're *safe*. And their mothers don't have to worry about them."[302]

On the Land girls whose mothers have not restricted them to *Sprouts* or *Gaia Girls* can move freely around the Festival. They hop on and off the shuttles as they please, but many just enjoy riding around all day. They can also go to concerts unaccompanied. They can head over to the Kitchen for a piece of watermelon in the afternoon, or they can inspire adults like Julianne to help them build an imaginary home for fairies under a shade tree.

Julianne: "The other day I was walking by and saw these two little girls creating their own fantasy out of a stump. The day before I probably looked at it and saw a stump. But these girls saw a world of fantasy – amazing things – there were fairies that lived there, and they were making a home for the fairies. I'm not sure if the fairies were there or not, but the girls were inviting them to live there. They had this little acorn cap for the baby fairies' bath. They had some jewels to lure and attract the fairies to this wonderful home. And I just saw that and I smiled, and thought that's our future. We all need that. That's the imagination that will keep this festival going. These babies came and experienced the love of women and the security, the *safety* net – they can do anything."[303]

Most womyn on the Land embrace mothers and their children, and often feel as if they are "community mothers" raising a unique and enlightened group of children. As Lindsy van Gelder and Pamela Robin Brandt claimed, "one of the Michigan festival's most inspiring experiences, even childless festies will tell you, is watching girls arrive on the Land grafted to Mom's leg, and within hours, metamorphose into self-confident, free-flying little beings,

---

[301] Chelly. Personal Interview. August, 2005.
[302] Veronica Jones. Personal Interview. August, 2005.
[303] Julianne Meyerle. Personal Interview. August, 2001.

strutting around like they own the place, hitching rides all night on the shuttle, and hold spitting contests with their official festie water bottles. This is one place where their mothers don't have to worry about them ending up on a milk carton.[304]

Mothers do not have to worry about their children because they believe that if their child has a need, every other womyn will do whatever is necessary to help their child. This is not an irrational or idealized belief on the part of these mothers. I have personally witnessed the "butchest dyke" transform herself into a soft and gentle "nurturing mother" when a child started to cry. For womyn who have never had children, the opportunity to care for and love another womyn's child is a precious experience. But often what is even more precious is the love these womyn receive from children. Receiving the unconditional and unreserved love of a child heals many womyn's wounds. For womyn who have lost custody of their children because the patriarchy deemed them "unfit mothers," sometimes Festival children provide them with meaningful, if temporary maternal relationships.

Such was the case for Bobbie, who lost custody of her one-year-old daughter and three-year-old son when the court awarded her former husband full custody. Bobbie never saw her children again because her ex-husband ran away with them. Yet I saw her practiced "tough butch" exterior melt away when a little three-year old African American girl tugged on her pant-leg and offered her a half-eaten, soggy, Oreo cookie in exchange for her chair at the opening ceremony. Bobbie accepted the used cookie with a smile, and in that moment she and the little girl bonded in a way that enabled them to share loving moments throughout the rest of the Festival week. They became so close that the following year, when the little girl spotted Bobbie walking along the path, she began shouting her name from the passing shuttle. When Bobbie heard her name, she looked over just in time to see the little girl's mother pulling her back into the shuttle before she could jump out into Bobbie's arms. Neither Bobbie nor the little girl's mother could believe that she remembered Bobbie from the previous year, but she did. Once again, Bobbie and the little girl were able to share special times at the Festival and this also gave the little girl's mother some much needed adult time. For womyn who are full time mothers, receiving free and safe childcare from thousands of womyn means they get the chance to heal their own wounds in an environment that nurtures them as adults. For these weary mothers, everyday life as breadwinners and caregivers can be extremely lonely and overwhelming, and even getting to the Festival can be a traumatic experience, as it was for one womyn that Kip told me about.

Kip: "Yesterday, there was a woman who flew in, and came in on the shuttle from Grand Rapids – she had a four month old baby – and no gear. She had gear, but it didn't get here. Well, let me ask you this. Where else could she

---

[304] Van Gelder and Brandt, 78.

have gone where the *community* would have grabbed her, cocooned her, taken care of her emotional needs, played with the baby, and said, 'Ok here's a blanket, here's what you need.' And by the time she got down to Triangle she was feelin' better, and as she was sittin' there waitin' for somebody to guide her down to where the camp was, you know I went over to her and I said, 'You know you're *home* now! You're Ok, we got ya.' And she like bawled, and the baby was like [giggling]. But where else could that happen but here?"[305]

Ironically, what Kip did not know at the time of her interview was that this womyn and her baby had spent the night in my camp. When I stumbled out of our tent that morning, Bobbie "shushed" me with a whisper. "Be quiet. The baby is asleep." I was quite surprised by her statement because when I had gone to bed the night before, no one in our family had a baby. As I poured myself a cup of coffee she explained. "Beth went down to the campfire last night at *Triangle* and she found this womyn and her baby. They came in on the shuttle but the airline sent her gear on to New York. She and the baby needed a place to stay so Beth brought her *home*." When my mind finally registered what Bobbie was saying, I just smiled to myself and thought how wonderful it was that our family had just had a baby. Another perfect Michigan moment!

Children who grow up on the Land often end up having several community mothers, as well as sisters, and this is even more meaningful for kids who are estranged from their families of origin because of their sexual orientation. In an interview with Linna Due, a young lesbian said "I don't think there is anyone more isolated than queer kids. You don't see yourself anywhere. At least racial minorities have their families. With queers, oftentimes our families are who we're the *most* alienated from. So what do we have? Maybe a room. A room and nothing."[306] Likewise, as Tamsin Wilton argues, elderly lesbians are also often invisible in the lesbian and gay community. "We have no means of knowing how many elderly people are lesbians, but it is likely that many elderly lesbians are living in hardship and loneliness and, given the refusal of the lesbian and gay community to consider the needs of its elders, this is a group likely to remain invisible for a long time."[307] But at the Festival "queer kids" and lesbian "elders" find families that welcome them and care for their needs. Just as Akosua's mother became a "celebrity" in her Festival family, Julianne was adopted into her mother's Festival family at the "coming out party" they threw for her.

Julianne: "The twentieth anniversary festival was my first year. That was my coming out year actually. I came out to my mom for mother's day. I gave her this card and I told her. My *family* knew years before, but it's not about when, it's about recognizing in your heart and feeling the strength of it, and the power of knowing who you are. So that Festival was an eye opening

---

[305] Kip Parker. Personal Interview. August, 2003.

[306] Linnea Due. *Joining the Tribe: Growing Up Gay and Lesbian in the '90s.* (New York: Anchor Books, 1995), 118.

[307] Tamsin Wilton. *Lesbian Studies: Setting an Agenda.* (London: Routledge, 1995), 200-201.

experience. And Mom decided to have a coming out party for me. We had a whole bunch a people, and it was just a wonderful experience. It was just a joy."[308]

Even though Julianne has her biological mother at the Festival, Bobbie and I have developed such a close maternal relationship with her that she makes our camp her home base. Julianne drops by almost every morning for hot chocolate and she usually comes home for dinner, especially when we are serving apple and chicken sausages. She even introduces us as her "other mothers" when she brings her friends home to meet us. Her love has empowered us to claim her as our adopted daughter even though we know she already has a loving and supportive parent at the Festival. We have also adopted Julianne's twin sister and all of us have regular "family reunions" together with their biological mother, Connie. But what makes our relationship even more complex is that I also claim Connie as my adopted mother.

*Julianne – 2004*

While this relationship may seem an incontinent kinship, it appears so only in contrast to the patriarchal model of the nuclear family. Festival families are not defined by hierarchies of power that limit membership or relationship roles. Rather, they are based on "lines of affinity" and on the choice to love. In other words, the love and respect of family members determines the role an individual will have within the Festival family, rather than the role obligating the love and respect of family members. Because Festival families are not based on economic, religious, or biological investments, they radically redefine and restructure familial roles and relationships, allowing womyn to have multiple mothers, daughters, and sisters.

Marissa: "It's like they're redefining family. And I know my family at home would, you know, mostly drop everything for me, but these women

---

[308] Julianne Meyerle. Personal Interview. August, 2001.

would do that no matter what. And that's so wonderful, to feel loved and welcomed after only a week of knowing them. It's like I don't feel like I need to hold anything back. They're there, and they're not leaving. I gained five sisters, and four moms, and not like the old definition of mom and sister. This is extra. I don't want to say real – but it's like no holding back, non-biological, unconditional love. And Michigan creates the environment to be able to do that."[309]

In Marissa's case, her Festival family crosses race, religion, sexual orientation, and social class lines. Through their Festival experience they formed what Barbara Myerhoff might call a "bricolage" family that meets their "present circumstances."[310] *Love* holds bricolage Festival families together and the Festival is the bank where they make emotional investments according to their present circumstances. Often womyn come to the Land with emotionally depleted bank accounts and during the Festival they engage in emotional transactions that carry them through the coming year. Lorraine thinks of the Festival as a "family reunion" and the place where she "recharges" her emotional batteries.

*Cindy & Marissa – 2005*          *Kate & Marissa - 2005*

Lorraine: "We were both in the medical field and we had to be closeted. This was back in the 70s. So when I came here, it was like I was with lesbians! It was the most lesbians I'd ever been with all year. We lived in New Jersey, but all of our friends were in Manhattan, and so we'd run to Manhattan to see our friends, and then we'd say 'we'll meet you in Michigan,' and we became like a big *family*. And then, as the women from New York moved across the country, they'd come back one year or the next. So it really was a *family* reunion. But to me it was more of a *spiritual* thing, because it was almost like I replenished my batteries – so I could face – I could see the good of the whole lesbian community, because we were not in a community in New Jersey. We had one or two other friends, but it wasn't a community."[311]

---

[309] Marissa Corwin. Personal Interview. August, 2005.
[310] Myerhoff, "Life Not Death in Venice: Its Second Life," 264.
[311] Lorraine Alexis. Personal Interview. August, 2002.

Like Lorraine and Kathy, many womyn experience extreme loneliness outside the Festival. They feel they must remain in the closet, isolating themselves for protection against the everyday insults and injuries that lesbians experience in a homophobic and misogynistic culture. And while there is more public awareness today about lesbianism and more images of lesbians in popular culture, these do not necessarily mean that womyn feel safer in their everyday lives, nor does it help them find love and support within their families of origin. This is one of the main reasons womyn at the Festival guard its boundaries so closely. Creating a "safe space" allows womyn to make themselves vulnerable to each other, vulnerable enough to let their guards down long enough to give and receive the love that gets hidden in the closet the rest of the year. Several of the womyn who participated in this project suggested that this feeling of safety manifests as a feeling of being at "home," and the love that they invest in each other during the Festival manifests as a feeling of family.

This feeling of being safe in a family was particularly important for Susi. Although she had come with three friends, they returned to Australia after the Festival, leaving her to travel around America alone for three months.

Susi: "We had no idea how to set up tents. None of us had ever set up tents before, and then Kate's girls [my research team] came along and we just felt so *safe*. They adopted me, and now I'm a part of their *family*. I mean, look at me, I'm alone in America! But I've met so many women, and that's really been important to me. I think I knew going to Michigan first would be a good move. I've got quite a lot of addresses of women I can go and stay with now. People have been incredibly friendly, and come up and wanted to talk about where I come from, what I was doing, and where I was going next. Probably a dozen people just basically gave me their card and said, 'ring me up,' or 'come and stay.' Pretty much, women from all over America. They have been so welcoming. That experience will always stay with me. Well just look at us [she and I], we are *family* now!"[312]

The feeling of safety also manifests doubly inside specific spaces of the Festival, particularly for womyn of color who, at times, feel marginalized within the larger Festival community. Both Mary and Veronica felt that being at the Festival was safe for them, but that the *Womyn of Color Tent* was where they found home and family.

Veronica: "Being on the Land is a measure of *safety*, but being amongst Black womyn on the Land, well that's a complete feeling of coming *home*. It's very different outside, because it's just like going to some party, or game night, or event, or whatever, with lesbian women, or Black lesbians, where you're just there for an hour or a day. This is like a whole week-long experience, so you come with maybe the walls from the outside world, and so you come in here for six or seven days and those walls break down. And by the time Friday or Saturday comes you're totally comfortable and immersed in the experience, and

---

[312] Susi St. Julian. Personal Interview. August, 2005.

so it does feel like *home*. So like the first year it was all about that – finding my way around, getting comfortable, blah, blah, blah – and now this is like a *family* reunion. It's like seein' people year after year, seein' people get older, seein' teens actually become adults. I have met so many women every year, and even though I might not keep in contact with them for the rest of the year, when I see them here, I know this is my *family*. We speak like we never left off. It's like people will come up to you and like, 'Hi Veronica, how was your year?' So you go through that, and you just pick up."[313]

Colette: "When I come here, it's like a *family* reunion. And immediately we make connections again. I think because there's such a sense of familiarity, you know, I go in the Womyn of Color Tent and lay on the floor – and it's like what I'd be doing at home. Waiting to see what's goin' on."[314]

Mary: "The Womyn of Color Tent means I have a *family* to come back to. Before, I didn't have that. Now I have a *family*. Now I have people I know I can connect with. You know one year I stayed with Pat and her sister, and they took care of me. And I stayed after the Festival and helped tear down, and I was part of the *family*. You know, and there are women I touch often, like Isis. I call her and she rides up here with us. We touch each other often – we love each other. I encourage every woman to come. It's like being on another planet, another world."[315]

This world that Mary describes is a world where the patriarchal model of the nuclear family is transformed into a web-like structure with multiple points of connection based on love. It is a world where womyn adopt each other as mothers, daughters, grandmothers, and sisters, and through their kinship networks they heal each other. For many womyn, their Festival families are more loving and more meaningful than their families of origin, and during the Festival they make emotional investments in each other that are just as "real" and just as powerful as those in any "normal" family. But often the Festival is the only place that they are safe enough to touch each other as sisters, mothers, daughters, and as lovers.

## Couples

One day while Bobbie and I were strolling through the Crafts Bazaar we saw smoke rising over a crowd of womyn gathered in a circle outside one of the large vendor tents. Curious about what was going on, we edged into the circle and saw Shirley Jons (a Native American spiritual leader) performing a wedding ceremony for two womyn. Afterward we learned that the couple had just purchased rings from one of the jewelry makers and had gone to show them to Shirley, who then decided a celebration of their relationship was in order. Joy for the couple quickly spread through the Bazaar and within

---

[313] Veronica Jones. Personal Interview. August, 2005.
[314] Colette Winlock. Personal Interview. August, 2005.
[315] Mary Sims. Personal Interview. August, 2005.

moments random womyn were gathering at the impromptu ritual to watch Shirley smudge the couple with burning sage, and to hear their vows. After each of the womyn said "I do," and Shirley pronounced them united in the bonds of love, the crowd erupted with applause, offered congratulatory hugs, and then dispersed as quickly as it had formed. I stayed to talk with one of the brides who told me that although she and her partner had lived together for years, they had never had the opportunity to formalize their relationship in a ceremony, and that the Festival seemed like the ideal place to do it because, as she put it, "our *family* is here."

As safe as individual womyn feel on the Land, couples feel it even more so. In their everyday lives, few couples live in communities where they can touch each other in public or discuss their relationships openly at work (ironically, today, as I am working on revising this chapter for the second edition of this book, the Supreme Court has, in effect, recognized gay marriage). But when they get to the Land they are free to express their love and affection for each other openly, proclaiming what Bonnie Morris calls their "coupledom." "A primary attraction for festiegoers is the freedom to walk hand in hand with another woman.

*Cindy & Marnie – 2005*

This public affirmation of coupledom cannot be overestimated. Where in the 'fake world,' as Alix Dobkin says, there are very real penalties for lesbians who come out to their families and employers and schools [for regardless of what the Supreme Court ruling means to lesbian couples and the law, it cannot force families of origin to love their lesbian daughter or American society to embrace lesbian womyn as a group], at festivals we have carte blanche to enjoy the normative functions our straight friends take for granted: holding hands, sweet talk, cuddling under a tree on a beach towel, watching a concert with her head on your shoulder. These simple public actions pose real dangers in homophobic society, and observing otherwise closeted lesbians experience new liberty is a bittersweet phenomenon. Some couples attending their first festival demonstrate a positive mania of public togetherness by dressing exactly alike throughout the weekend, right down to their matching fanny packs. . . . Some couples ostentatiously make love on the ground in an open field. Some begin every sentence with 'My partner and I…' or 'Where we live…' These mannerisms may not be at all indicative of how the two live and behave all the rest of the year. Instead, they often signify the burst of relief many lesbians feel at 'coming home' to festival space, where love between women wins approval and sanction, not punishment and ostracism."[316]

As much as it embarrasses me to confess it, Bobbie and I are one of those lesbian couples that dressed alike on the Land. After our first Festival and experiencing the tremendous freedom to be *seen* as a couple, we went the following year with matching everything – except the fanny packs. We did not need them because Bobbie made us matching vests with pockets to carry our "stuff." But as cute as matching couples are, as Morris noted, seeing them is "bittersweet" because their matching outfits often signify the desperation they feel to be *seen* as a couple. Susan Krieger wrote, "It seems to me that for all the assimilation and acceptance that appears on the surface to be our new lesbian reality (we are the couple next door), our kinship as well as our existence is still repeatedly denied. Our care for one another is largely invisible, as is our different kind of love, our different life, and our different vulnerability in the world."[317] When I talked with Cindy and Marnie they were wearing contrasting tie-dyed t-shirts that clearly signified their "coupledom." They talked about the reality of hiding their relationship in the outside world and the relief they felt being somewhere they "belonged."

Cindy: "At first, it was hard for us to get used to being able to express who we are. To let people *see* who we are. Like out in the real world you can't walk around and hold your partner's hand, or stop and give her a kiss. You can't do those things in the real world."

Marnie: "You can't sit next to her in the car [laughs] – unless you've got the dog on the other side. We play those tricks. But here…"

Cindy: "Here it's ok. It's ok to be who we are."

Marnie: "It's the feeling of belonging. And for one week out of the year we can be exactly who we want to be. We can kiss in public, hold hands in public, and smile at each other, and not get stared at."[318]

For lesbian couples, the Festival may be the only time throughout the year that they get to celebrate their relationship publicly, and as Morris suggests, the Festival community gives them numerous opportunities to do so.

---

[316] Morris, 21.
[317] Susan Krieger. "The *Mirror Dance* in Retrospect," *Journal of Lesbian Studies* 9, no. 1/2 (2005): 8.
[318] Cindy Avery and Marnie Keifer. Personal Interview. August, 2002.

"Standard festival workshops address a range of sexuality topics, including presentations on what works for long-term couples. Role modeling along these lines is much appreciated at festivals, since the outside world hardly honors the sanctity (or tenacity) of committed lesbian relationships. Stage announcements at festivals invariably include tributes to couples who are celebrating seven, ten, 15, 20 years together – and powerful applause follows. One may catch a glimpse of a proud producer wiping away a tear as a beaming pair tell the story of how they met at that very festival on a windswept night X years ago."[319] Although we did not meet at the Festival, Bobbie and I are one of those "long-term couples" that our Festival family celebrates , and even now at the time of this writing, our family is planning a 25th wedding anniversary party for the 2006 Festival. And at the time of this second edition we have just celebrated our 32nd anniversary.

Weddings and anniversaries are common on the Land even though lesbians are known for being the "queens of serial monogamy."[320] But many Festival couples end up spending the rest of their lives together. During our second festival we were invited to the wedding of an older lesbian couple who had met at the Festival several years prior, but because they lived in different states they always left each other at the end of the week. That particular year, they decided it was time they left together, so one of them sold her house, quit her job, and arrived at the Festival with all of her worldly possession packed in a U-Haul. On the last day, after the couple recited their vows, their Festival family blessed them with a wedding reception. Bringing whatever food and decorations they could scrounge up, about 15 womyn gathered under a big blue rain tarp to offer the couple gifts they had purchased in the Crafts Bazaar. Then they feasted on barbequed chicken, baked beans, watermelon, and wedding cake that one of the womyn had gone into town to buy. The next morning, like all the other festiegoers, the couple packed up their tent and headed back into the "real" world, but this time they had each other as they headed out into the diaspora.

**Families in the Diaspora**

For many womyn, leaving the Land means leaving their families and returning to the loneliness of exile in their everyday lives. As womyn pack up their gear and load their cars, they fight to hold back their tears, knowing that in a few minutes they will have to say goodbye to their sisters, mothers, daughters, and grandmothers, whom they will most likely not see again until the next Festival. Then, as the steady stream of cars winds its way out to the highway, they head off in every direction. But womyn replay special Festival moments in their heads to stave off the pain of having to trace their fingers along the map that leads them back into the diaspora.

---

[319] Morris, 123.
[320] Vandenburg, "Home-phobia," 55.

What then do these Festival families mean in the context of the "real" world? Are their families simply utopian fantasies that carry no weight or responsibility in everyday life? If these Festival families are not based on biological, economic, or religious structures, how do they function the rest of the year, and what purpose do they serve? As suggested at the beginning of the chapter, womyn use the word "family" to signify multiple meanings. For some womyn who remain close to their families of origin, the term is a metaphor for "community." For others, it is a word used to describe membership in the lesbian community. Still others use it to name their specific partner and children. But for many, the word "family" signifies the loving familial relationships they invested in during the Festival. For these womyn, their Festival family is just as "real" as any other and they care for it throughout the year in the same ways that "normal" families do when they live in separate states.

Like "normal" families, members of Festival families send holiday cards and birthday presents through out the year. Those that can afford to travel visit each other as often as possible. They call each other on weekends to catch up. "How are the kids doing in school?" they ask. "What did the doctor say?" "Is there anything I can do? Do you need anything?" They also talk about the mundane chores of life. "Well you need a Philips screwdriver for that" or "I hate my boss." But most of all they call just to say "I love you."

Others keep track of, and even create families on the Festival Bulletin Board. Like the telephone, womyn use the Bulletin Board to discuss everything from what happened on *The L Word* to what they are doing in their courses at college, to what a beloved pet's symptoms mean. But "talk" is not all that womyn *do* to maintain their families across space and time. Like "normal" families, they also provide tangible economic and spiritual support for their members, and the Bulletin Board helps them do that. Below is only a small portion of one Bulletin Board conversation that lasted several years. It was called "V's Healing Thread."

This conversation revolved around a womyn named V, who was terminally ill with cancer and suffered multiple complications due to treatment problems. V worked at the Festival for several years and she always brought Parker (her young son) with her. Over the years, the thread became a place where V's Festival *family*, as well as other community members, offered their words of comfort, prayers for healing, and calls for help. Womyn from around the world have used the thread to keep track of V's day-to-day medical and financial situations. At times the thread became a place to organize their very real efforts to provide for V's physical needs.

When V was too sick to write her own posts, those closest to her kept everyone else in the loop by informing them of V's condition. Sometimes posts were written on a minute-by-minute bases as womyn gather in sacred circles to pray and perform magic for V during critical moments of her treatment. Others came minute-by-minute when the womyn around V thought she was about to die. The posts were so numerous on "V's Healing Thread" they could have filled an entire book. What follows are only a few posts I copied between 5/19/04 and 5/13/05. I left the posts unedited for the most part. They demonstrate the love, tenacity, and magic that transformed V's life in concrete and tangible ways before she died.

**5-19-04  Planetearthgirrl:** *Still here, in the circle, grounding the energy, rooting it…holding it for all.*

**5-22-04  V:** *been spending most waking hours at the hospital. I got platelets just before surgery to have a second midiport put in. Maybe you remember that the original port got infected. Thus the removal. After surgery they gave me a pint of red blood. Today they gave me 3 more pints in hopes that I'll have enough energy for the trip to New England. I also decided to take on another round of chemo. I want my quality of life to be good while I am here. I already throw up so much and for unexplained reasons that taking chemo won't be any worse. I'm already bald so couldn't be any worse there – with the possible exception of losing my eyelashes and eyebrows or my nails again but even those are so superficial. This chemo is every 3 weeks and if we could possibly send the darn cancer into remission I could have remission and my release as well.*

**5-22-04  Danni:** *I send out my energy and waves of blessings.*

**6-6-04  Whitewolf:** *I talked with V the other day – she has a fungus or a viral infection in her esophagus. They are treating her with antifungal and anti-viral drugs. She seemed to be in good spirits when I talked to her, but I am sure that this set back is difficult. The doc's in Portland are [taking a] different approach – trying to get her white cell count up, rather than treating the caner. Since I am no longer in the middle of the medical situation, its hard to tell if this a good move. Treating the cancer means treating the pempigus – and her white cell count is suppressed to keep the pempigus in check – although her white cell count is soooo low at this point that trying to increase it is probably not a bad idea.*

**6-7-04  Tessa:** *sending energy from down under…straight through the earth's core…up again through to the other side…where it will find V.*

**6-20-04  Babs:** *As I sit in my new office and unpack my belongings, I come across a beautiful photo of V & me from one of the earlier uniform parties [at Michigan]. V is clad in a sexy Viking garb (complete with horned metal helmet)!*

**7-1-04:  V:** *Hi all – Coyote Song's updates were right. . . . They finally got my medication the IVIG some 6 weeks late! But with all the open lesions in my mouth I am grateful and hope I might find some relief.*

**7-12-04:  Womyn2me:** *I am picturing the Sunday healing ceremony [at Michigan] in my mind, beautiful blankets on the ground, V lying comfortably in the middle, all of us around her, waves of energy gently lifting her spirits and bringing her relief from pain, worry and fear…*

**7-14-04  Scout_in_Rhode_Island:** *I'm agreeing, right now it seems like V really needs some material support, she's really struggling with issues like housing, kidcare and even food. I talked to her about trying to do a bit of a fundraising campaign at Mich somehow…She was very appreciative but said there's some problem with anything that hits her bank acct, they use it to reduce her benefits. So, thinking about how this can happen with* *some type of flowthru. But I'm sure it can happen.*

**7-15-04 paducahjenn:** *Don't know if this is crazy or not...but how about cold hard cash that she doesn't have to "put through the system."*

**7-15-04 Beth:** *What is that address for V at her sister's? Also, I would like to buy some raffle tickets in V's name - - I'd like to hear her name called from the stage, and have her receive a gift or two from the Festival via Chance.*

**7-15-04 Coyote Song:** *Alright, all those who gather here to offer support --- now is the time to come to action. I am putting out a desperate plea to each and every one of you. We MUST pull together. V is tired. She is losing her will. But only we can bring her the peace she needs now, to know that all is well, because she is not able to count on what may come. PLEASE send money orders to... People who would rather send checks, e-mail me and I'll try to take care of that aspect. I also want to hear from womyn in the New England area who may be able to step in with childcare for Parker. We need a plan, and we need one now. Especially people that Parker knows and has spent time with [at Michigan].*

**7-15-04 ramonajane:** *Is V hooked up with a hospice program in her location?*

**7-18-04 Traficmama:** *V as time grows near to leave for the Land you are in my thoughts on a daily basis. You are and will be in my heart from now until eternity.*

**7-19-04 V:** *Hi everyone, ... I appreciate all your support. Parker will probably be at Brother Sun, if you want to stop in and say hi. But as you know, I won't make it this year.*

**7-21-04 po:** *I hope to see Parker this year at Brother Sun. My dad made bird house kits for us to put together and paint/decorate. Does that sound like a camp activity or what?*

**7-24-04 Babs:** *I was looking through some old festival papers last night and came across the "Raffle Manifesto" that V wrote when I was looking for advice the first year I was on raffle crew. Her spirit and love for festival shine so brightly in her words!*

**7-27-04 Traficmama:** *V, I haven't posted as of late but please remember that you are always with me and on my mind. Especially at this time of year as I am packing to go to the fest and will be missing you something awful this year. I do have a festival package made up for Parker so that he will have plenty of cool things to do while there.*

**8-3-04 bunnyfemfem:** *My thoughts have been wandering to fest, which means I can see V with her pink lace slip and her Viking helmet. I hear her voice reverberating through the belly bowl, louder than any PA system.*

**8-5-04 Coyote Song:** *Once again, a heads-up to all who haven't yet left. There is a "V Donation Fund" happenin when you get to the Land.*

**8-17-04 Travelintomboy:** *This is my first day back to work [after the festival] I just wanted to share with you what an amazing experience we all had at brother sun....We all love you and Parker so much and I just wanted to say thank you. I know I am rambling but I am filled with emotions right now...since emerging back into this way of life.*

**8-26-04 V:** *Hi Galz! Here I am...I want you to know how floored I am that womyn raised money for me, remembered me and carried my spirit around fest. I gobble up stories and feel like I can picture it all. Well, all except Grandpa Lorraine in Queenies' chaps at the worker auction. That might need Kodak proof for me to believe! But I can picture Traffic Mama with a bucket at Triangle, and Nance selling kisses in the femme parade, and Trish's beautiful charms enticing donations. I can picture Scout networking and Po, sick as a damn dog and still supporting me behind the scenes. And the proof is that $2,000 was raised. I* *cried and smiled and lifted my hands to the sky. There were sooo many wet [from a week of rain] crumpled one dollar bills. That's what really got me. Imagine the stack of ones it takes to make that much money. I am incredibly grateful for the larger bills – don't get me wrong! – but it was the ones that represented one woman at a time, all that love coming from a wet, cold patch of ferns in the forests of Michigan. No words can match my joy. Thank you. Love, V.*[321]

     V's thread represents only one of the many ways the Michigan Bulletin Board transforms individual womyn's lives through their *family* networks. Another came after hurricane Katrina when womyn from around the country gathered to offer tangible support to displaced Festival workers from New Orleans. Below are just a few of their posts.

**8-30-05  Puma:**  *Dear all, I have started an Emergency Fund for Michigan workers who have been affected by Hurricane Katrina. All the info you need is here:...[Puma set up a PayPal account]  NOTE: I need folks to e-mail me the information about workers who need help and their contact info. Please e-mail this info to me at ... If you have any substantial questions about this, PLEASE do not comment here but send ALL correspondence about this to... [Puma's personal email address]. Thanks a lot! The reasoning is: People will not have homes or jobs for a long time and will need funds to keep them going. The reason for this being worker-only is that we work with these womyn in the woods for a month each year and they are our community.  I encourage anyone who wants to start a fund for festies from NOLA [New Orleans, LA]. Love and hope to all the folks affected by Katrina.*

**8-30-05  ohboyhowdy**  *hi puma, thanks so much for starting this fund. i'll donate asap. also, i'm wondering if you know anything about a few of the workers who live in no - mesha and justin. they're friends of mine and i'm hoping they're ok. -bryan*

**8-31-05  Fae**  *Mesha's in Chicago with Scorcher...she's fine.*

**8-31-05  Puma**  *Dear all, I have some contact info for people now. I know nola phones and cell phones are not working but I now have e-mail addresses for Mags, Deuce, Kiki, Mesha, Cherie, Dix, Val, Kristen, Justin, Debra and Karen. If anyone knows about anyone else please let me know... Thanks a TON to all who have donated, these girls really appreciate it. Keep those donations coming and please send the info out to everyone you know. Your rich or even not so rich uncle could give his money to a worthy cause. More Nola workers are always coming out of the woodwork every moment and lots of them need help badly.*

**9-4-05  LZBN69**  *You rock for doing all that you are...also... I feel like I want to offer housing for a lesbian or 2 here in the Bay area of CA. I was tremendously concerned about Debra...so relieved that I found the post that she is ok. When you go to MWMF for 23 yrs it is hard not to be bonded to those who work yr after yr.*

**9-9-05  Puma**  *Dear all, We have received a bunch of donations, over $2900. Thanks so much to everyone who has donated. Some news about the fund: I spoke to PayPal today and this is the deal: I cannot accept donations until I get a federal Tax ID number. This means we kind of have to become a real organization, which is probably best anyhow since there is a bigger benefit in the works here in NYC where I live. This means the PayPal is down for the*

---

[321] "V's Healing Thread." [online], accessed between 5/19/04 and 5/13/04. Available from www.michfest.com/ubb/Forum7/HTML/000048.html.

*forseeable future while I make this fund a legit charity. SO I have changed the webpage to tell people that we are currently only accepting donations by check in the mail. Please pass this info on and keep forwarding this to people… I will try today or next Monday to get the wheels in motion to become a real charity. We are gonna be legit, gals! Thanks again to all who have donated, keep passing this info on as these girls are trying to get by with very little right now. Lots of love to you all, Puma.*[322]

**Festival Families are Democratic**

These types of Bulletin Board threads demonstrate the very real ways womyn love and support their Festival families across time and space. "Bonded" through telephone lines, bank accounts, and cyberspace, these womyn are what Chela Sandoval calls "multiply displaced figures" who form families that are not "quite as imperializing in terms of a single figuration of identity."[323] Festival families may not share bloodlines or family structures that resemble the patriarchal model, but they do provide the love and support that is often withheld from womyn whom the patriarchy has no use for. Furthermore, I would also argue that they *do* meet Valerie Lehr's criteria for democratizing the private life of the family in such a way that its care becomes a "function of community."[324]

Festival families are democratic and their care is a function of the community because rather than sharing a bloodline they share what I have called an Amazon consciousness, which allows them to transcend patriarchal models of family and claim each other as sisters, mothers, daughters, and grandmothers in a web of familial connections that support them throughout the year. In other words, Festival families are structured in a matrix of ideas held together by the "apparatus of love."[325] The Amazon represents the idea of an origin from which all womyn can claim a familial or spiritual lineage if they choose to. For many womyn, imagining a familial lineage of matriarchal clans is a comforting *idea*. Elana Dykewomon wrote after visiting Emma Goldman's grave, "Seeing her grave was important to me. The experience told me that more than blood defines ancestry. We have an ancestry of ideas, of place in the work for a better world. We need to be able to bury our dead in a place that the descendants of our ideas can find, so they can feel us reaching out to them in love, over time."[326] When Dykewomon asks, "Where are our lesbian cemeteries?" she is talking about "building spaces," real and tangible where womyn can find their imagined "ancestry."

---

[322] "Emergency Relief for Mich Workers Affected by Hurricane Katrina." [online], assessed between 8/30/05 and 9/09/05. Available from www.michfest.com/ubb/Forum9/HTML/000624.html.
[323] Sandoval, 172.
[324] Lehr, 10.
[325] Sandoval.
[326] Dykewomon, "Lesbian Quarters: On Building Space, Identity, Institutional Memory and Resources," 37.

This longing for the tangible motivates womyn to build families at the Festival and it drives them to build family homes where they share their ideas as they pound down their tent stakes. In their tents and around their kitchen tables, and where they bury their dead in the shade of oak trees, womyn are investing their love in each other at the Festival. While the word "family" has multiple meanings and is richly complex with ideas, looking at what womyn *do* to build homes at the Festival is perhaps the best way to understand what they mean when the call each other *family*.

# ⚔ 5 ⚔
# Welcome Home

For lesbians who have been rejected by their families and kicked out of their homes, the whole concept of "home" becomes a complex notion fraught with longing and loss. Like Chandra Talpade Mohanty, many lesbians ask "What is home? The place I was born? Where I grew up? Where my parents live? Where I live and work as an adult? Where I locate my community, my people? Who are 'my people?' Is home a geographical space, a historical space, an emotional sensory space?"[327] Like Mohanty, many lesbians argue that "how one understands and defines home – is profoundly political."[328]

Several other feminist scholars including Biddy Martin, Laura Levitt, Patricia Hill Collins, Amber Hollibaugh, Susan Fox Rogers, Bonnie Zimmerman, and Gloria Anzaldua have explored the meaning of "home." Their political analyses reflect the feminist ambiguity around the concept of home, particularly as it maintains patriarchal and colonizing systems of inequality and oppression for womyn. The popular concept of home as a loving and safe place is, as Martin and Mohanty argue, a social construction based on "the exclusion of specific histories of oppression and resistance, and the repression of differences even within oneself."[329] For Patricia Hill Collins, home is closely connected to the concept of "nation," where systems of race and gender are maintained through "blood ties." Collins wrote that, "Overall, by relying on the belief that families have assigned places where they truly belong, images of place, space, and territory link gendered notions of family with constructs of race and nation. In this logic that everything has its place, maintaining borders of all sorts becomes vitally important. Preserving the logic of segregated home spaces requires strict rules that distinguish insiders from outsiders. Unfortunately, far too often, these boundaries continue to be drawn

---

[327] Chandra Talpade Mohanty. "Crafting Feminist Genealogies: On the Geography and Politics of Home, Nation, and Community." In *Talking Visions: Multicultural Feminism in a Transnational Age*. Ella Shohat, ed. (Cambridge: MIT Press, 1998), 487.
[328] Ibid.
[329] Chandra Talpade Mohanty and Biddy Martin. "What's Home Got To Do With It?" In *Feminism Without Boarders: Decolonizing Theory, Practicing Solidarity*. (Durham: Duke University Press, 2003), 136.

along the color line."[330]   As already argued, boundaries are also drawn along sexual lines that keep many lesbians from crossing the threshold of the family home.

These boundaries force many lesbians to maintain what Bonnie Zimmerman calls, "a multiple subject position that is neither comfortable, coherent, nor easy. It means being a gadfly everywhere, constantly questioning and deconstructing the metaphor of home."[331] Many types of womyn maintain multiple subject positions and as Laura Levitt suggests, they learn the "process of reconfiguring home on many fronts."[332] Levitt explored the intersections of a Jewish feminist identity and home, and found that "the knowledge that home could be both de/ and re/constructed was visceral."[333]   She argued that "location matters" in any analysis and that it is "crucial to theorize out of the contingent places we call home."[334] Rather than being a permanent place of stability and comfort, these scholars argue that home is a "contingent place" that constantly shifts as multiply positioned subjects move through different social locations.

For multiply positioned and multiply marginalized womyn, home is often, as Mohanty suggested, an "imaginative, politically charged space, in which the familiarity and sense of affection and commitment lay in shared collective analysis of social injustices, as well as a vision of radical transformation."[335] In this way, Amber Hollibaugh found home among the women she "came from," the working-class lesbians in prisons, reform schools, mental institutions, bars, the military, and auto factories "who had mostly been left out of the current feminist exploration," but who offer critical commentary among themselves about the forces that demand they live in constantly shifting realities.[336] These spaces of shifting reality are what Gloria Anzaldua called "nepantla."

Like liminal space, "nepantla" lack boundaries and according to Anzaldua, "living in this liminal zone means being in a constant state of displacement – an uncomfortable, even alarming feeling. Most of us dwell in nepantla so much of the time it's become a sort of 'home.'"[337]   Anzaldua describes "nepantla" as "bridges [that] span liminal spaces between worlds." [338]

[330] Patricia Hill Collins. "It's all in the Family: Intersections of Gender, Race, and Nation." In *Decentering the Center: Philosophy for a Multicultural, Postcolonial, and Feminist World.* Uma Narayan and Sandra Harding, eds. (Bloomington: Indiana University Press, 2000), 163.
[331] Bonnie Zimmerman. "Placing Lesbians." *The New Lesbian Studies: Into the Twenty-First Century.* Bonnie Zimmerman and Toni A. H. McNaron, eds. (New York: The Feminist Press, 1996), 272-273.
[332] Laura Levitt. *Jews and Feminism: The Ambivalent Search for Home.* (New York: Routledge, 1997), 2.
[333] Ibid.
[334] Ibid., 3.
[335] Mohanty, "Genealogies of Community, Home, and Nation," 128.
[336] Amber Hollibaugh. *My Dangerous Desires: A Queer Girl Dreaming Her Way Home.* (Durham: Duke University Press, 2000), 206-207.
[337] Gloria Anzaldua. "(Un)natural Bridges, (Un)safe Spaces." *This Bridge We Call Home: Radical Visions for Transformation.* Gloria E. Anzaldua and Analouise Keating, eds. (New York: Routledge, 2002), 1.
[338] Ibid.

For womyn at the Festival, liminal space is everything off the Land. Once they leave the Land they drive out onto the "bridges" of time that span the 51 weeks between Festivals. There they pass through the year as decentered subjects, marginalized womyn living in a "constant state of displacement" that they also call *home*.

However, Elana Dykewomon argued that "we need physical places. That's what I come back to. A church is a physical place where like-minded people can gather and discuss both their spiritual and physical needs. A theater is a place where we hold the mirror of art up, to show our reflections. A school is a physical place where history and literature are actually created – the importance of events and words is made real by the work of teachers. A graveyard is the place where we honor our dead, and our connection to each other through life. If lesbians need each other, and I believe we do; if we are in the constant and fluid process of working out our senses of community; if we are to move forward while creating a past we can pass on – then we need to build."[339]

Dykewomon called lesbians to build physical spaces that institutionalize their memories, values, and resources. And although Michigan is temporary, womyn at the Festival do build physical spaces. More accurately, they "bring place into being." Jonathan Z. Smith argued, "It is the relationship to the human body, and our experience of it, that orients us in space, that confers meaning to place. Human beings are not placed, they bring place into being."[340] If we think about the concept of bringing place into being, womyn at the Festival are creating a place rather than occupying space. In other words, what if rather than building spaces that mark significant events, spaces were built for significant things to happen?

Womyn at the Festival are tired of living in the margins, in interstitial spaces, in the liminal borderland. They are weary from working to keep their balance on swaying bridges that constantly shift their realities. They are tired of constantly deconstructing and reconstructing home, feeling continually displaced and perpetually homeless. They want a home and homeland where they can truly love and support each other in families and communities, and create lineages of ideas and institutions that maintain their values and their histories. They want some ground to stand on, where they can sink their roots, so they return to Michigan each year pulling wagons of "stuff" to build their homes.

At the Festival, womyn bring "place into being" by building a space where significant *experiences* are meant to happen. Womyn know that the only permanent thing about Michigan is the *experience* they will carry home with them when they leave the Land, so they build spaces where they can *experience*

---

[339] Dykewomon, "Lesbian Quarters: On Building Space, Identity, Institutional Memory and Resources," 42.
[340] Jonathan Z. Smith. *To Take Place: Toward Theory in Ritual.* (Chicago: University of Chicago Press, 1987), 26-28.

themselves fully and freely. Red-faced and panting for breath, they schlep tons of gear across the Land because they want to *experience* family, home, community, and sacred traditions in the flesh. Womyn call Michigan *home* because of what they *experience* there, in *corpora*, in the *body*, in the relationships they build in living rooms and dining rooms and bedrooms, in parades and workshops and work shifts, in symbol, myth, and ritual, in music and dance and theater. The remainder of this chapter focuses on womyn's narratives and the places of *experience* they build. It pays particular attention to how they experience themselves in *corpora*, in their bodies and communities, and the places they build to offer each other the ritual greeting of "Welcome Home."

**Bringing Place Into Being**

Every year at the end of the Festival, as exhausted womyn lug their gear to the *Triangle* and wait for shuttles to the parking lot, the Land crews, loading crews, traffic crews, and shuttle drivers sing their mantra, "less stuff, more womyn." But every year womyn return to Michigan with more "stuff." This "stuff" represents the tangible elements in the "apparatus of love," the tools for building home, family, and community.[341]  Womyn use this "stuff" to implement their ethic of care and demonstrate their love for each other.

On the first day of the Festival, steady streams of womyn cover the terrain, moving back and forth over every road, sidewalk, and footpath on the Land. Like columns of army ants marching over hills and through gullies, carrying loads four times their weight, womyn march back and forth from the parking lot to their campsites, pushing wheelbarrows and pulling red wagons, hand trucks, and every other type of yard cart imaginable. In sometimes 100° heat, thousands of womyn make the mile-and-a-half round trip several times, pulling carts loaded with plastic bins, cardboard boxes, suitcases, folding chairs, tents, tarps, water jugs, rolled carpets, musical instruments, cameras, and ice chests. Back and forth they "schlep" their wagons as sweat pours from their beet-red faces, down their backs, and between their breasts, where it mixes with road-dust to form little pools of mud. They pause only long enough to offer each other a greeting of "Welcome Home" or to help each other through deep patches of sand, over narrow footpaths covered in thick bark, or around impertinent tree stumps that stand in their way.

Shuttles loaded to the breaking point also create a steady stream of movement, kicking up road-dust as they snake their way up and down *Lois Lane*. Tractors pulling surreys, rented vans, DART buses, and private pickup trucks stuffed to overflowing make their continuous loop transporting womyn and their gear between the *Front Gate* and the *Triangle*. But because the road is only wide enough for one vehicle, the shuttles have to pull over or back up and pull over, to make room enough to pass each other, which means that using the shuttle service on the first day can take even longer than schlepping gear in by

[341] Sandoval.

140

hand. Either way, once the gates open, everyone is in a race against the sun because no one wants to set up camp in the dark. So rain or shine, womyn march on, never stopping until their tents are up and their homes are secure.

*Bobbie with our Family Gear on the Flatbed Tractor - 2006*

The first time we went to Michigan, I stood out on *Lois Lane*, amazed as I watched what seemed to be a never-ending line of red-faced, out-of-breath, exhausted womyn struggling to pull wagons loaded with more "stuff" than I ever thought anyone could use. When one of these red-faced womyn paused long enough to catch her breath, I offered her some water and asked how many people she was camping with. "Just me," she replied. "Then why," I asked, "do you need so much stuff?" "Oh, this isn't all for me. I bring a lot of extra stuff because someone in the *family* might need something." When I asked her whom she meant by "family," she just waved her hand and puffed, "any other dyke on the Land." So what kind of "extra stuff" did she bring? "Oh, I've got an extra tent and sleeping bags, a few blankets, and of course my footlocker of stuff for the Femme Parade," she laughed. "I've also got an ice chest filled with med supplies. I'm a nurse. I always bring meds with me, just in case. So if you need anything, and you don't want to walk all the way to the Womb, come see me. I've also got extra tarps and flashlight batteries too, in case anyone needs them. Just let me know. Well, I better get moving. Gotta set this condo up before the sun goes down."

At the time I could not imagine what she meant by "condo," but as Bobbie and I made our first tour of the Land we were astonished to see the elaborate campsites womyn were setting up. Some had two and even three room tents that did, in fact, look like small apartments. Some womyn erected large canopies under which they rolled out carpets, arranged blowup couches and armchairs, and strung battery powered lights to create homey living rooms. Others used canopies to create dining rooms, where they would eat burgers and steaks fresh off their large gas barbeque grills. Some womyn even erected two canopies, one for a living room and one for a dining room. In effect, they created homes without walls, but had tarps at the ready to create walls just in case it rained. But beyond the structures themselves, womyn brought other stuff to make their house a "home." Unpacking their plastic bins, they placed "little things" around their campsites that infused them with a homey ambiance. Homemade banners hung from trees that welcomed visitors, flowers in vases, a wedding album on the dining room table, an American flag on a stick stuck in the ground, toys in the yard, and a saint's candle on a tree stump all served as little touches that transformed campsites into homes.

But why go to all this back-breaking work when the Festival only lasts a week? Why waste time and energy schlepping in two, three, four, or even five wagon loads of plastic bins to just turn around and schlep them all back out again? Why not simply set up a small tent and hurry off to enjoy a concert or workshop or parade? For most womyn the answer is simple. The Festival is the only time they get to be with their families, and families need homes. Like Festival families, Festival homes are often more real and more important because they represent the love and support many womyn do not experience in the outside world.

In essence, womyn feel "homeless in the most profound sense of the word." Margaret Vandenburg argued that it is "no wonder we [lesbians] are the queens of serial monogamy. The divorce rate among lesbians is second only to the birthrate of the moral majority. Try building a lasting relationship without having a home to hang your hat in, let alone your heart."[342] In her essay titled "Home-phobia," Vandenburg wrote, "Lesbians are such a terrible threat to the whole notion of home itself that once we wreck the home of our birth, we are forever punished by not being allowed to establish our own homes as adults."[343] Because lesbians are perceived as "unproductive," "rebellious," and "dangerous threats to family values," there is no role for them in the patriarchal model of home, and therefore lesbians find themselves excommunicated from their homes of origin. Like Vandenburg, many womyn find that after being "crucified on the cross of sacred family values, and having been branded the scapegoat not only of [their] family but also Public Enemy Number One of

[342] Vandenburg, "Home-phobia," 55.
[343] Ibid., 54.

142

homes everywhere, without a doubt, home is the most inhospitable place [they] have ever been."[344]

Yet, as Vandenburg notes, "The homing instinct is strong, even when there is no home to return to."[345] Like the other authors in Susan Fox Roger's anthology, *Chasing the American Dyke Dream*, home is a place lesbians long to return to, but are always in search of.[346] "I will never forget," Vandenburg writes, "the feeling of finally wanting to go home and knowing that this place – whatever it was – did not exist for me."[347] Vandenburg argued that most lesbians live transient lives because, "Mere mortals cannot create something out of nothing."[348] Having had their root cut from the family tree, lesbians find they have no ground on which to build a home.

## Building Homes

One evening in late July 2004, Cindy and I were engrossed in one of our regular Sunday evening chats over the phone. We were discussing our packing lists for Michigan, and she made the remark, "we have everything but the kitchen sink." I immediately replied that Bobbie and I had the kitchen sink covered. On a recent trip to our local sporting goods store, we had seen a kitchen unit that folded up into its own neat, self-contained aluminum case. This kitchen unit came complete with a working sink and drain hose, a spice rack, shelves for pots and pans, a dish drying rack, and a counter top to set the camp stove on, plus a paper towel rack. We made that purchase a surprise for our Michigan family, which by then had grown to four couples. When our family rolled into camp to find a complete kitchen ready and waiting, they were thrilled. Cindy was as giddy as a schoolgirl and squealed, "Now we really do have everything, including the kitchen sink!" Beth was so excited that before she even set up her tent, she ripped through her plastic bins to find the surprise she had brought for us; a Mr. Coffee drip coffee maker designed to fit over the grates of a camp stove. We laughed and laughed as each couple added their "surprises" to our family home. The following year, during one of our Sunday evening chats, Cindy informed me that she and Marnie had purchased a set of plastic cabinets. "We need a cool place to store the food!" she exclaimed. So now, our Michigan kitchen is built under its own canopy and is complete with a working sink, counter top, stove, overhead lantern, four ice chests to refrigerate perishables, and cabinets to store our eating utensils and dry goods.

While kitchens are arguably the most important room in any home, other rooms are also built with loving care on the Land. For instance, Bobbie and I have a full size airbed with its own pedestal frame. We also have two small folding canvas tables that make nice nightstands on either side of the bed.

---

[344] Ibid., 59.
[345] Ibid., 58.
[346] Susan Fox Rogers. *Chasing an American Dyke Dream: Homestretch.* (San Francisco: Cleis Press, 1998).
[347] Vandenburg, "Home-phobia," 59.
[348] Ibid., 58-59.

We pack flannel sheets, pillows, and a down comforter into a plastic bin, which then serves as a dresser at the foot of the bed. We have even considered schlepping in one of those plastic drawer units for this purpose, but we did not want to "get too carried away." A couple of years ago we restricted ourselves to bringing only those things that we could transport to the campsite in two trips with the yard wagon, which gets parked in the driveway next to Cindy's and Beth's yard wagons. Alas, those plastic drawers would require another mile and a half of wagon pulling, and neither of us is getting any younger.

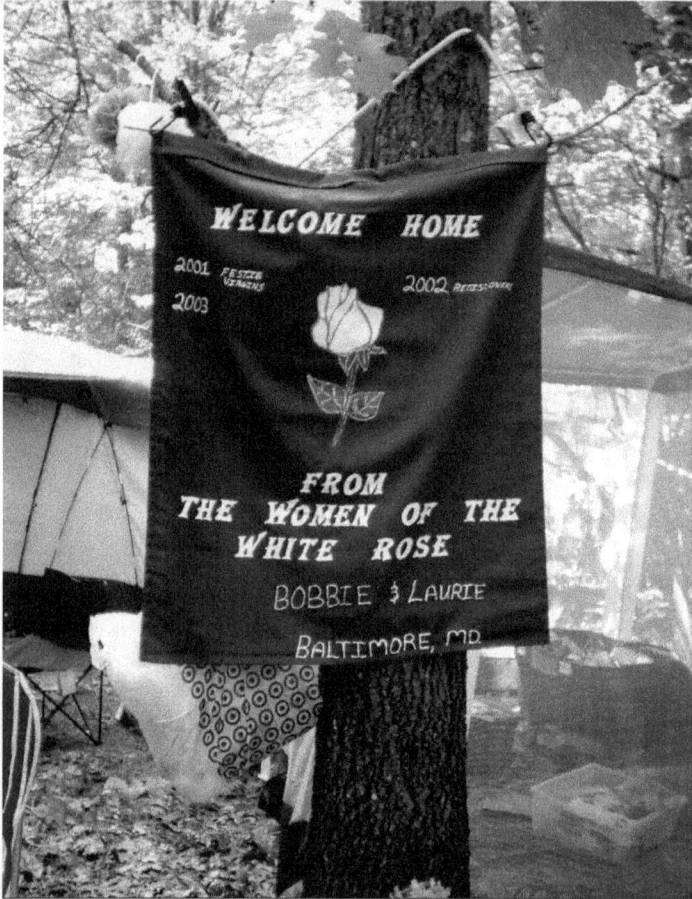

*Laurie & Bobbie's Welcome Home Sign - 2003*

As for the living room, well that is another family effort. Each couple brings a dining canopy that we "bungee" together to form a large living/dining room combo. In this space we have three tables and an assortment of chairs. Our living room/dinning room is approximately 10 x 20 feet, and most of the time it is overflowing with womyn and children, and their stuff; coffee cups, hats, toys, Festival programs, hairbrushes, towels, munchies, flashlights, water bottles, various articles of clothing, etc. Between the living room and the kitchen we tie a rope between two trees to hang our wet towels. This space becomes our bathroom, and Cindy even brings a mirror for this space, which she usually hangs from a tree branch. This area is where everyone brushes their teeth in the morning, and where we dress for the Femme Parade. Like sisters in the bathroom, Cindy, Beth, and I jostle in front of the mirror to put on our mascara and lipsticks, check our hair, and help each other zip up our dresses. One year, Cindy even brought tiaras for us to wear in the parade.

We have also worked on creating a nice yard for our home. After our first year, when it was unbearably hot, we decided to bring a little kiddy pool. To cool off on hot summer afternoons, we can sit around with our feet in the pool, but more often it is use by neighborhood kids, whose mothers bring them by to take a dip. In addition to our pool, we also decorate our yard with banners that welcome visitors, and candle lanterns that provide a warm glow in the evening. There has even been talk about bringing a portable propane heated hot tub, but that really would be "over the top" because we would spend all week hauling water to fill it.

Still, as nice as our home is, it does not begin to compare with some of the more luxurious ones in our neighborhood. As describe earlier, some womyn bring area rugs, and blowup couches and arm chairs to furnish their homes, but other womyn bring luxurious RV's, which means they only have to unpack their yard decorations. Nevertheless, every year we are inspired by the imaginative ways so many womyn create actual homes at the Festival, with each womyn bringing her own vision, and then constructing it as concretely as possible.

Akosua: "It's camping, you know. But you can be as minimalist or as luxurious as you want to be. Because some of these women, you know, even though they're in tents, you'd think you were in their living rooms. I tell women that it's really important that at least once in their life they come and experience what's not really describable."[349]

*Home, Sweet Home – 2004*

[349] Akosua. Personal Interview. August, 2005.

Van: "The women I always camp with were talkin' last night about how much I've changed, and commented on my bringing an airbed and a coffee pot. And I said, 'Look, just because you're camping doesn't mean that you can't have a decent life here,' and they all laughed."[350]

Of course not everyone wants to schlep in so much gear, and not all womyn can afford the expensive equipment it takes to build such comfortable homes. Like the outside world, comfort usually comes with a steep price tag, but because the Festival is so important to them, womyn save money all year to make their experience as comfortable and empowering as possible. But as womyn have grown older or wealthier, some have traded in their camping gear for homes on wheels.

Akosua: "It's just really empowering. And I guess there are a lot of women who don't feel the need in their lives for empowerment. They might feel like they've already got that. But you know, there are women who come here who have no jobs. There are women who come here who make a million dollars a year. And you never know. You might know – maybe out in R.V. There are two hundred thousand dollar R.V.'s out there. But by the same token, they might be rented. So you really don't know who's who. So the issue of class – I don't think it goes away completely, but that's largely reduced in place like this."[351]

Other womyn fly to Michigan, which means they are restricted by the amount of weight airlines allow them to carry. These womyn bring only the basics, but quite often find themselves comforted in the homes of other womyn who invite them to join their families.

Susi: "We experienced that here. Like we arrived with nothing more than a tent, a sleeping bag, and a chair. And we are walking along the road, and then we stopped at the midway toilets, and we were discussing where we should camp because we didn't have a lot, and we thought we should keep going toward the kitchen. But we were so tired from the flight from Australia, and then the flight to Michigan, and then the bus ride here. And then there was Kate, and she heard us and told us that 'this is the place to camp because these girls have got everything that opens and closes, and if you've got nothing, this is the place to stay.' And it was like oh my God, we couldn't have picked a better spot. And then some other girls arrived from Pittsburgh and we helped them carry their gear up, and we were so thirsty because we didn't have any water yet, and they gave us a cold beer each. And that was the last thing we expected was a cold beer. But it was fantastic on that first day."[352] Festival lore has it that you only have to speak a need out loud and it will be provided by someone, somewhere, usually by someone you do not know, and will possibly never see again.

---

[350] Van. Personal Interview. August, 2005.
[351] Akosua. Personal Interview. August, 2005.
[352] Susi St. Julian. Personal Interview. August, 2005.

Kip: "This *community* is built on the fact that we trust each other. It's built on the fact that we will care about each other, and that we trust that it will be Ok. And that has remained the same. No matter what kind of crap has happened over the years, or what kind of political shit, what's the same is that if you're walkin' through the woods, you'll hear a voice sometime during the festival, and somebody will shout 'I need some women over here.' And all of a sudden you're surrounded. And they don't know what you needed, or what you wanted, or what your problem is, but they're there and they've got hands, and 'what can I do for you?' And they help. And they don't know you from Adam, and they're never gonna see you again. Well, their gonna see you next year. But that's what this is about. It's not about the music. The music is wonderful, the culture is wonderful, the drums are amazing, the workshops are great and thought provoking, and bonding. But that's not what this is about. It's about them. It's about that. It's about 'hey, we're pickin' up this sign over there and we need some hands, come help,' and people who don't know what you're doin' or who you are, just come help. And it's Ok. That's what it's about. It's about the *community*. It's about building something. And I don't know what it was like 30 years ago, but by the time I got here that was very solid."[353]

Marissa: "I was told by friends that all you had to do was say what you need out loud, and it would come to you. But I was a little skeptical until it happened to me. I went down to the phones the other night, to call and check on my flight back. I'd forgotten which day I made the reservation for. Anyway, I got down there and realized I didn't have the number. It was dark and I said, "Oh shit, I don't have the number for Northwest Airline." I was really upset because I thought I was gonna have to walk all the way back to camp, and then all the way back out to the phones. But then a voice came out of the darkness, "It's 1-800 blah, blah, blah." And I was astonished. What are the odds that right then and there, some woman out in the darkness just happened to know the number for Northwest Airlines right off the top of her head? I never saw her, but I just called out, "Thank you!" And she called back, "No problem," and just kept on going. I was just amazed! I guess things like that happen all the time here."[354]

Kip: "And lots of things have evolved over the years – policies – you know there's always a problem. Every year there's some crisis. You can't bring six thousand women out into the mud, under sometimes adverse weather conditions, and teach 'em how to get along in a week. But somehow it works. And there's rough edges and stuff happens, and we deal with it."[355]

Part of how womyn deal with crises is by bringing enough extra stuff to share with womyn who do not have much to begin with, as when the mother and infant arrived on the Land without their gear. Indeed, things like this do

---

[353] Kip Parker. Personal Interview. August, 2003.
[354] Marissa Corwin. Personal Interview. August, 2005.
[355] Kip Parker. Personal Interview. August, 2003.

happen at the Festival, and often womyn find themselves in real physical need. Thus, a nurse hauls in extra medical supplies, Beth brings extra sleeping bags, and Cindy and Marnie bring extra food. But whether they bring special skills and knowledge or extra "stuff," womyn build homes on the Land to care for each other, mind, body, and soul.

## Home Bodies/Bodies at Home

In her essay, *"Foucault, Femininity, and the Modernization of Patriarchal Power,"* Sandra Bartky explored the many ways women are told their bodies are inferior. For instance she wrote, "the strategy of much beauty-related advertising is to suggest to women that their bodies are deficient; but even without such more or less explicit teachings, the media images of perfect female beauty that bombards us daily leave no doubt in the minds of most women that they fail to measure up. The technologies of femininity are taken up and practiced by women against the background of a pervasive sense of bodily deficiency; this accounts for what is often their compulsive or even ritualistic character."[356] Bartky argues that because women live in patriarchal cultures, "woman must make herself 'object and prey' for the man: it is for him that these eyes are limpid pools, this cheek baby-smooth. In contemporary patriarchal culture, a panoptical male connoisseur resides within the consciousness of most women; they stand perpetually before his gaze and under his judgment. Woman lives her body as seen by another, by an anonymous patriarchal Other."[357] This is particularly true for some lesbians who find themselves under the gaze of fathers, priests, male employers, and even gay male friends who usually feel free to comment on their lesbian friends dress, hair, and weight, and are often more harsh and hurtful than their heterosexual counterparts.

Therefore, women engage in the "disciplinary practices" by which "the ideal body of femininity – and hence the feminine body-subject – is constructed."[358] Some of the disciplinary practices that Bartky outlines include perpetual dieting and exercise, with women being 90 percent more likely than men to join self-help groups like Weight Watchers and Overeaters Anonymous. In terms of exercise, women are more likely to "sculpt" specific "problem areas" of their bodies in order to fit the perfect patriarchal female body type. Furthermore, women discipline themselves to take up as little space as possible, sitting with their "arms close to their bodies, hands folded together in their laps, toes pointing straight ahead or turned inward and their legs pressed together. . . The 'nice' girl learns to avoid the bold and unfettered staring of the 'loose'

---

[356] Sandra Lee Bartky. "Foucault, Femininity, and the Modernization of Patriarchal Power." In *Feminist Philosophies.* Janet A. Kourany, James P. Sterba, and Rosemarie Tong, eds. (Upper Saddle River: Prentice Hall, 1999), 125.
[357] Ibid., 126.
[358] Ibid., 125.

woman who looks at whatever and whomever she pleases. Women are trained to smile more than men, too."[359]

The final set of disciplinary practices that Bartky explores are those that "ornament" the female body. Because women's faces are supposed to be soft, supple, and hairless, and their bodies are not supposed to show signs of "wear, experience, age, or deep thought," they engage in disciplinary practices that are often painful and expensive.[360] Bartky argues that even when women succeed in sculpting and painting the "ideal" feminine body, they fail because the "practiced and subjected" body they produced was originally and forever a woman's body, a "body on which an inferior status has been inscribed."[361] When womyn cannot meet the patriarchal standard of feminine beauty they often become "homebodies," secluding themselves in their houses and going out in public only when absolutely necessary. When I talked with Kathy, she described the pain of going out to dinner with Lorraine to celebrate their anniversary and being ridiculed by a stranger in the restaurant. She told me that experiences like that made her somewhat of a recluse.

Kathy: "I just don't want to go out anymore. I mean, people are so rude. They feel like they can just say anything they want to a fat woman. Like when we went out for our anniversary, this guy just walked up to our table and said, 'do you really think you should be eating that cake?' After that, and other experiences like it, I just didn't want to go out anymore. And I know it's been hard on Lorraine, not going out a lot. But that's one of the reasons Michigan is so important."[362]

During the Festival, womyn experience their bodies differently. They have created a safe space and a discourse that rebels against patriarchal beauty standards, and redefines all types of female bodies as beautiful, regardless of their weight, shape, color, facial hair, or scars. For instance, some womyn think the bearded shuttle driver is "hot" and that the portraits in the Crafts Bazaar of womyn who have had mastectomies are beautiful works of arts. Rather than letting their mastectomy and cesarean scars, or their facial and body hair, or their cellulite and fat make them homebodies, the safe space and the beauty discourse at the Festival empowers womyn to feel at home in their own skin. As soon as some womyn hit the Land, they rip off their blouses and bras, and some even strip down to their birthday suits. Most of the womyn I spoke with commented on the beauty of *all* the womyn, including those whom the patriarchy would deem aesthetically deficient.

Kathy: "But here, it's different. I think it's more something within, a sense of your own personal identity. Your own visualization of yourself. I mean certainly, I'm a larger size woman and that's not a pleasant sight, so it

---

[359] Ibid., 122.
[360] Ibid., 124.
[361] Ibid., 125.
[362] Kathy Davis. Personal Conversation. June, 2003.

took a while for me to get comfortable with myself before I could get out there and expose myself. But I've never had anybody, regardless of whether I had a shirt on or not, say anything or make me feel uncomfortable. That uncomfortableness came from within. That was something I had to change in myself. And I do. I have a boss at work and she asked me what I was gonna be doing on my vacation, and I said 'I'll be walking around without my shirt on.' And she said, 'oh, how can you do that?' I said, 'real easy! I take my shirt off and I walk around.' She said, 'with all those people looking at you.' I said, 'who's looking.' And that's really how you think of it. I mean, because everybody is naked in some form. I mean, there's a lot more to look at than boobs."[363]

Although it takes most "festie virgin" several days, or sometimes even years to shed their patriarchal ideals and feminine disciplinary practices, it becomes easier to do when they finally acclimate to the feeling of safety. The safer womyn feel, the more at home in their bodies they become, and like their relationships, they make their bodies more visible.

Lorraine: "This is like the only *safe* place I am ever in, outside of my own home. You can be totally nude here if you want too, because it's *safe* here, there are no men. Nobody's gonna rape you. It's emotionally *safe*, not just physically *safe*."[364]

Ro: "Women can appreciate other women's bodies, whether they are interested in them sexually or whether they are just appreciating them. But it's not a power over kind of thing. It's not like, 'because I see you I have to possess you' or 'I have a right to grab you,' or 'I am raping you with my eyes.' You know, it can be sexual. It can be assertive. It can be alluring, or exciting. But it's not the same thing as men having power over you. And you know, women are so beautiful and there are so many types of us. I went to an art museum after I left Michigan, and I saw this painting with lots of naked women, and all their breasts were the same shape. I thought if anyone had ever seen a bunch of women together they never would have painted it that way. And going back home again, it really is hard. It's a shock. Even little things like when you see men without their shirts on. Even if we changed the laws and women could take theirs off, we wouldn't because we'd get stared at. We'd get looked at differently. Like I remember saying to someone here, you could look at as many breasts as you wanted too, because I think women look in a different way than men do. I said that to a male friend and he said, 'so you mean I can look, I just have to pretend like I'm not looking.' So he didn't really get it. But going home again is hard because it's a different sensibility. It got cold the other night, so I took off my shorts and put on a pair of pants right there at the concert. And there's no way you could do anything like that back home. I mean you might be able to be like that with your group of friends, or in your

[363] Kathy Davis. Personal Interview. August, 2002.
[364] Lorraine Alexis. Personal Interview. August, 2002.

own home, but not really. And it's not like nudity is a goal for spiritual development or anything, but it's a level of comfort and *safety*. It's *safe* here. The festival is a *safe* place. And that's not in everyday life."[365]

As well as the feeling of safety on the Land, part of what makes womyn feel at home in their own bodies is the discourse that *all* womyn's bodies are beautiful and unique. On the Land, womyn feel safe enough to make their bodies visible, and as individual womyn begin seeing the uniqueness of other womyn's bodies, they become more comfortable in their own. It is often said that "if you have a body image problem when you come to Michigan, you won't leave with one."

Van: "Like I said, the first thing that Michigan gives me is being able to touch my partner in public. But the second piece of that, for me, is the whole body image thing. I'm from a family where, very much, thin is in. I went through some eating disorder issues when I was in high school. When I went from a size three to a size five, my mother said she was going to put me on a lettuce diet. So that has always been in the forefront of my mind. And I got sick with a pretty serious disease about seven years ago. And I was put on a medicine that had me gain a hundred and twenty pounds in six months. And for me, that forced me to kind of deal with, 'I'm more than just what my body looks like.' And I get that reaffirmation here when I come. There are just so many women of different sizes and colors and shapes. And a lot of them are comfortable with who they are, and that just helps me center myself. And I've had friends here who have brought their daughters, and this has just helped them so much in terms of body image. It just reaffirms that there's something about a woman's space. Going back out there is always tough."[366]

Womyn do not judge themselves in a better light simply because they see larger womyn than themselves, or womyn with more scars and cellulite than they have. Rather, their body image changes because of the body discourse that redefines individual "flaws" as badges of strength, survival, and beauty.

Julianne: "I admire just the uniqueness of all the women. There's nobody the same. I remember observing just the other day how this one woman was very muscular, and I was thinking 'wow, there's a lot of strength there, but how unique.' And I was also noticing some other women. They were, well as society would put it, they were over weight. But ya know, I wouldn't have known. Unless I would have thought about it, but I didn't see that. I was just amazed at their beauty – they were just so beautiful because they had an air about them, a confidence. They had – it's like they were free. They had all the baggage, the worries that they have at home, the worries that they are over weight. But you didn't see that. They walked like they owned the world. They were lighter than light. And I loved it. It made me love women more, and it made me love me more. And it made me proud of who I was, because I

---

[365] Ro Rasmussen. Personal Interview. August, 2002.
[366] Van. Personal Interview. August, 2005.

see so many women and they are so proud of who they are. And they don't care if they have rolls – they may – but they don't think about it here. I think there is a difference between the way men and women gaze. They are just so different. There's women who see someone and find them attractive, and they may look at them sexually, but the way they look, it's gentle – it's a gentle gaze – in comparison to men. With men, it's like a power. And it's not like that with women – it's just an admiration and joy. Believe me, I have tried to explain the nudity to so many people, and they never understand how I feel. I explain about the spirituality of it, of the land, and how it's not really – we don't need to stare at women's breasts or their bodies. We don't need to do that. It's not an in-your-face type of thing. It's a gentle beauty, that's natural. And I don't know how to explain it, but they don't understand that it's not about sex. Granted, there's a lot of sex going on in this gorgeous place! It's hard not to – there's so much energy – so much sexual energy that goes through because we're four thousand women. And there's energy there. It would be hard not to have that going on, but it's not the sole focus. To some it might be, but that's not what the festival is about. There's so much more, there's the *spirituality*, the energy that goes from the ground up."[367]

Cindy: "But you desensitize [to the nudity]. You know, it's like maybe for the first hour you notice it, but then you don't notice it any longer. Somebody can take their shirt off and..."

Marnie: "It's no big deal."

Cindy: "It's like you don't even notice that they've done it."

Marnie: "After we got back, we talked about that. About all the different sized women. It didn't matter what size they were, they were all beautiful. They carried themselves with so much grace and dignity."

Cindy: "So much confidence. And you know back in the world, they don't do that. Back in the world I'm not able to do that a lot of times."[368]

Back in the world, womyn often walk with their heads down, never making eye contact with others, and they hide their bodies beneath baggy clothes so no one will notice them. However, during the Festival, womyn make their bodies as visible as possible, particularly under the body-painting tree and in the annual parades. The "Femme Parade," the "red-head parade," the "Butch Strut," and the "Chocolate Womyn's Streak" put every shape, size, color, and scar on public display. Womyn line both sides of *Lois Lane*, from the *Triangle* to the *Kitchen*, and cheer the womyn who have hauled in wagon loads of "stuff" to make these parades an experience to remember. Butches, who are usually reviled in the outside world, dress in kilts, tuxes, police uniforms, military uniforms, and Amazon attire. Together they strut their way up *Lois Lane* to the cheers of appreciative "femmes" who make them feel loved and appreciated.

[367] Julianne Meyerle. Personal Interview. August, 2001.
[368] Marnie Keifer and Cindy Avery. Personal Interview. August, 2002.

Asa: "I just love being surrounded by all these people. And just being able to feel comfortable in my skin, and being appreciated, and - I don't know – I actually hold myself a lot better here [pulls back her shoulders]. I feel so much more centered here – I don't know, I just feel a whole lot more visible here, as a butch dyke, than I do at home. And a lot more appreciated by the people around me, so, I mean, that was my experience here. I mean, I was in the Butch Parade and people were goin' crazy. And I was in the burlesque show last night, and there were screamin' people. So, I just feel much more confident here than I do at home. And in straight culture, media, body image, you know, that's not such a big deal here. And everybody's beautiful here, and they know it. That's really fabulous. I just feel really good in my skin here. I mean, it's not totally gone, cause the outside culture doesn't disappear, but it's a much more affirming place for me. Like nobody's giving you creepy looks. And it's *safe*, and I think people underestimate that out there."[369]

*Beth & Laurie in Femme Parade*   *Heather & Lauren in Femme Parade*

The Femme Parade also brings every size, shape, and color of womyn to flaunt their "feminine wilds" before the waiting throngs of festiegoers who line each side of *Lois Lane* from the *Triangle* to the *Kitchen*, waiting with anticipation and cameras at the ready to snap shots of the most outrageous womyn in the most outrageous feminine attire imaginable. Womyn actually haul in footlockers loaded with garter belts, corsets, feather boas, make-up kits, high heels, evening gowns and mirrors. These trunks would make even the most glamorous Hollywood movie star envious. On the day of the Femme Parade, womyn gather at the *Triangle* and help each other dress and apply liberal amounts of bright red lipstick so they can mark butches with their kisses along the parade rout.

Veronica: "You know, I go to the Femme Parade every year and I identify as femme. But outside of here I don't feel comfortable dressing femme. I really don't. Because it brings on this unwanted attention. And it

[369] Asa Bartholomeu. Personal Interview. August, 2005.

becomes this huge, kind of lecherous weird feeling. And so here, I feel completely comfortable just goin' completely high femme, and wearing what I want, and doin' my makeup and my hair. I get to explore facets of myself that I don't get to out there."[370]

One of the most inspiring things I ever saw at the Festival happened in the Femme Parade. In 2001, the most beautiful womyn by far was the Femme Parade Queen. She was about 40 years old and had long blond hair. She rode on the hood of a black convertible, waving and blowing kisses to the crowd. She wore a tight black corset that accentuated her large voluptuous breast on one side, while exposing her thick red mastectomy scare on the other. In one brave and defiant performance, she redefined the patriarchal constructions of beauty, femininity, and womynhood for all who saw her. Furthermore, the adoration she received from the crowd helped her see herself as a beautiful and sexually desirable, whole womyn.

Performances like hers have helped many womyn over the years feel more at home in their own bodies. Avril Flanigan wrote to *Lesbian Connection* about being similarly inspired:

> One woman who had a complete mastectomy walked topless proudly in the midst of the young bodies; the whole parade was a human chain of desire and survival.[371]

Kiki, from New Orleans, also expressed similar feelings in her letter to *Lesbian Connection.*

> When I went to my first <u>FESTIVAL</u> several years ago, it changed my life. I was particularly moved by the women with surgical scars, mastectomies, stretch marks, cellulite and other 'blemishes' who were enjoying themselves without an ounce of shame.[372]

Like drag shows, both the Butch and Femme Parades are exaggerated gender performances done for fun, but they are also ways the community challenges and redefines patriarchal beauty standards. For instance, womyn like 64 year-old Patricia, ride along in their motorized wheel chairs and receive kisses from Butches who tell them how beautiful and sexy they really are.

Yet it is not just that womyn are redefining patriarchal beauty standards in special events like parades, they are also redefining "disability" and "age appropriate" behaviors. For instance at the 2005 Festival, I was with some of my students at the body-painting tree when Patricia came rolling up on her scooter. After introducing my students and catching up on the year's events, Patricia told us she was doing things at the Festival that she had never done before. Part of her plan was to "crowd surf" in the mosh pit during Tribe 8's

---

[370] Veronica Jones. Personal Interview. August, 2005.
[371] Avril Flanigan. "Womyn's Festival Strikes Harmonic Chord." *Herizons.* Fall 95, Vol 9, Issue 3.
[372] Kiki. *Lesbian Connection.* May/June, Vol 20, Issue 6, 1998, 53.

performance at the *Day Stage*. She wanted to know if we would help her out of her scooter and support her in the air while she was passed, hand over hand, above the heads of the crowd. At age 44, I was not thrilled with the idea of attending Tribe 8's concert – I like my music a little softer and easier to dance to – but I felt that if Patricia, a 64 year old womyn with MS wanted to "crowd surf," then by God, I was going to help her do it. On the day of the concert, Bobbie and I, and one of my students met Patricia in the mosh pit. She was already standing beside her scooter, gripping the handlebars, and bobbing up and down with enthusiasm to the pounding rhythm of the radical thrash music. The three of us immediately formed a circle around her to protect her from the crowd of slam-dancers who were just getting warmed up. But Patricia was fearless as the womyn in the mosh pit began crashing into her bodyguards. That day, the slam-dancers never seemed interested in starting a wave for crowd surfing, but Patricia had the time of her life regardless, and she danced the entire concert. Although her bodyguards walked away with bruises and crushed toes, Patricia's zest for life and her refusal to let her age or disability stop her from living, was inspiring to those of us who were feeling the pains of middle-age setting in.

Womyn like Patricia, and the blind womyn who gave directions to the bus driver, and the Femme Parade Queen, inspired every womyn who saw them. I do not think I ever saw the definition of "womyn" more clearly demonstrated than it was in these womyn's lives. Each of them stood in defiance of patriarchal constructions of beauty, ability, and age, and each womyn who saw them was transformed.

Though womyn who transform "disability" into "desirability" inspire womyn without disabilities, few of us actually see what these womyn go through on a daily basis, either inside or outside the Festival. However, it may take several years before some are at home enough at the Festival to feel at home in their own bodies. Therefore, the communities that specific groups of womyn build inside the Festival (DART, Deaf Way, Womyn of Color, Jewish Womyn, Twilight Zone, Over 40s, and Over 50s) are particularly important because they also provide the safe familial communities that heal womyn to the point where they can feel at home in their own skin.

## Building Communities

In American culture, "community" is usually defined in a couple of different ways. One way is to conceptualize it as a neighborhood, village, town, or city. Yet as everyday life becomes more and more mobile, transitory, and global, the less Americans ground community in specific neighborhoods or towns. Rather, communities are more closely associated with specific groups of people. One can be a member of a professional community, a social community, a spiritual community, or even a virtual community. Today, when families, friends, coworkers, and members of religious groups live, work, and worship in different parts of the world, the internet becomes a "virtual" community where Americans gather to share their lives, skills, and prayers with each other.

Like the larger culture, most womyn at the Festival connect home and family with specific locations and people, including womyn from specific ethnic, spiritual, professional, and social groups.  On the Land they build centers for the S & M community, the deaf community, and the differently abled community.  Different womyn find themselves at home in communities of womyn of color, Jewish womyn, Christian womyn, and Wiccan womyn.  They also build communities of musicians, crafts womyn, and scholars.  They can even connect with the virtual communities they build in cyberspace.  One such community is called "Lesquire's Pub."

On the Michigan Womyn's Music Festival Bulletin Board, a Boston attorney named Lesquire opened up a virtual Pub in cyberspace, where she invited womyn to "say hello, pull up a stool, tell me what you are drinking, and let's talk about life."[373]  On its opening day in May 2000, Lesquire never imagine so many womyn would make her Pub their home.  A thread on the Michigan Bulletin Board holds only 300 posts, and then it must open a new thread.  By 2004 Lesquire's Pub reopened 44 times on new threads, which totaled over 12,800 posts.  For Carolynn Sween, Lesquire's Pub is an important link to her Michigan community.  "Living in a city of about 110,000 people in northeast Iowa does not afford me a large community of lesbians with which to identity.  The Pub *is* my lesbian community – the community that embodies the Festival all year long.  In the words of one of my cherished pub friends, 'Swennie, this is your culture.'"[374]

The womyn who visit Lesquire's Pub call each other "publies," and after two years of creating community together in cyberspace, the Pub was so important to them that they actually built their "Pub On The Land" at the 2002 Festival.  "In August of each year, when the Michigan Womyn's Music Festival finally rolls around, Publies from coast to coast flock to the Michigan woods and the Pub materializes in real life.  Complete with a six-foot wooden bar, hauled all the way from Massachusetts, the Pub OTL [Pub on the Land] is an amazing creation set up under some of the largest suspended tarps anyone has ever seen.  Circles of chairs and coolers, and even a generator, help to make the Festival expression of Lesquire's Pub cozy and cushy."[375]  While it is hard to imagine hauling a six foot bar up and down hills and through deep puddles of sand, it is not hard to imagine the love and gratitude that over 40 publies showered on Lesquire for building the Pub on the Land.  Together, these womyn pooled their funds to buy Lesquire a celestial star, which they presented to her at the Pub OTL's anniversary party.  "Be it known that Star Number

---

[373] Frances Wasserlein and Carolynn L. Sween.  "Lesquire's Pub – An Essay on Virtual Community Building," *Journal of Lesbian Studies* 9, no. 1/2 (2005): 113.

[374] Wasserlein and Sween, "Lesquire's Pub – An Essay on Virtual Community Building," 118.

[375] Wasserlein and Sween, "Lesquire's Pub – An Essay on Virtual Community Building," 117.

004243 with the celestial address of 00Hrs.50Min 18.166 Sec and the Declination of +7633' 34.000" Epoch 2000 in the Constellation of Cassiopeia shall henceforth be known by the name: Lesquire's Pub. The Power of Womyn, The Power of Love, The Power of Shine Forever!"[376] For such a temporary home built in the intangible realm of cyberspace, it is amazing that these womyn chose to express their love in such a permanent and tangible statement. But there are other communities that womyn bring from the world outside, and reclaim and recreate during the Festival. During her interview, Ro cried when she told me how much it meant for her to find a community of lesbian Girl Scouts among the festiegoers.

Ro: "You know, the women who were better at camping, a lot of us were old Girl Scouts. But at the time [in the 1970s] it wasn't really cool to talk about that. But then, one year I came, and there was a Girl Scout reunion. And I went! And we sang Girl Scout songs! And I cried and cried! Finally we were able to say that we were Girl Scouts and that's why we knew not to leave the tarp stickin' out from under your tent. I guess that was the best workshop I ever went to – the Girl Scout reunion."[377]

This story demonstrates all of the little ways womyn form *communitas* in their everyday lives, and how at the Festival these *communitas* transform into communities that once again become meaningful to the womyn who live their everyday lives in hiding. Michigan may not be the utopia that womyn describe, but as Lisa Vogel said, in the beginning "we were all discovering that – if we did it in our likeness – it looked different."[378] What Michigan looks like is a matriarchal community where womyn and children are free from the patriarchal constraints and disciplinary practices of everyday life. This community looks different because collectively it has redefined and revalued *all* womyn as strong, intelligent, and beautiful. Communities like these do not tell womyn they are powerless to change the system. Rather, they empower womyn to build systems that place their bodies, relationships, and experiences at the center. Alison Bechdel wrote, "The theory I accepted at 19 about a matriarchal utopia may have been a romantic fiction, but the Michigan Womyn's Music Festival is a real, working model. It's easy to ridicule its minutely parsed anti-oppression politics or its own failure to always live up to them, as evidenced by the regular eruptions over race, class, and gender. But without these debates, 'Michigan' wouldn't be the flawed, practical, perennial utopia that it is, nor would it continue to provide stupefied young women with a new take on how the world could work."[379]

Julianne: "Oh, I love the unity this place has. Because it reminds me of a community. We're like a tribe of women. We all help each other out. We're a

---

[376] Ibid.
[377] Ro Rasmussen. Personal Interview. August, 2002.
[378] Sandstrom, 133.
[379] Alison Bechdel. "Michigan Womyn's Music Festival." *Advocate*. Nov. 12, 2002, Issue 876.

big family. Women at the festival will let you know if you're doing something that's inappropriate - and that's just the way of living in a community. We all take care of each other. We're all sisters. And that's what I love about this place. We take care of each other."[380]

Ro: "I think that so many issues have been worked out, and there's just a certain respect. I know there's a lot of controversy, but it's funny, when you go back, and you read something in LC [Lesbian Connection] that happened at the festival, and you didn't even know some of those things went on. Or the reactions to it – how upset somebody got by a performance, or the food. But it didn't bother you. There's just a whole range of women. And everybody has a different feeling about that performance, or what was said in a particular workshop. It might not have bothered you, but then when something does bother you, you really want it to be addressed. I think Michigan really tries to address as much as they can, and sometimes it's really razzed – it's really joked about. You know, 'chem-free,' all the little different areas, but that's so we can all respect each other and still all get along as much as we can during this time. And I think that has happened. It's so wonderful to see so many young women working on the festival and making it their own. They work so hard. And, it's like a whole culture. It's a lot of work. And it's so great to see so many young women, because we wouldn't be able to do it without them. You know, once you're 50, you're not luggin' all that stuff as much. So it's good to see young women coming up."[381]

Akosua: "I tell people all the time that A: there's no place like it. And B: that the sense of community is overwhelmingly powerful. Sometimes the music doesn't do much for me, but really, I'm not coming for the music, I'm coming for the community."[382]

Mary: "We brought a woman from Miami with us, and when she got here she was pissed [because she perceived the culture as geared toward young women], and we told her to go hang out with the older women. 'Go to the Over 40s Tent,' we said. And a few days later that woman came back, and she had all her hair cut off, and she was nude. The only thing she had on was a backpack. Those women freed her up. That's what Michigan does for us, it let's us be who we want to be. That's why I think all the women bring those costumes. Cause you can make the statements you want to make, that you couldn't out there in the 'real world.' I guess that's what they call the 'real world,' but I'm doubting it. This must be the real world. Yeah, this gotta be the real world."[383]

Carol: "What I found here is that you have a microcosm of the outside world, but you can find a *community* in here – whether you're straight, whether

[380] Julianne Meyerle. Personal Interview. August, 2001.
[381] Ro Rasmussen. Personal Interview. August, 2002.
[382] Akosua. Personal Interview. August, 2005.
[383] Mary Sims. Personal Interview. August, 2005.

you're gay. It doesn't really matter. Women in here come from every walk of like. They are from every economic level. There's something here for everyone. Every year, it's just a sense of *community*, where I can meet women from all over the world. Women that I would not normally meet. And this is what brings me back every year, being able to connect, being able to network with women of all ages, of all nationalities. Basically, you get more than you bring. When you go home, you've met a new person, or discovered something new about yourself. So for me, I come for no other reason than just to enjoy *community*. Like this year, I met a woman from Canada. She road her motorcycle here, and she's sixty years old! And you hear people tellin' you that anything is possible and then you meet women, and you hear their stories, and then you know anything really is possible. I also met a fifty-year-old power lifter. I mean, I've met doctors and lawyers, so it's not just radical feminists out here. You get what you need each year. And they have the Womyn of Color Tent here, and the Womyn of Color Tent is what you make of it. One of the things I've learned here is that so many women in America, whether we see them as such, don't identify as such. Some Asians, some Latinas. So one of my things is just to embrace people and get them to come to the Womyn of Color Tent. We don't ask questions in that tent. If you are a woman of color, and you feel you need to be there, come. So that's what Michigan is about to me, it's about reaching out to other women."[384]

As much as Michigan is about connecting with *family* and friends, and building communities, it is also about building a culture and practices that maintain communal harmony and a sense of home where everyone can feel safe and valued.

Kip: "Culture is collective practice. Collective assumptions. To me, culture is collective agreement of premise. You know, our premise is that everyone here wants to help each other, and everyone here wants to trust each other. And we're all here to love each other. And then, we have these practices that we follow. We have a philosophy that all women are valuable. And to me, that's what culture is. It's shared premise, and shared practice. You know there's stuff you shouldn't do. You shouldn't throw cigarette butts on the ground. That's a shared cultural practice. The drums go on till one o'clock. Why? Cause after one o'clock people want to sleep. Everybody on the Land knows that. And you almost never have to go tell the drummers to stop. It's just a shared practice. Everybody buys into it."[385]

The philosophy that "all womyn are valuable" is a guiding principle of the Amazon culture. This philosophy is always in the forefront as womyn try to define what their differences mean in the context of their culture, and as they care for each other's needs even when they may not agree on specific issues. They are committed to loving each other even when they challenge each other's

---

[384] Carol. Personal Interview. August, 2005.
[385] Kip Parker. Personal Interview. August, 2003.

attitudes and assumptions, and even when their differences might mean carving out new spaces and building new community homes.

Mary: "The whole Festival is *home* for me. I worked in the kitchen and I met women from all over the country. Cause I think, if you're here, you're of like mind, in a lot of respects, no matter what color you are. It's about women of like minds. That's what Michigan is about – you know, the gathering of women from all over the world. It makes you have goose pimples when they have the opening and they start speaking all of these languages that you don't even understand. . . . And that's what makes me sad; our Black sisters don't understand that we're all one. . . . But I'll be back next year with my granddaughter – she'll be six – and she'll just have a great time. And I'll feel *safe*. It's like my friend whose mother is here. She's seventy-five years old and runnin' all over with dementia. We just feel *safe* here. That's a beautiful thing. And someone was saying, "I hope that's not because we don't have men here." And I'm sayin' that's the one reason we don't have violence here. You know, when we have disagreements we seem to want to sit down and talk about it."[386]

Cindy: "This is the most accepting place there is in the world. The women here just accept you for who you are."

Marnie: "They accept that you don't know all the answers and they all share their wisdom freely."

Cindy: "We can celebrate being women. When they have that sign out there that says 'Welcome Home.' That's exactly what it is; this is *home* for a week. It's *home*! On our trip here this year, I was just so excited and I said to Marnie, 'We're going *home*! We're going *home*!' Cause it just feels like *home*."[387]

Even though the population is quite diverse in terms of age, race, gender expression, sexuality, and religion, and even though there are perpetual controversies and issues that have to be dealt with, Bonnie Morris claims "women return again and again each summer, declaring that festival time is sacred."[388] Part of what makes the Festival sacred is that womyn are not only willing to redefine their definitions of family, home, and community, but that they are willing to work across lines of difference to include different womyn in their families, homes, and sacred traditions. This willingness to work is rooted in a matriarchal ideology of love, where love is an act of will and a tool for building homes and communities. And no, the Festival does not always succeed in creating a utopia for all womyn, but most womyn are determined to create a living model, or at least a living room where different bodies, communities, and traditions are valued.

---

[386] Mary Sims. Personal Interview. August, 2005.
[387] Marnie Keifer and Cindy Avery. Personal Interview. August, 2005.
[388] Morris, 10-11.

# ⚒ 6 ⚒
## Sacred Traditions

Given that concepts of family and home are closely connected to religious ideologies that mark them as sacred institutions, it is understandable that womyn at the Festival would transform the material structures of their sacred traditions. Women are often designated as the keepers of the home and family, as well as the angelic keepers of the family's sacred traditions. "But given the rigid dichotomies of Western culture," as Margaret Vandenburg argued, "if you're not an angel of the hearth, technically speaking you're a murderer, a feminist, a siren, a Medusa, a witch, or, worst of all, a lesbian. Where the angelic mother rocks the cradle, we rock the boat. Though the angel seldom ventures beyond the sacred threshold of her home, we are forever hopping onto our broomsticks and other symbols of transgressive mobility. But are we liberated from the confines of home, or doomed to wander forever and ever without even a closet for our brooms, let alone a whole house to call home? Why do you think they burned lesbian witches at the stake? Because the grave is a final resting place, a home for the corpse to sleep until final judgment unites body and soul in glory. No such heavenly home for the lesbian's disembodied spirit, all that remains of the martyred specter of female desire. When the Wicked Witch of the East, who was a lesbian in real life, was murdered in The Wizard of Oz, she was squashed by Dorothy's home plummeting from the heavens. There's no place like home to kill a lesbian dead in her tracks. I rest my case."[389]

Because home and family are so bound up with concepts of the sacred, many womyn at the Festival redefine and reconstruct sacred traditions right along with their families and homes. Like their intention to experience family and home, many womyn come to Michigan with the specific intention of experiencing the sacred. But what they mean by "sacred," and how they create the "sacred" is a complex weaving of personal, political, and spiritual traditions that generate imaginative and uniquely gendered symbols, myths, and rituals.

This chapter takes up the discussion of sacredness and how womyn's personal and political identities are intertwined with their concepts of the sacred. In her study on the religious thinking of women, Mary Farrell

---

[389] Vandenburg, "Home-phobia," 57.

Bednarowski found five themes that run through feminist theological writing; 1) ambivalence toward religious communities; 2) an emphasis on immanence; 3) the ordinary as sacred; 4) a view that relationality is the ultimate reality; and 5) that the function of religion is to heal both the spirit and the body.[390] These themes were also prominent in the spiritual narratives womyn shared with me at the Festival. Furthermore, their spiritual narratives and practices run parallel to the "two dimensional" project of feminist theology that Natalie Watson defined as "critical analysis and constructive re-reading and re-writing that involves a commitment to transformation."[391] Like their academic counterparts, "Festival theologians" construct a feminist theology that is critical, contextual, constructive, creative, and draws on multiple traditions and perspectives while keeping womyn's bodily experience at the *center*.

Like feminist theologians, "Festival theologians" struggle for a libratory and "holistic" theology that materially transforms sacred concepts, methods, language, and imagery.[392] Feminist liberation theology, as described by Ada Maria Isasi-Diaz, centers itself in the daily experiences of Latina women, and is not so much a theology for Latinas, as much as it is a *place* for Latinas to speak their own theological understandings from their experiences. Isasi-Diaz argued that mujerista theology is community based praxis that "helps our people in their struggle for survival, not a theology that receives the blessing of the status quo because it follows traditional patterns."[393] Like mujerista theology, womanist theology places black women's lived experiences of slavery, sexual abuse, and economic deprivation at the center of theological conversations. Stephanie Mitchem defines womanist theology as "a creative human enterprise that reflects the social and political realities of human groups. . . .Womanists generally view theology as 'God-talk,' a way of thinking that keeps the human dimension front and center."[394]

Lesbian theologians are also concerned with lived experience and placing the body at the center of "God-talk." For instance Lisa Isherwood and Elizabeth Stuart argue that the Protestant Reformation "shifted the emphasis from sensual engagement with God to mental communion through the word of the gospels."[395] While traditional Protestant theology actively devalued the body and fleshly experience, Isherwood and Stuart demonstrated through feminist, liberation, and queer theologies that all knowledge of the sacred begins in the body.

Womyn at the Festival experience the sacred through their bodies, through their physical and psychic senses and through the tangible arts and

[390] Mary Farrell Bednarowski. *The Religious Imagination of American Women.* (Bloomington: Indiana University Press, 1999), 1.
[391] Natalie K. Watson. *Feminist Theology.* (Grand Rapids: Wm. B. Eerdmans, 2003), 2.
[392] Watson, 3.
[393] Ada Maria Isasi-Diaz. *Mujerista Theology*, 79.
[394] Stephanie Y. Mitchem. *Introducing Womanist Theology.* (New York: Orbis Books, 2002), 143.
[395] Lisa Isherwood and Elizabeth Stuart. *Introducing Body Theology.* (Cleveland: Pilgrim Press, 1998), 12.

rituals they create. During the Festival womyn actively redefine their childhood traditions, explore other cultural traditions, and create new sacred traditions to satiate their spiritual hunger. For instance, Christian womyn sing praises to "God the Mother" in a Gospel Choir on Sunday morning. Jewish womyn embrace Shekinah during their Friday evening Shabbat service. Native American womyn from several tribes pray together in a Sweat Lodge ceremony. And Wiccan womyn carve a Goddess statue and cast ritual circles in her shadow.[396] Even womyn who have no religious traditions at all find themselves spontaneously building altars on tree stumps and creating imaginative rituals to mark the special moments of their lives.

*Altar – 2002*                    *Altar – 2007*

Kip: "Just like in every other *community*, there's all these legends that you'll hear over the years, like the bubble. The bubble – the legend goes like this. There is a coven that meets only here – of powerful priestesses – that are each in their own right leaders of their own covens. And the only time this coven meets is here. And they have this huge amethyst crystal. This big rock. And every year, the night before the Festival – the night before the festies come – they have a ceremony at the Goddess statue and they put that in the Earth,

---

[396] Sandstrom, *Performance, Ritual and Negotiation of Identity in the Michigan Womyn's Music Festival*, 244. According to Sandstrom, the head of the goddess statue was carved on the old land, but her body rotted so they buried it in a gully and kept the head. This upset many of the workers, who sought to locate and exhume the body, but they could not find it. "A woman named Bear, who was the coordinator of inventory and in charge of carvings, started a group project to carve a new Goddess figure. It was housed near the coordinator's tent for the crafts area and women would stop by and work on it. The unveiling during the opening was of this new carved figure with the head from the old Land."

they bury it. And they do a protection bubble over the Land. And after the Festival, a different one of them takes it home and guards it for the year. I can't say whether or not that's true, but it's what many people who have been coming here for a long time believe happens."[397]

As distinctive as individual womyn's traditions are, what makes them even more unique is the cultural tapestry they create when their threads are woven together using the "apparatus of love."[398] In this tapestry the social, political, economic, sexual, gendered, ecological, and spiritual threads create an image of the divine female that nurtures and empowers womyn to become their own priestesses and to imagine their own sacred connections in the web of life.

From the very first day I stepped foot on the Land, I had a vague awareness that something "spiritual" was going on; something sacred, although I could not articulate what it was at that time. I noticed the Goddess statue on my first walking tour of the Land, but I had very little understanding of what she symbolized. I also took note of the workshops in the Festival program that focused on things like "Creating Sacred Space," "Goddess Yoga," "Singing In Sacred Circle," "Hawaiian Goddesses," "Drumming for Spirit and Ritual," "Business Plan for the Goddess." But these types of workshops were not the only ones listed under the heading of "spirituality." There were also workshops and services for womyn with more "traditional" interests, including a "Friday Night Shabbat Gathering," a "Quaker Meeting for Worship," and a "Unitarian Universalist Celebration." Christian womyn were invited to attend an annual workshop titled "Hurt by the Christian Church/Organized Religion," where participants were asked to come and discuss their views concerning spirituality and their relationship with their religion.

Over the past five years I have watched the "spiritual" section of the Festival program grow from 21 offerings in 2001, to 28 in 2002, 35 in 2003, 50 in 2004, and 66 in 2005. As discussed in a previous chapter, symbol, myth, and ritual play a large role in creating Amazon culture. While these are not necessarily always associated with religious or spiritual matters, what is clear from a casual perusing of the Festival program is that womyn attend to their spiritual needs on the Land.

For many womyn the ritual elements of the opening ceremony bring them into "sacred space." The ritual blessing of the Land and the singing of "Amazon" create what Boden Sandstrom called "a budding spirituality."[399] Sandstrom suggested that the lyrics "I am" in "Amazon" are particularly significant because they reference a Hebrew name for God, thereby redefining and implying womyn's sacred relationship with the divine.[400] While this "loosely defined spirituality during the opening did not try to replace each

[397] Kip Parker. Personal Interview. August, 2003.
[398] Sandoval.
[399] Sandstrom, 212.
[400] Ibid.

individual's religious or spiritual practice or non-practice with a new religion," the non-denominational setting "helped women feel united and to feel their own power by linking them with their mythic past." [401]

In her discussion of women's music festivals, Bonnie Morris wrote that festival culture is "…as tribal and ritualized and sustaining to the participants as any spiritual movement, and this is because the diverse contributions of the women involved have forged a sum of art and politics that is richly nourishing."[402]  Indeed, because most womyn at the Festival do not draw firm boundaries around their sexuality, politics, esthetics, or spiritual practice, they have shaped a unique spiritual culture that, like the writers that Mary Farrell Bednarowski studied, are mostly ambivalent about traditional religious institutions; placing more emphasis on the eminence of the divine and on the sacredness of the ordinary.  Perhaps more than anything else, womyn at the Festival see all things as being connected in the web of life or what Bednarowski calls "relationality as the ultimate reality."  Like the womanists, mujerista, and queer theologians, womyn at the Festival place their bodily experience at the center of their "Goddess-talk."  The remainder of this chapter focuses on womyn's narratives and what they *do* to experience the sacred.  It explores how they experience Judaism, Christianity, Native and nature based traditions, feminist spirituality, and an emerging religion that fuses multiple traditions into a practice called the Dianic Tradition.  Finally, the chapter concludes with a discussion of the rituals womyn with no particular traditions create to mark the Festival as sacred space and sacred time.

## Judaism & Christianity on the Land

One of the early theological projects feminists undertook was reinterpreting Biblical texts using feminist methodologies and modes of thought.  Christine Blair suggested that the imagination was an important hermeneutical tool that allowed women to find themselves between the lines of Biblical texts.[403]  In the context of Michigan, however, womyn are not so much interested in reading themselves between the lines as they are placing themselves up front in sacred texts.  For instance, in one workshop titled "Let Thy Kingdom Come," womyn were invited to create new Biblical verses to help them survive the "Bible thumping, gay hating, modern day zealots."[404]  But workshops are not the only places womyn write sacred texts.  As already discussed, musicians write songs like "Amazon" that become, in effect, sacred texts in womyn's culture.  Artists like Nedra Johnson also write songs that actively redefine "traditional" Christian concepts and perform them for Michigan audiences, who respond enthusiastically with thunderous applause.  At

---

[401] Ibid.,205, 230.
[402] Morris, xiii.
[403] Christine E. Blair.  "Women's Spirituality Empowered by Biblical Story." *Religious Education*, Fall92, Vol. 87:4, 536.
[404] 2005 Michigan Womyn's Music Festival Program, p. 38.

the 2005 Festival, Johnson performed her song, "Any Way You Need Her." This song represents Johnson's own attempt to reinterpret the gospel message and place her own bodily experience at the center of the text.

> Jesus is a lesbian,
> And any way you need her she will come.
> And if for you to see the light, it's got to be male, long blond hair, and white,
> Sing hallelujah, I know she'll come.
> (Chorus)
> Any way you need her, she will come.
> Any way you need her, she will come.
> By the intensions of your heart, know that you can call on God,
> And any way you need her, she will come.
>
> Jesus is a fierce gay man,
> And any time you can't, I know he can.
> But if for you to see the light, it's got to be asexual and white,
> Hallelujah, halleluiah, he will come.
>
> Jesus is a lesbian,
> And any way you need her she will come.
> Now if for you to see the light, she's got to be a crunch granola dyke,
> Birkenstocks and all, I know the lord will come.
>
> Ya see, the bible says that Jesus had dark complexion and hair like a lamb's wool.
> But we see images like Da Vinci's *Last Supper*, and the Sistine Chapel. Even in the illustrated Bible, that's not how they portray him.
>
> So we can follow the lead of mainstream Christianity, and we can visualize God in the way that we need to see God.
> So if for you to see the light, it's got to be male, long blond hair and white, Sing hallelujah, I know she'll come.[405]

Biblical reinterpretation is not the only tool womyn at the Festival use to empower themselves spiritually. They also reinterpret ritual practice. At the Festival, Bonnie Morris coordinates the Jewish Womyn's Tent, where she often leads workshops designed to meet the spiritual needs of Jewish womyn. Morris is the facilitator of the annual Shabbat service on Friday evening, held under a huge oak tree on Old Workshop Walk. Morris wrote that the service "attracts more Jewish women (and onlookers) than any other event in Jewish women's

---

[405] Nedra Johnson. "Any Way You Need Her." *Nedra*. ft David H. Johnson. (Big Mouth Girl Records: TMI, 2005).

programming at festivals, [and] of course includes the mourners' Kaddish, where those attending are specifically invited to name loved ones lost in the previous year. Interestingly, because the Michigan Shabbat is so profoundly a Jewish 'family' space, the loss of gay Jewish men to AIDS is mourned quite openly, compared with other festivals and rituals where the focus stays on women. One Jewish Michigan festiegoer annually offers a prayer to Oscar Schindler in honor of his efforts to save Jewish lives."[406] Along with the Shabbat service, Morris has also led a "Jewish Service of Shalom: Seeking Wholeness and Peace," and various other workshops meant to empower the spiritual lives of Jewish womyn. For Marissa, Michigan helped her think about her own Jewish concepts and practices in new ways.

Marissa: "I think it's about women helping women. And I think it's important because you help and you don't expect anything back. You just do it, and go on. I kind of think the karmic balance of the universe centers here. It will come back to you, and not that that's why you do it initially, but if you do, it will. I was thinking about different experiences growing up Jewish – they have popped into my head – and there's something called tikkun olam, which means repairing the world. And that really struck me here, a lot. Repairing the world can mean anything from leaving the space more beautiful than you found it. It can mean lending a shoulder for somebody to cry on. It can mean helping somebody unpack the trolley. Where you kind of give yourself. Other things that popped in were tzedakah, which is like giving alms to the poor, but the highest form of tzedakah is when you give anonymously. And so when you're doing things for somebody else, you're not expecting anything in return. I think that's as close as you can get to giving anonymously. And so knowing that's such a good thing, it felt extra special here. When we were walking toward the *Triangle* and women were unloading one of the tractors, and so like all of us just formed an assembly line, unloaded it, and then we just kept walking. And women were yelling 'thank you ladies,' but it just felt good. We didn't know each other. It was just part of what you do at Michigan. Because you can, and you do. And I think those kinds of moments were – not exaggerated – but given extra importance, like there was a little star attached because of my upbringing. And there is always this little battle like – are you doing this because of yourself, but none of that came up here. It kind of makes me more able to help people when I wouldn't have, and now I'm going to do it with the Michigan consciousness. Which is what I'm gonna take away from Michigan. It's like the battle axes [labrys] we're all wearing, it's the energy from women. How can I explain to other people how close we are?"[407]

For Asa, Michigan helped her find a space where she felt comfortable being both Jewish and "gender queer." However, Asa was also very skeptical

---

[406] Morris, 144.
[407] Marissa Corwin. Personal Interview. August, 2005.

about the various multicultural expressions of spirituality on the Land, particularly when they seemed to appropriate Jewish traditions.

Asa: "I haven't really found a Jewish home, a space where I can really be myself, or be the kind of Jew I am. But I really want to learn more. Being Jewish is always there. I had an interesting experience once when I was working for a Hasidic rabbi, doing an addition on his house. And he thought I was a man. That's not that unusual for me. But I didn't know that Hasidim don't touch people of the opposite sex, and he was like shaking my hand and touching my shoulder, and trying to be my friend. And I was like, ok, he thinks I'm a boy. That's nothing unusual. I'll just continue letting him think I'm a boy, because that's the easiest thing to do, to do my job. But then, one of the painters on the job said to him, 'that's not a boy, that's a girl.' And then he was really uncomfortable with me. And I felt really bad because he must have felt really violated. And he didn't recognize my name because it's a male name. He kept saying, 'You need to get a nice Jewish name, like Rivka.' And it was funny, because that is my real name. And I wear the Hamsa. I call it the 'hand of Miriam,' and it just makes me feel kind of grounded. I mean, I have a little discomfort with Judaism because of the sexism, so just having that makes me feel like, ok. It helps me feel a little better about being a woman in Judaism. And also being a very masculine woman. There's not a lot of space for being gender queer in Judaism. And the reformed temple is trying, but there's a lot of work to be done. There's just not really a space within Judaism that's all about gender queer. I have a good friend who's trans and Jewish, and so that's been a real blessing for me. And I met another trans man who's Jewish [female to male]. And actually, my friend in college was gender queer. And I really appreciate those Jewish gender queer people in my life. I don't know where the fuck I would be without them. None of them are part of my daily life anymore, but I still need their images. I still need to know they are there, and that they are struggling with the same things I am. So yeah, that's been a struggle for me within Judaism, not finding representations of myself. I've found it in little pockets, but not within institutions.

"And here at Michigan, I went to Shabbat last night. And it was really nice. And there were a couple of young people there. But they appeared to be married, and that's just not where I am. I mean, I'm kinda like married, but it's different. But one of them appeared pretty gender queer, and that was really nice. But it was just like being around a lot of older women and butch women, and they were really nice to me, and really affectionate toward me. And they made me feel really comfortable. I think that outside this space, if people had just grabbed me around the shoulder while we were singing Kaddish, you know, she just grabbed me around the shoulder while we were singing. And in any other space, I don't think that would have been Ok with me. I felt like I was totally wanted there, and it wasn't like that 'in spite of thing.' It was like 'you totally belong here.' And that was great. That doesn't happen to me every day. I think that Michigan is the closest I've come to finding a space where I just feel 'alright.' Because it's just a bunch of Jewish dykes, and Jewish butches, and Jewish gender queers."[408]

The Festival has also become a place where Christian womyn "feel alright." In early March 2005, a couple posted a message on the Festival Bulletin Board requesting the services of a "lesbian minister" to baptize their son during the Festival. Several womyn wrote back suggesting that the couple perform the ceremony themselves because they believed the couple could be their own "ministers," and that they should feel worthy of the role. The couple, however, was intent on locating a licensed minister to perform the baptism because they believed in the sanctity of Christian ordination. Eventually several of the regular Bulletin Board readers contacted female Christian ministers who all replied that they would be happy to perform the ceremony for the couple sometime during the Festival. Still, as welcoming and inclusive as the Festival community is for Jewish and Christian womyn, their traditions are much less visible at Michigan than other spiritual traditions. Without a doubt, the most visible traditions are those of Native peoples, and those with a nature based, feminist, or Goddess focus womyn.

## Native & Nature Based Traditions

Native American, African, and Polynesian traditions are the most visible traditions on the Land because most womyn believe they are more "natural" and their symbols, myths, and rituals are more closely connected with the cycles of the seasons and womyn's bodies. These traditions are also influential because they use drums in their ritual performances, and as Bonnie Morris suggested, "For many festiegoers, falling asleep in a warm tent to the sound of distant drum rhythms evokes an immediate sense of caring, of a tribal community wherein music is always a part of the landscape of creation and expression. Others liken the sound and feel of the drumbeat to a heartbeat and, specifically, to the sound of the mother's heart surrounding a fetus in utero, a comforting, life-giving background pulse."[409]

The drums influence womyn from nearly every tradition and are literally everywhere on the Land. Their deep resonating rhythms are heard almost every hour of every day and night. Drums are played in nearly every ritual ceremony, as well as in parades, from stages, and even in the food lines and on shuttles. There are workshops for every type of drumming imaginable, with the most influential being Ubaka Hill's intensive workshop that trains the Drumsong Orchestra. The Drumsong Orchestra plays with the One World Inspirational Choir on Sunday morning. In an interview with Dee Mosbacher, Hill described the spiritual connections between womyn and drumming. "I'm African American. I've never been to Africa. But there's a knowing. There was a knowing inside of me that women have always played the drum, and the

[408] Asa Bartholomeu. Personal Interview. August, 2005.
[409] Morris, 161.

women of all cultures at some point or another in our herstory, we have had the drum as the central part of our community, in ritual, in ceremony, in celebration, in completing cycles, recognizing cycles, births, deaths. I like to make a connection through the heart, that the drum in almost every indigenous culture, whether it's sacred or secular music, has been called the heartbeat. The heartbeat of the mother. Of the great mother. Whether it's the Earth Mother or the greater goddess. In almost every culture. And that women, as women we have a very profound relationship to the heartbeat and the heartbeat of the mother and the drum as the metaphor, as the symbol of that heart. And that is through birthing."[410] Taz, a Brazilian womyn I interviewed, has played with the Drum Song Orchestra for the past five years. For her, drumming enhances the "magic" of her spiritual practice.

Taz: "One of the girls in the group that I just met – which they adopted me by the way – she is getting ready to take a test to be accepted for medical school. I also know how hard these things are – I'm an EMT and I'm also going through school to be a medic – and I understand the pressures. It's a very hard thing. So these wonderful women decided to give me the honor of making a circle of women and doing a positive energy circle to give this wonderful person the strength, and the hope, and the memories of something so beautiful so she can really focus on passing this test in her life. I picked up a stick, and each of us blessed it, so she could carry our blessings with her, and I gave her a leaf to carry the spirit of this place with her. But the drums are magic, because most of the energy has to do with the drumming. And it has been an honor for me to play with Ubaka Hill."[411]

Although I have never performed in the orchestra, I have attended several of Hill's workshops. During these sessions, she taught the rhythms and lyrics of several songs that asked drummers to "trust the rhythms in your body – all the rhythms in your mind, body, and soul," and to remember that we were "living in the beat and drumming out the rhythm of our ancestor's feet." In one song, "She's Been Waiting," the lyrics suggest that all womyn are daughters of a long forgotten Goddess, but that she is still intimately connected to the life stages of womyn.

> She's been waiting, waiting.
> She's been waiting so long.
> She's been waiting for her children to remember - to return.
>
> She's been waiting, waiting.
> She's been waiting so long.
> She's been waiting for her children to remember - to return.
>
> Blessed be, and blessed are the lovers of the Lady.
> Blessed be, and blessed are the Maiden, Mother, Crone.

---

[410] Sandstrom, 244.
[411] Taz. Personal Interview. August, 2005.

Blessed be, and blessed are the ones who dance together.
Blessed be, and blessed are the ones who dance alone.
Blessed be, and blessed are the one's who work in silence.
Blessed be and blessed are the one's who shout and scream.
Blessed be and blessed are the movers and the shakers.
Blessed be and blessed are the dreamers and the dream.[412]

Many womyn feel these lyrics are calling to them specifically, and asking them to not only remember their ancient connection with the Goddess, but to return to the practices of ancient Goddess religions. "She's Been Waiting" is particularly meaningful to Ann, who was a devout Christian before leaving the church that inflicted horrible pain on her when she "came out." During that time Ann's minister demanded that she endure an exorcism to "drive out the demon of homosexuality." I asked her if she could talk about what being a Christian had meant to her and how she has dealt with the pain of being called an "abomination unto the Lord." Even though the exorcism was almost thirty years ago, the wound of rejection and excommunication was still too painful, though Ann did speak about her anger.

Ann: "I am so angry with the church – with 'killer Christians,' as I like to call them. Especially the right wing Christian Republicans who use the government to do their dirty work. Those types of Christians preach nothing but hate, and they would just as soon kill me as look at me. I hate that they say things like 'we love the sinner but hate the sin.' That's so hypocritical it makes me want to puke. And it's not just whackos on the streets that commit hate crimes – fundamentalist Christians are the ones I fear the most. They are the one's killing in Jesus' name – in the name of a supposedly loving God. And if they don't kill us outright, with their fists and their guns, they're killing us with love, and their politics, and their wars. And it's not just gays and lesbians they're killing. They're killing everyone who doesn't believe in their version of God – their version of the Bible. I mean, look at the killer in the White House [Bush]. He claims to be a Christian, and look at who he's killing in his holy war [Iraq and Afghanistan]. Christians have used God and the Bible to justify everything from slavery to beating women and children, to their current wars. When really it's about oil, and increasing their own profits. That's not God! That's not love. That's not about forgiveness or freedom, or democracy, or anything else. It's about their own power to take what they want and kill who they want. And they use God to do it. If that's really God, then I don't want any part of him. I'd rather believe in a Goddess."[413]

As for the way she feels about the drum songs, Ann said that when she hears songs like "Amazon" and "She's Been Waiting," she remembers "what it's like to be filled with the Holy Spirit."

---

[412] Paula Walowitz. "She's Been Waiting." *She Changes.* (Heartway Productions, 1991).
[413] Ann. Personal Interview. August, 2004.

171

Ann: "Just hearing them makes me feel like I'm in a sanctuary again, just praisin' and worshippin' again. It's the only time I feel at *home* enough to worship – in my own way. I get fed here, by those drum songs. I'm not African-American or Native American, but the loving Mother they sing about comforts me. She tells me I'm ok, and that she loves me even though my family and my church, and my country have rejected me. This is my *spiritual home!*"[414]

In whatever way womyn conceptualize the sacred, what is clear is that they have transformed the dominant concept of a white male God into a loving and nurturing Mother Goddess who comforts them. In one of the drumming workshops I attended, Ubaka Hill said, "this song is about the Goddess, and the way I like to experience her. It's a way that each of us gets to celebrate the Goddess, in whatever way we identify with the Goddess. Whatever her name is to you, we get to celebrate her. We return to the great yoni [the female reproductive triangle] in the sky. So the idea is this – Marija Gimbutas, an archeologist who wrote the only book, the only book right now on women's drumming traditions; she followed a European path – archeologists have found images, artifacts, of women in temples, in ritual form, images of the Goddess; European Goddesses, Asian Goddesses, African Goddesses, Latin American Goddesses and so forth. And we are the present day Goddess. ["Amen," someone shouts from the drummers]. We are the artifacts. We are the present day ancestors. And just like we have, in various ways, done research and walked the path, and crossed the seas to Europe and Africa, and Asia and Latin America to find the ancestors, and to learn about who they were, how and why – to get a clue about ourselves – guess who those who have yet to be born on the planet are gonna be lookin' for? Us! Us! We are the present day ancestors."[415]

Polynesian and Native American traditions are also quite visible on the Land. Often Native American womyn give the blessing in the opening and closing ceremonies, and Polynesian womyn dance the sacred Hula as an offering to the Goddesses. During one opening ceremony Nancy Brooks asked everyone in the audience to join hands as she began a Native blessing:

> Now then, please close your eyes for a minute and picture this land a few thousand years ago. The women who I am quite sure came here then were from the tribes named Pottowatomie, Ojibway, Ottawa. And their tradition, as is tradition in many religious practices, was to salute the directions or to call forth spirits from the directions and to remember the elements – air, fire, water, earth. So we will turn and face the directions and stay connected all at the same time. So let's all breathe together once and we turn first to the East.

[414] Ibid.
[415] Ubaka Hill. Quoted from the Drum Song Orchestra intensive workshop, 2004.

To the East - away from the setting sun. We call upon forces we cannot name and those forces and spirits who have many names in many different traditions, we turn to the East - to the sunrise - to the beginnings and we remember the sweet air breathing deep together. We turn then to the South - grateful for heat, for Fire, for our passion - the fire of our passion for each other, for our work, for this Earth and for life itself. We turn then to the West - to the setting sun. Looking to the West we think of Water, the water under the Earth, the water in the skies. We send to places around the Earth in drought at this time, the water that flows through us, as do all our emotions, to connect us one to another in community. And we turn then to the North. Thinking of Earth - that great mother Earth beneath our feet, in gratitude for this land, for this planet, and asking the forces for healing for her and for all of us. And we turn then again to the East - making then a circle reminder of our cycles of beginnings and endings and beginnings and endings.[416]

Then, in this same ceremony, before Vicky Nobel offered her blessing she asked the audience to make the connections between African, Native American, and European traditions:

Sometimes those of us with European ancestry feel as if we are orphaned or in someway bereft, like we don't have a tradition of Shamanistic or nature-based religion. And in a way we don't, in the current times. And we have this incredible debt of gratitude to our native and tribal sisters for having a living tradition and sharing it with us. I would like to point out, and help us remember, that we come from a European nature-based religion that wasn't so long ago. It goes way back into the Paleolithic and the Neolithic periods of old Europe, when the witches, the women healers were wiped out in the Middle Ages. So was our tradition, to a certain extent. But we can remember it in our bodies. And so much of the work that I do with women is about coming back into our bodies and remembering our own genetic tradition, so that we also have something to offer that comes from within us. So I'm going to ask you to sing a chant with me tonight, I'm not a singer, I'm a healer, so I want you to really sing the chant with me "Isis, Astarte, Diana, Hecate, Demeter, Kali, Inanna."[417]

---

[416] Nancy Brooks. Quoted by Sandstrom, *Performance, Ritual and Negotiation of Identity in the Michigan Womyn's Music Festival*, 198-199.
[417] Vicky Nobel. Quoted by Sandstrom, *Performance, Ritual and Negotiation of Identity in the Michigan Womyn's Music Festival*, 229.

For womyn who have been hurt by traditional patriarchal religions, but still hunger for spiritual expression, seeking a new spiritual path can lead them to the more "natural" or nature-based Native traditions. Vicky Nobel's suggestion that white womyn from European ancestry have had their own "shamanistic" tradition has helped these womyn revive and embrace "Celtic" type traditions at the Festival. It is not unusual to see womyn wearing Celtic knots or ancient Rune letters on clothing and jewelry.

But whatever tradition they come from, images of Isis, Astarte, Diana, Hecate, Demeter, Kali, Inanna, Mother Goddess, and Spirit Grandmother are visible all over the Michigan landscape. Crafts womyn carve their images into pottery, emboss them on leather goods, paint them on canvases, print them on fabric, set them in silver, sculpt them in metal, and carved them into wood. In the *Crafts Bazaar* womyn can also purchase psychic, Tarot, and Rune readings from those who practice these traditions. However, Bonnie Morris cautioned that some womyn may not "fully understanding how white ethnic consumerism exploits first peoples on the earth."[418] In their thirst for spiritual sustenance, white womyn often fail to recognize the way ethnic consumerism is linked to neocolonialism, which is based on the white privilege of cultural appropriation. For this reason some workshops and community spaces are reserved for womyn of color only, and white womyn are asked to understand and respect these times and places. One such space is, of course, the Womyn of Color Tent where African American womyn gather in workshops and ceremonies to honor and learn from their ancestors. In a workshop titled "Another World is Possible," Akiba Onada-Sikwoia led womyn of color to "extract wisdom from the experiences of our ancestors."[419]

Another reserved space is the Native Sweat Lodge that was built by a group of womyn led by Charlene O'Rourke in 1990. There, "native, indigenous, First Nations womyn" gather in traditional Native sweat lodge ceremonies, where they pray to the spirits, honor ancestors, and recall cultural traditions.[420] In these ceremonies, Shirley Jons often "pours the water." Shirley is from the Eastern Band Tsalagi, (Cherokee), where she received extensive training by elders in her community. Her role in "pouring the water" means that she is the spiritual leader and facilitator of the rituals that take place inside the lodge. Over the years, Shirley has called the spirits of the four directions and given the blessing many times during both the opening and the closing ceremonies, and has helped womyn with Native ancestry reclaim and place themselves in the center of their Native traditions.

Teresa: "I wasn't raised within the Native American culture, but my grandfather was Iroquois. He used to talk about the old ways with me and my sisters, but after he died we just kind of lost that part of ourselves. But going

---

[418] Morris, 155.
[419] 2005 Michigan Womyn's Music Festival program, 27.
[420] Ibid., 44.

into that sweat lodge, although I was really uncomfortable at first with the heat, and the feeling of claustrophobia, once I got past that, I – I just felt – I mean, it's really hard to articulate. I can't explain it. It was just really important for me to do it. It made me feel connected again, *spiritually*."[421]

Even for African American womyn who primarily identify with African traditions, but who have Native American ancestors, the sweat lodge ceremonies are important part of their Festival experience. When asked about her favorite memories of the Festival, Colette's first response was going into the sweat lodge. Unfortunately she was unable to articulate what that experience meant to her. However, after working in the Womyn of Color Tent Patio for several years, where womyn gather before and after sweat lodge ceremonies, I found that womyn with both African and Native ancestry are spiritually empowered by the experience.

Mary: "It's the energy. It's *spiritual*. It's a *spiritual* happening, really. And it enriches your mind, and your body, and your soul. In fact, my daughter is gonna spread my ashes somewhere on these hills. I mean I told her; you gotta go back to Michigan and take part of my ashes. But I can relate to the paganism because that came from Africa. And I know if you look in our herstory, I think it's the same Goddess their worshiping. We just call it a different name. The Mother Goddess can be any of our African deities. So I practice the African religion. So it's back to Earth, Mother Earth. But you gotta realize that I have Indian in me too. Native American Indian. So I can sweat along with my Native sisters."[422]

Still, other womyn of color conceptualize the sacredness of Michigan in more generic terms. For them the sacredness of the Festival is not specifically linked to ethnic traditions or religious concepts.

Colette: "I can see where this is a *sacred* space, because one, you have nothing but women's energy that created this whole event. And it's more than just the six days that you and I are here. And when I look at the major construction, it's very *sacred* because women are thinking about what the needs and desires of women are. Because, women, we are very special people, and when you get this many of them together, you're gonna have all kinds of magical, mystical things goin' on. I think it's real important for all women right now to explore their spirituality, and to get a sense of how they're connected to each other, to their world. And I'm not speaking about Christianity, or anything like that, but it's a spiritual battle we're in on the planet. It truly is, and that spiritual battle is about where I will take my energy. I can't say that I had a religious upbringing, or that I have a church home. My community is a spiritual community."[423]

---

[421] Teresa. Personal Interview. August, 2004.
[422] Mary Sims. Personal Interview. August, 2005.
[423] Colette Winlock. Personal Interview. August, 2005.

Veronica: "I'm not very spiritual in my regular life. But the feeling I get here is just of *safety*, of being completely comfortable. And not having expectations about being guarded, or what I should wear, or say, or do. I know that every other woman here has that sort of spiritual connection to the Land, and you know, I love that, but it's not that for me personally. But I can't imagine this in the outside world. I don't know. Being free from cattiness and defensiveness, and being able to be that open with other women. I don't know. So maybe it is. Maybe it is a *spiritual* thing. Maybe it is actually getting in touch with the Land. A Land that's been consecrated for thirty years with the blood, sweat, and tears of all these women who have put things in. You know - it is a *spiritual* thing."[424]

For other women the sacredness of Michigan is associated more with art, politics, philosophy, and esoteric practices than with specific traditions. Yet these do overlap with "traditional" religions, Native and nature-based traditions, and generic spiritual concepts and practices to form what some of the womyn I spoke with call "feminist spirituality."

## Feminist Spirituality

Feminist spirituality has more to do with praxis than with a particular tradition or theological perspective. While drawing from and blending several traditions, including Christianity, Judaism, Wiccan, and Native and nature based traditions, feminist spirituality is grounded in feminist political, environmental, and economic theories, and puts these theories into practices through political protests, art, literature, and performances inspired by female images of the divine.

Patricia: "I see it all as a piece of music, but an improvisation. And I don't mind dissonant notes. In fact, I like them. Dissonant notes are very interesting. But disharmonious notes are not what I want. And now, I have begun to be able to discern when something's disharmonious, within me, or in an action, or a thought, or an attitude. To me, if there were a golden rule, it would be to be within the harmony of the song and in dissonance. Definitely in dissonance. And as far as my spiritual practices, that's just living. Certainly I've gone through all the different phases, meditation, art. The older I get, I'm 62, and the older I get the more simple it gets. It just pares away, pares away. Now, it's just living. But that's the hardest part. And, it's attempting to be fully present. Fully present wherever I am, with who ever I am. And following my gut. I guess I'd say, where I'm supposed to be, when, with whom. What I'm supposed to be doing. 'Intentionality' is very important to me. 'Intentionality.' But not intentionality of the outcome - never the outcome. Intentionality of the being there. Of the process - this moment, what we're doing right now. You know, this to me, what we're doing is deeply *spiritual*. And our encounter at the ritual, deeply *spiritual*. And the talk I had with Falcon River and Ruth Barrett in

---

[424] Veronica Jones. Personal Interview. August, 2005.

front of the porta Janes, where they were laughing and said, 'you do pick an interesting place to have a conversation,' yeah, deeply *spiritual,* you know.

"I have this sense that it's either all or nothing. That there's no such thing as the sacred and the secular. That if everything isn't sacred, than nothing is. To me, it all is. Even the things that seem so counter to any image of the divine, or belief system. I mean, it's easy to say that this tree is *sacred* and that the Earth is *sacred,* or Michigan is *sacred,* or the women. That's easy. And yet, what I've had to do for myself is then say, Ok, does that mean that the Pentagon is sacred? Does that mean that bombing Iraq is sacred? Does that mean that someone being shot to death in a domestic quarrel, is that sacred? And that's the hard part. That's the part I struggle with. Because I don't want to believe that it is, and yet, for me, if it isn't, than none of it is. So, then where that takes me is - my definition of the sacred is too narrow. It's not something on a pedestal. And it's not the nirvana. I guess I would say that now, my definition of the sacred has become what is. Just what is. Whether I like it or not. Whether I think it is good or not. Whether I think it's right or not. Just what is. That it's all sacred. Or none of it is. And for me, that means that it all has to be. But, I'll be growing into that idea for the rest of my life.

"I see feminist spirituality impacting the American culture on the whole, and I would love to see it impacting it more. But, I'm very active in the peace movement and have my website, and I keep in touch with people from all over the world. It is happening. It's just that the patriarchy is the last to know. And, what we do here is totally subversive. What we do here is very subversive! And, if they knew it - I mean Michigan. I mean, something like Michigan, which is the beating heart of the women's movement, in the world, globally, now, is beating here at Michigan. The accumulated woman energy that is in this Land, I mean all you have to do is think about it and your heart beats with it. And this is the most subversive place on the planet. And if they knew it, they'd close us down in a minute. But you see that's the joy of it – that's the wonder of it - that they're so ignorant, because all they can see is their own system. They don't even think we are worth bothering with. That's what will save us. That they don't know how dangerous we are to them. It's already been happening. It's a process that was begun long ago now, decades and decades, well yes, I mean, look at the suffragettes, on and on, back and back, the women on whose shoulders we're standing. It's a consciousness.

"And it isn't just women. There are men who share this consciousness. So it isn't just a genital gender thing. But it's a way of being in the world. You know, just in terms of image, it's circle as opposed to pyramid. I mean, it's just real simple. There it is – circle as opposed to pyramid. The pyramid being hierarchy – the patriarchy. That's total pyramid. And ours is circle. But not just circle, it's spiral circle. And it weaves in and out of itself. We're always passing the same places we've past before, we're just going deeper. Whether it's personal, communal, or societal. And these things are happening. Yes, they are happening in churches. In your classroom, it's happening. It is happening in people's living rooms. It happens a lot here, in talks on the Land."[425]

Gretchen: "There's this family saint, and works particularly with the oldest daughters of my mothers linage. I've got Mary. And I've also got a family saint. And when my mother died four years ago, I was given Saint Anthony. He's the patron saint of lost souls. He's like a soul retriever, Saint Anthony. I always had Saint Anthony to play with. My mother was always very psychic. We have a linage of very psychic women. So that was always there. I went to psychics with her when I was very young, and heard how we'd been together in other life times. She was a powerful soul. She was very aware of the other worldliness of things. Of what is in between the spaces. So I've always had this pantheon of divines. And I think that suits my astrology.

"So much has happened at this Festival that it's going to take a whole year to understand - to get it, to bring it into me. And a couple of things I thought about – I just watch what comes flying through my head – and in many traditions of women, they talk about 'a year and a day.' The taking on of a study or a teacher for 'a year and a day' – and I thought about that with you, Laurie. I thought, ah, maybe there is something to that. It takes a year and a day to bring it all in and understand it. This is a *sacred* Land. Oh, I just want to cry. I cried so much. It's so phenomenal, this place. It's so very true, isn't it? It's this Land. These ancestors of this Land. These trees. All of it. [Crying]

"So I find the divine keeps moving around, it keeps surprising me. My mother died four years ago and I find her now, as she has spread out, in her passing. Over these past four years she has spread out into it all, so much more. And she leads me and she teaches me, and it's not like it's her, but it's that divine feminine. That comforting place. And I think it's like, where do I find God? I find God where I can find refuge. I find refuge in a field of hypericum. Like here we are Laurie, and as we were looking for a place to sit [for the interview] I said, 'ah, let's sit right in the middle of the hypericum, the St. John's wart, the light bringer. Because that's where I find spirit.' The more alert I can be to what is informing me, what is flirting with me, what wants to be in relationship with me, so I do a lot of work with the plant world, with the animal world. I think it was from all those years of being sick to my stomach in church. So it's in the plants, like the hypericum, the light bringer, which is so good for people in despair. And it's growing all over this whole Land.

"So coming here, and the few people I've met, Ruth and Falcon, particularly the time with Falcon has been really helpful to me. To have companions who travel to the same places, because some times that other world is very, very hard. So the planets inform me. My dreams inform me. I thought I would become an artist, and I'd do fantastic Mandela's for people, and instead I spontaneously started reading tea leaves. They are a woman's scrying tool. A woman's well of wonder. And I love that what informs me are the things

---

[425] Patricia Lay-Dorsey. Personal Interview. August, 2005.

around women. The things that are simple and available to us, that can be hidden. I think that from perhaps in our bloodlines or our memory lines, something about being persecuted for what we knew, and for being powerful women, it continues. And so there's ordinary things around that you can pick up, so that you and I, Laurie, could sit here with a cup of tea, and probably should. We could add that to your study and see what comes up.

"And I love teaching kids. I love being here and teaching 'Hogwarts, the Real Divinatory Arts.' That's what I teach at a high school, back where I come from. I love that there's young women here. They are fabulous, and curious - they're belligerent, they're bold. And they only listen so much, and that's exciting. And I want to hear from them, and I want to give them enough of what I've got so that we can get into the conversation.

"Astrology is a symbolic language that goes way beyond reason. And right now, astrologically, Uranus, the great lightning bolt, the agent of change, the evolutionary force. On the last day of 2003, Uranus finally stepped into Pisces, solidly, where Uranus is going to travel for seven years. The last time that happened was in the 20s. And the 20s was the beginning of modern psychology. That's coming around again. So psychology is ready for more. We're ready for more. It's not the prevailing – we're dreaming up something else. Pisces has to do with the dream world. So it's the lighting bolt of change. This is a time when the intuition, when the deep cellular body wisdom is once again available to all of us. And Pisces has to do with dreaming, so deep water is where artists and musicians, and healers, and dreamers go naturally.

"So it's through women coming here and being introduced, and those waves of women saying, 'this has helped me, this has helped me,' going out into the world. So there's these gatherings, these *sacred* gatherings that happen, where women gather together and give each other permission to be other, to be on this wild continuum. So that's how it goes out. People are going to be sensitive to it coming through art and music. So imagery is going to be stronger. It's through the art, through the music, because that's where there's going to be passion and electricity. It's not going to be so heady. It's really a time of breathing in, and it's a time of surrendering, knowing that a lot is breaking down. But where we are going to catch it is through the imagery, through the things that evoke strong feelings. It's showing up in dreams, and women being willing to spend more time in their dreams.

"June 6th of 2004, there was the beginning of this incredible star. It is going to shape the sky between now and 2012, and it's the star of Venus, the feminine. Venus went across the front of the sun, which she does very, very rarely, but she made a big show on that day. So it's about the power of connection. It's about the power of relationships, the power of relationships between us. It's like you stepping forward. It's about the connections that we make, and the webs that we weave here. But not just about people to people, but about people to plants, people to animals. So there is something very subtly being dreamed up here."[426]

What is particularly interesting about feminist spirituality is the fluidity between artistic, political, philosophical, and spiritual concepts. For Patricia and Gretchen, art, spirituality, and politics are in perpetual motion and inseparable from each other. As I have come to understand it, feminist spirituality is about the process of making connections between everything in the web of life; between the socioeconomic political realms and the spiritual realms of the larger universe. When one conceptualizes or imagines everything as sacred, then the sacred becomes unfettered by dogma and institutional practice. However, many womyn have combined elements of feminist spirituality, traditional religions, and Natives and nature based traditions with ancient Goddess religions to produce a tradition that is a little more identifiable than spiritual feminism. The Dianic Tradition is an emerging religion that is uniquely appealing to womyn because, while being eclectic, it focuses on a Goddess exclusively and on womyn's bodily experience in ritual making.

## The Dianic Tradition

Although Zsuzsanna Budapest, the tradition's founder, wanted to make the tradition available to all women, the term "Dianic became synonymous with lesbian witches."[427] As Ruth Barrett, Dianic High Priestess and current organizer of ritual at the Festival, said in her workshop on creating Dianic ritual, "it's not that we don't acknowledge men, it's just that the Tradition is not about them. It's about women, it's about us, it's about lesbians."[428] Barrett describes the Dianic Tradition as "a Goddess and female-centered, earth-based, feminist denomination of the Wiccan religion revived and inspired by author and activist, Zsuzsanna Budapest in the early 1970's. The Dianic tradition is a vibrantly creative and evolving Women's Mystery tradition, inclusive of all women. Our practices include celebrating and honoring the physical, emotional and other life cycle passages women share by having been born female. Contemporary Dianic tradition recognizes the greater or lesser effects and influences of the dominant culture on every aspect of women's lives."[429]

Barrett carefully distinguished between the "Z. Budapest lineage" that revived and revisioned the Dianic Tradition and other "Dianic traditions" that focus on balancing the male and female, and include men in their circles. "It was Z's spiritual activism that eventually brought Goddess religion to second-wave U.S. feminists, being the first to coin the phrase, 'feminist spirituality.' Concurrently, feminist scholars, activists, writers, artists and musicians began to speak, publish, and create art, music, and song, inspired by Goddess

[426] Gretchen Lawlor. Personal Interview. August, 2005.
[427] Ruth Barrett. "The Dianic Wiccan Tradition." [Online] www.witchvox.com. May, 2005.
[428] Barrett, "Creating Dianic Ritual Workshop." (August 2004).
[429] Barrett, "The Dianic Wiccan Tradition." [Online] www.witchvox.com. May, 2005.

iconography, mythology, feminist politics, and/or intuitive knowing."[430] Barrett also wrote that the Dianic Tradition draws heavily on the Gimbutas research, "regardless of whether some believe she attributed more opinion than the evidence supported."[431] Even though scholars were extremely critical of the Gimbutas research on ancient Goddess worshiping cultures, Barrett argued that it was tremendously influential and inspirational to womyn in the feminist movement.

Barrett suggests that the Dianic tradition reclaims the Goddess as the source of all life. Its religious rituals, liturgy, and imagery include the use of "magick" and lie outside the "male/female or Goddess/God dualism within the self or our practices. Languaging and the primary reference for life is female."[432] For Barrett, and other practitioners of the Budapest Dianic Tradition, the Goddess is not conceptualized as an individual entity but rather as a metaphor for the entire web of life. Furthermore, prayer and worship are not conceptualized in traditional ways. Instead, they are thought of as focusing consciousness on specific strands in the web of life to influence and shape the web in ways that repair the damage done by the patriarchal forces that oppress women, children, animals, nations, and the Earth herself.

In this Dianic Tradition, the male aspect is conceptualized as a variation of the female. Womyn practicing this tradition neither invoke a male God in ritual or liturgy, nor allow men to enter their sacred circles. Rather, they focus on creating rituals that heal, honor, and restore dignity to womyn. Often these rituals focus on "women's mysteries." According to Barrett, "the five women's uterine blood mysteries are comprised of: being born, menarche, giving birth/lactation, menopause, and death. These Mysteries acknowledge and honor women's ability to create life, sustain life, and return our bodies to the Goddess in death. Whether or not a woman chooses to birth children, all women are Mother/Maker in acts of creating, sustaining, and protecting. Women's mystery rituals support and celebrate female bonding, honor other significant personal milestones and transitions in women's lives, and include rituals for healing from the effects of patriarchy, personally and globally."[433]

I was fortunate enough to interview Ruth Barrett, and her partner Falcon River, after they had concluded their workshops on Dianic Ritual and Amazon Survival Skills. Together, they shared their personal spiritual journeys with me, which helped me understand their role as priestesses in the Dianic Tradition at the Festival.

Ruth: "Fortunately, I was raised in a family where the term "God" was not an old man in the sky. In fact I was told, very specifically, that God could be whatever you want. I was raised with that, and so, metaphorically speaking,

---

[430] Ibid.
[431] Ibid.
[432] Ibid.
[433] Ibid.

it came to me very early on that what we call the creator, or the force of creativity in the universe, had to be female. Because this is what I experienced in life. Life comes from women. The female fruit trees give the fruit, we live on a female planet. Mother Earth. So if I was going to choose a metaphor that wasn't just a figure of speech, that would be it. To say 'she,' included he. Just like women give birth to males and females, 'she' holds all the diversity. So that sensibility made sense to me early on. But the idea of a male god did not, because that would be something I would have to take on faith. And with 'she,' with mother, with mother Goddess, it's something I could experience. I don't have to take that on faith at all."

Falcon: "When I was little, I was born with this blessing, and burden, of being able to see colors. It's a gift I got from my mother and her mother. I was fortunate in that my mother didn't make any difference about it. My mother could see spirit. She taught me when I was really young. I can remember when I was about three years old, my mother said, 'now honey, it's only polite to speak to the people in the room that everybody can't see.' But one of the first things that I noticed was that when the so called spiritual leaders and preachers, when we'd go to church and they'd talk about God, or the emanation of God, or the presence of God, I'd look around and I didn't see anything. And what I saw around them instead were the colors that indicate - there are certain colors that come into a person's energetic field when they are not speaking the truth, and there are other colors that emanate from them when they are - and so pretty early on I had a truth meter.

"And then, as I got a little bit older, when I was about six, beings came to me and they introduced themselves to me as the watchers. And I came to know them as the watchers that wait. They have been guiding me all along. They were guiding me before I was six, but about six is my first real conscious memory of them. And I am profoundly dyslexic, and I didn't really learn how to read until one day when I was twenty-three and I decided to teach myself, so I sat down with four books, and I didn't stop until I figured it out. So I read now. I don't think I read like anybody else does, because I can't tell you if the words are going forward or backward according to the rules, but I can read. And imagine my surprise when I started reading in the esoteric books, or the witchcraft books, that there are actually these beings called watchers. And they are the guardians of the four directions in many traditions. But they came and introduced themselves to me when I was a child. So they came and introduced themselves to me, and I was fortunate enough to grow up in West Virginia and spent most of my childhood either up in a tree or down below the earth, literally in a cave. And they were my teachers in those places. A maple tree taught me how to play the guitar. One note at a time. I was about twelve when my mother gave me a guitar for a Christmas gift. And the first bit of warm weather, I took my guitar and I climbed up my favorite maple tree, and the tree would give me a note, and I'd search and find it on the guitar, and then she'd give me another note, and I'd find that on the guitar. And after a period of weeks she'd give me all these different notes and then the notes began to flow as my fingers got more limber and accustomed to moving, and then she gave me my first song. So when I think about God, to tell you the truth, a long time ago I stopped thinkin' about God because the people who spoke of him emanated the colors of lies. So I think I am fortunate that way.

"And it wasn't the first festival, and I don't even think it was the second, but at one of the earlier festivals there was this woman who came, and her name was Z Budapest. And she had women circlin' underneath the moon light, and chanting, and callin' us witches, and talkin' 'bout how we was Amazons, and we was gonna rise. And that was the second time in my life that I knew that I was *home*. And it all came together. Yeah, absolutely. There is a place for me, a butch woman, a feminist, and a witch. And so from that moment forward, for twenty-five years, I've been a witch, a butch witch. [laughs] And there's no turnin' back, there's no turnin' back."

Ruth: "Again, we're talking years ago, before there was something called the Goddess movement, before there was something called the women's spirituality movement. I think it's so important for women who are able to see something, like what you are presenting for example, to see what goes into the beginning of something that becomes something else. You know, there were no books in the bookstores on the Goddess. There was nothing at all. There were barely any feminist books in the book stores, never mind books integrating feminist politics and spirituality. Nothing at all!

"So, I had my own spirituality, and then it was late 60s, early 70s, again, in that time in the herstory of the United States and the second wave of feminism where many different forces began to merge. Feminism meets the ecology movement, meets – I like to think about the Goddess movement and the origins of that, really, as an idea whose time needed to come again. And so women started getting messages, transmission. I mean, creating art that was about the sacred female. A lot of women were creating art, and they didn't have a clue as to why they were doing it. Writing songs, and ideas coming to them, and they had no idea how it came.

"Because in the early years, the feminist movement was not interested in spirituality. Because of the influence from the left. So, it wasn't like the feminist movement had this sensibility, or had this idea of the Goddess at all. In fact, in the early years, it was looked upon like, 'oh shit, what's this coming to distract us from getting the ERA passed.' But it's the core of who you are, and your behavior is sourced from what you believe in. Which is why spirituality and religion have always been inherently political. It's the battery, the energizer that propels you into your choices in the world – what you choose, who you vote for, frankly what you put in your mouth to eat. I mean everything. How you live. So, there is no division between politics and spirituality, as much as in patriarchy we like to compartmentalize. Patriarchy, the way I understand it, keeps itself going because it does compartmentalize. So you don't notice the connections between things.

"So part of what feminism has been about for me is noticing the connections between everything. And in the craft, the practice of magic is based on noticing the connections between everything, and using those connections to influence what you would like to see happen in the world, as well as changing one's self. I met my first teacher in the late 60s, early 70s. Her name now is Shekhinah Mountainwater. Before, she had a different name. She became my first formal teacher even though I had been writing poetry about the Goddess since I was twelve. But again, I was on my own. It was just me thinking I'm on my own with this. To find out later that, no there's other women who have just not been talking about this because we thought we were lunatics. With the emphasis on Luna, you know, the Goddess.

"So anyway, then I met Z Budapest in 1975 or 1976, and I began to work with the Susan B. Anthony Coven # 1. I was initiated into that coven, and eventually, before Z left to move to Northern California from Los Angeles, where she was having her ministry, she asked me if I would take on the work she had started, and continue it. So I said yes. And after being totally and unbelievably freaked out, she ordained me in 1980, and I continued in Los Angeles for twenty years. And eventually that became the Circle of Aradia, which continues to this day in Los Angeles. Falcon and I live in Wisconsin now, and we have an organization called the Temple of Diana, and we continue the work there. We are still connected to the Los Angeles community, but I ordained another high priestess there to continue on. Laticia Layson. And so it goes. Now there's a movement. Over these last decades this amazing thing has occurred. Many influences went into this, and now we influence. Everything kinda goes full circle."

Falcon: "If I might tag onto this, at that first festival that I met Z Budapest, she brought this little yellow book, *The Holy Book of Women's Mysteries.*"

Ruth: "Actually it was called, *The Feminist Book of Lights and Shadows*, in that incarnation."

Falcon: "Anyway, it was a little yellow book, as she said, *The Feminist Book of Lights and Shadows*, and I took that book home, and my partner at the time, and I got back to Kentucky, and we immediately started inviting women to come and gather with us under the full moon. And from that book – that book was like seeds scattering from the winds of Michigan. After that, covens sprung up everywhere, everywhere. We started leading women's circles in Cobhill, and then we hooked up with women in Cincinnati, Ohio, and formed a coven with them. And because there was no priestess to initiate us, we all initiated each other. I actually just met one of my coven sisters over in the crafts area just a few moments ago. It was just a sweet moment. They're still doin' their work in Cincinnati, and I've moved on. And now that book, in its new incarnation is called *The Holy Book of Womyn's Mysteries.*"

Ruth: "For me, ritual is the main focus of my practice, and to a huge degree, assisting others in the creation and facilitation of personal and group ritual. And I'm happy to say that I'm finally about to publish the book that I've been writing for a really, really long time, which is *Women's Rights, Women's Mysteries: Creating Ritual in the Dianic Wiccan Tradition.* It is a book really to empower women to take care of their own needs for rites of passage, rather than telling you, Ok you must do this, this, and this, in this order, and all of that. Part of the Dianic Traditions has been to really empower women to meet their own needs that are not validated by the dominant culture. So, everything from physical rites of passage – from birth to menarche to menopause to dying. I mean all of the different physical rites of passage regarding women's life cycle events, to anything that a woman might consider significant in her life, that she might register as an important moment that needs to be treated in a sacred manner in order to be conscious in her life. Instead of going through our lives and all this shit happened, and kind of, well here I am, and how did I get here. And meanwhile there are all of these events that have happened, and decisions that have been made unconsciously most of the time, along the way. And yeah, how did I arrive at where I am.

"And so, for me, ritual – as a medium, is to be conscious. To be fully conscious, and to remain conscious has been the focus of my personal work. It's probably the most significant thing I can think of doing, personally. But I think besides ritual making, what I have certainly been learning to do more of, since Falcon and I have been together, working together, is I've been doing very consciously more noticing. Just noticing nature in deeper ways than I ever had before. Just knowing how to be still and notice. Not just with my eyes, but with every sense I have access to. Just the nuances of things. And I consider that, really, just practice."

Falcon: "Being with Ruth, she has helped me deconstruct what it is that I have always done intuitively – or instinctually – so it can be taught. So for instance, I mentioned earlier that the watchers came and introduced themselves to me, and they taught me a lot of things. Most of what I know about magic. I wasn't fortunate enough to have actual people teach me. So what we do now is, Ruth brings her wealth of knowledge from her teachers, and I bring my wealth of knowledge from my teachers, and we put them together and teach people.

"So, what I consider to be a spiritual practice is just being with my folks, and listening to the trees. To be able to walk by and just notice. For instance, this morning as I was busily walking towards the restroom when I was stopped in my tracks, not by something I saw, but by something I felt on my shoulder. And I turned, and there was a covey of quail on the ground not too far away. And they were looking at me as if they were asking if there was a reason for fear here. So I turned and I addressed them. I said, "Blessings and thank you," and they looked at me and perked up, and went on about their way. I consider that to be a spiritual practice. That when you feel that touch, it's validated. That you know that another being has reached out to you, and you turn to address them in an appropriate fashion. It takes a great deal of practice. It's a cat's whisker touch. It's the touch of a quail's eyes. It's very light. But no less valid than a touch of a lover. A few days before that, here at the festival, a friend of mine said, 'did you see that little creature run up that tree?' And I said, 'no, I didn't.' So we waited until the little creature came back down, and it turned out to be a small mouse. I don't know the mice here, so I can't name it. But we watched her as she was in the tree above me, and I noticed that she had large breasts. So I said, 'this is a mother, and she has concern.' So my friend and I stayed with her, because it was right in the middle of the food line, and there were cars going past, and she seemed like she wanted to cross the road. So we spoke with her, and told her it was dangerous to cross the road here, and we asked her if we could help her. But she wouldn't have any of it. So we kept backing up, but we kept a container around her so that she wouldn't be disturbed. What we discovered was that right at my feet she had a nest of children. So my friend and I held space for her as she came one by one, grabbed a child, stuffed it in her cheeks, and went up this big old oak tree and put it in a new place. She did that four times. This mother mouse, facing all of these people, all of this traffic, all of this danger, to save her children. She is my teacher. She faced me down. I was between her and her children. And she wouldn't leave them. So when I realized that, I backed up. So I consider that to be spiritual practice.

"To hone my skills of discernment to notice, to pay attention and honor, and be curious with respect. Other folks might call it inter-species communication. I think of it both as a gift and a huge responsibility. So that's my spiritual practice. The Goddess is everywhere. She's even in television ads. So Goddess consciousness is coming. She's emerging, she's rising. It's not always the way I'd like, but she's there."

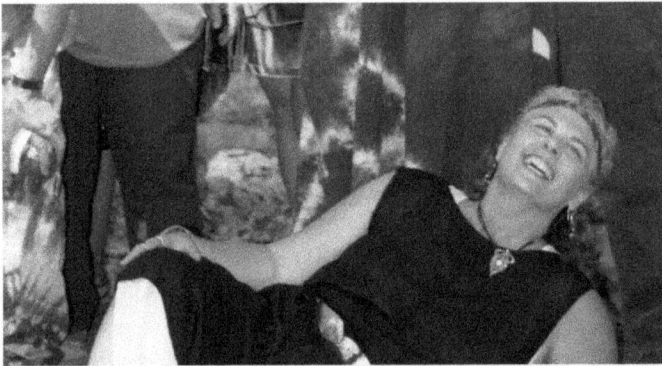

*Ruth Barrett – After the 1ˢᵗ Michigan Croning Ceremony in 2007*

Ruth: "What I think of, especially in the last 30 years, whether we like it or not, is that there are choices. Oh there's this option to consider, there's that option to consider. What I like about it is the diversity of belief, especially if it's not enforced through fear – that people can come to what truly resonates with them. Instead of what you are told you should feel, or should believe. The more information that's out there – and what I mean by information is in the spoken word, in the visual, in the arts, music, spoken word – the more choices women have. They can say, 'Oh that's an interesting thing to think about. I never thought about that before. Wow, there's that image of a woman with her hands raised to the moon. That really resonates in kind of a primal place for me. I'm curious about that, why might that be.' You know, then you can translate it to death. Some call it a primal resonance, or some say it's what they experienced in a previous life. I just like to think that each woman can have her own spiritual experience, and it is profound for her. Here she is, outside in nature, and she's having a profound spiritual experience. And there's no one interceding for her. There's no one telling her how to be with her creator. There's no one telling her how to do that. She's priestessing herself. She's facilitating her own spiritual experience. And then you place that in the context of some religious traditions and that's inherently heretical. You know, that she should feel empowered enough to have that connection on her own. And yet, we know, from all the research that has been done, that is her birthright.

Women used to do this for thousands of years, before God the father came around, and we are doing it again. The Goddess, and all of her reverberations are reaching into all the places, you know. Some people call it the feminine divine, but I don't like that word. I don't use that word myself. I would rather say the divine female than the word feminine. Which I mean, what attributes go with that? Who makes that up? So I don't use the word feminine like some do. So, the influence of this is reaching everywhere, or it wouldn't be so threatening. I mean, my own experience since the early years, is that this information, and the experience of when a woman can look in the mirror and say, 'I see the Goddess there, I see her reflected in me,' her life changes. It can never be the same. And she will never let herself be treated in a way that is demeaning when she really has that paradigm shift. That shift in consciousness, where she sees herself as *sacred* – where she sees all women as *sacred*. Where all the diversity of race and age are all the different facets of the diamond. She has this profound experience and her life will never be the same."[434]

In all of the interviews where womyn shared their spiritual narrative with me, but particularly with Ruth and Falcon, I could see the five themes that Bednarowski outlined. Their narratives articulated the ambivalence they felt about organized religion and the emphasis they placed on "immanence" and the sacredness of the ordinary. Ruth was also very clear that everything is connected and that ritual is about healing both the spirit and the physical body. And because so many womyn, and lesbians in particular, have been abused or neglected by their original traditions, having a ritual practice like the Dianic Traditions helps them connect to the sacred in ways that a male centered religion or God never could. But Ruth and Falcon do not just represent a small

---

[434] Ruth Barrett and Falcon River. Personal Interview. August, 2004.

group of womyn. On the contrary, priestesses and witches of the Dianic
Traditions circle the globe.

*Bobbie was Croned at the 1ˢᵗ Michigan Croning Ceremony – 2007*

Susi: "In Australia, where I come from, there are a lot of witches. And
it's not unusual to have circles. They are advertised, in fact. My friends have
circles all the time. And we dance in the moonlight. But it's not on the level of
Michigan."[435]

Yet, regardless of what traditions womyn bring to Michigan, they are
eager to express a years worth of joys and sorrows in spiritual services and
rituals. As Bonnie Morris suggested, "there is a heightened awareness of ritual
in festival culture, not only because of the profound woman-centered spirituality
and Goddess ceremonies regularly invoked onstage by artists such as Kay
Gardner and Ruth Barrett. Most urgent is the need to repeat, or reclaim, critical
life-stage celebrations – because 'out there,' in a homophobic society, our own
partners may not be welcome home for holidays, at synagogue, at funerals, or at
graduation parties. Those women who burst out of the closet only at festivals
bring accumulated joys and milestones in their backpacks and recreate the past
year's highlights in the good company of festiegoing allies. And where rituals
from childhood haunt those emerging from dysfunctional families, festivals
offer the chance to begin again, to design new rituals that can be anticipated
annually without stress."[436] While womyn from all backgrounds are free to
attend or facilitate workshops, services, and rituals that focus on their particular
traditions, womyn without specific traditions simply enjoy the Festival as a

---

[435] Susi St. Julian. Personal Interview. August, 2005.
[436] Morris, 122.

generic sacred space and time where they imaginatively create the celebrations and memorials that mark the stages of their lives.

*Kay Gardner's Chair served as the Altar for the 1ˢᵗ Croning Ceremony at Michigan*

**Sacred Time, Sacred Space**

"Life-stage" rituals often revolve around the three phases of a womyn's life. The first stage (maiden) is the time before a woman enters puberty. The types of things most often celebrated during this phase relate to academic and skill achievements. The second stage of a womyn's life (mother) is her child-bearing years, when things like college graduations, first loves, first jobs, weddings, pregnancies, child-births, divorces, new careers, and "coming out" are celebrated. The third stage of a womyn's life (crone) is her post-menopausal years. These years often bring a mixture of rituals, including celebrations and memorials. While most "traditional" religions have no ceremonies to acknowledge the three phases of womyn's lives, most womyn do feel the need to mark them with some type of ritual or celebration, even if they do not have a specific spiritual tradition.

Such was the case with Cindy and Marnie, who wanted to celebrate their daughter's entrance into puberty. Months before the Festival, their daughter asked if she could start shaving her legs. Cindy kept putting her off because she wanted to mark the occasion by doing something special at the Festival. One Sunday evening she called me on the phone to talk over her plans. She asked if Bobbie and I would mind not shaving our legs until we could all do it with her daughter in Michigan, around our kiddy pool. Cindy purchased a couple of cans of perfumed shaving gel, as well as several new shaving razors because she wanted her daughter's first shaving experience to be with the womyn in our family. Bobbie and I thought it was a wonderfully creative idea, so we agreed to stop shaving for a few weeks before Festival.

189

One afternoon during the Festival, we filled up the pool and about six of us gathered around while Cindy and Marnie brought their daughter into our circle. Cindy said a few words about how wonderful it was that her daughter was becoming a woman, and about the hazards and hassles of shaving. Earlier that day, Beth had gone into town to buy a special razor for the occasion. It was a new style of razor with shaving soap around the blades. She thought it might be fun and nick proof. When Beth presented the special razor to Cindy's daughter, and all of the womyn in the circle started performing our shaving rituals. We each lathered up and began gently scraping the hair from our legs. After rinsing off, each of us gave Cindy's daughter ritual items that symbolized her entrance into womynhood, including tampons, sanitary napkins, and bottles of perfume. Each of us, in our own way, talked to her about what it meant to be a womyn. We told her what strengths we saw in her, and that she should never be afraid to be her own womyn or do the things in life that she really wanted to do. That day, Cindy's daughter was welcomed into womynhood by a circle of loving and supportive womyn, and the ritual changed the way she saw herself. Several months later, Cindy called to tell me that her daughter had stopped obsessing over every little thing she ate, and that she had become more confident in her everyday life.

Even for those without a particular spiritual tradition, the Festival does heighten womyn's awareness of the sacred, which helps them create imaginative rituals even if they do not have the language or tradition to express what is churning in their consciousness's. For some, a growing spiritual awareness may prompt them to have their bodies painted. For others, it may mean that they buy a drum and learn a few licks. For some, removing their shirt and going topless may be a ritual act. For others, attending a workshop or buying a book on the Goddess in the Craft Bazaar may signify their emerging consciousness of the sacred during the Festival. Some womyn feel that learning to walk on stilts is a spiritual practice. Others may attend the Friday night Shabbat Gathering or a ritual at the Goddess statue, or both. Whatever way a womyn chooses to express her spirituality, what is clear is that their spiritual lives are being transformed and nurtured on the Land.

On top of the more jubilant ways womyn express themselves spiritually on the Land (building altars, painting their bodies, dressing as Amazons or in the robes of various spiritual traditions), they also bring with them all the pain and hurt from the preceding year. If womyn have spent their entire life in the closet and hiding their relationships, mourning becomes a difficult process, particularly when friends and lovers become ill or pass away. Many of these womyn wait for Festival to express their grief and begin their healing process. Most receive no bereavement leave from work and few have families that understand the depth of the love they feel for lovers and friends, or the anguish and pain they feel when those lovers become ill and die. Often their grief is bundled up with their camping gear and carried to Michigan along with their tents. For these womyn Michigan is a *sacred* time of mourning and the *sacred* ground where they bury their pain.  Bonnie Morris wrote, "As we get older, lose our parents or partners or other loved ones, and cope with illness, festivals take on new meaning as healing spaces and resting places.  I once expressed a desire to have my ashes scattered around the land of the Michigan festival.  When I confided this wish to Alix Dobkin, convinced that my plan was original and daring, she gave a knowing snort: 'You think women haven't been doing that privately for their friends and partners for *years* in those woods?'"[437]

Morris' wish has been express by several womyn, including Mickey, from Chicago, Illinois who wrote to *Lesbian Connection*:

> The Michigan Fest is the only place in the world where I feel free. . . . In fact, I have requested that when I pass on my ashes be buried on the Land.[438]

As Dobkin asserted, womyn have always performed the *sacred* act of scattering the ashes of friends and lovers on the *sacred* ground of Michigan.  In private ceremonies with close friends and Festival family members, womyn lay their dead to rest, and heave out their sobs in each other's arms.

Because so many womyn believe the Land is *sacred* ground, and that the Festival is a *sacred* time, they cannot think of a more appropriate place to find eternal rest.  Even Bobbie and I have designated the Festival grounds of Michigan as our final resting place.  For womyn who were excommunicated by our families and churches, there is no other meaningful place for us.  Moreover, for those who survive, the *sacred* time and space of the Festival provides spiritual healing.  In the sunshine of meadows and in the shade of oak trees, womyn release their pain and grief in the loving arms of their Festival families as they lay to rest their lovers and friends, at *home* in Michigan.

[437] Morris, 143.
[438] Markko, Mickey (Marsha). *Lesbian Connection.* May/June, Vol 20, Issue 6, 1998, 50.

# 7
## This Changes Things

One of the last things Ro said to me was, "Michigan just penetrates so much of your life. This changes things!"[439] Looking back over the last thirteen years, I can honestly say that "Michigan" changed me. It began changing me in that women's studies classroom, when I first heard the song "Amazon" and saw those bare breasted womyn drumming their way across the Land. *Stolen Moments* was the name of that video, but for me it was more than just a moment. It was an epiphany; one of those moments in life when consciousness is crystallized and for a split second everything seems clear. Barbara Myerhoff described that kind of moment as a "transformation of consciousness," a "conversion in awareness."[440] For me, transformation came in the spring of 1999 when I was introduced to the Michigan Womyn's Music Festival for the first time. I was 38 years old and finishing the last year of my undergraduate degree when I was suddenly presented with the possibility of belonging, of having a home. Silent tears streamed down my face.

In the postmodern paradigm, locating one's self within one's work, or offering a reflexive analysis is paramount. Reflexivity, according to Victor Turner, is "the ability to communicate about the communication system itself."[441] This process usually begins with locating the foundations on which one has constructed their identity and world view. Race, class, gender, sexuality, age, ability, ethnicity, and religion all inform our particular worldview and shape our identity, but the foundations that usually ground these are located in the social structures of home, family, school, church, and government. But how does one locate one's self when, because of gender and sexual orientation, one has been excluded from the very foundations that inform an individual's identity, history, and worldview? This question is one I have struggled with most of my life, and the one that frames my perspective on the Michigan Womyn's Music Festival.

Like many third-world women who live in "borderlands" or the diaspora, many lesbians struggle with the concepts of home, family, and the

---

[439] Ro Rasmussen. Personal Interview. August, 2002.
[440] Myerhoff, "The Transformation of Consciousness in Ritual Performance: Some Thoughts and Questions," 245.
[441] Turner, *The Anthropology of Performance*, 73.

sacred. For me, like Chandra Talpade Mohanty, defining home and family is extremely political, but it is also deeply personal. It is political because as a lesbian couple, the family Bobbie and I have created is considered illegal and immoral by powerful social institutions that ground their definitions in rigid ideological concepts. It is also extremely personal because these rigid ideologies have informed the families, churches, schools, communities, and governments we grew up in, causing them to withhold their greeting of "welcome home." Sitting there in that dark classroom, I finally heard the words I had longed to hear for most of my life.

My ethnographic work at the Michigan Womyn's Music Festival, and my subsequent work in the Women of Color Patio and as Crafts womyn has been more than an academic enterprise. Both the personal and the political are deeply intertwined in my being, and both have shape my analysis of the Festival. At times I struggled with staying "objective." I had to ask myself if my own lesbianism and experiences of oppression influenced my interpretation of what womyn were saying and doing at the Festival, and I was forced to answer that "of course it did." How could I disentangle myself from the memory of my step father molesting me, and mother kicking me out of the house at age 15? How could I erase the memory of her further rejection when I came out. How could I realistically forget about being discharged from the Army because of my lesbianism? How could being asked to leave several churches not have affected me? How could I forget about loosing a job because coworkers were "uncomfortable" around me? How could I forget the poverty, the humiliation of needing a Salvation Army food box because there was no food in the cupboard? How could I forget the fear that I lived with, knowing that ideologies and institutions of "my culture" branded me a sinner, a deviant, an outcast, a danger to home, family, faith, and country? How could I systematically extricate myself from a lifetime of experience and the situated knowledge that those experiences informed? The answer is, I could not. Because of this, I can make no claim of "objectivity." But as Melissa Wilcox argued:

> Perhaps we should not bemoan the loss of pure datum; perhaps we should instead accept the limitations of our own humanity and turn them to the best or most ethical use possible. Given the frequency with which socially non-dominant groups have been abused, misinterpreted, and exploited by researchers, it seems only just to reverse the process.[442]

I am aware that my own experience and human limitations influenced the shape of this text, and the analysis it offers. Would the text offer a different

---

[442] Melissa M. Wilcox. "Dancing on the Fence: Researching Lesbian, Gay, Bisexual, and Transgender Christians," in *Personal Knowledge and Beyond.* James V. Spickard, J. Shawn Landers, and Meredith B. McGuire, eds. (New York: New York University Press, 2002), 59.

perspective if the researcher had been heterosexual, middle-class, or African American? Certainly. I am quite willing to admit that my own needs have tinted my rose-color glasses as I painted this cultural portrait. Yet, my own profound need for "home," "family," and a connection with the "sacred" is not that different from many other womyn's needs. Hopefully, my work has given voice to those needs and the very real ways womyn are fulfilling them at the Festival.

My work at the Michigan Womyn's Music Festival is more than just an academic project. It has changed the way I define home, family, and the sacred. It has changed the way I conceptualize history, religion, and culture. And finally, it has changed the feelings of homelessness and isolation that Bobbie and I have lived with for most of our lives. Because of our experiences at the Festival, we have gained a new home, a new family, and new sacred traditions that strengthen us and help us survive the everyday liminality of our lives. But ours is not a unique experience, because as Ro said, "this changes things."

What Michigan changes is that womyn leave the Land knowing they have a place in a matriarchal culture with rich traditions. The Amazon culture built at the Michigan Womyn's Music Festival is a unique culture based on feminist principles, socialist/egalitarian values, and womyn's spiritual traditions. It is a culture that values all womyn, children, and the Earth. It is a culture where womyn's lives, bodies, and experiences are reflected in the art, music, and literature of the culture. It is a culture rich with symbols, myths, and rituals that heal womyn's minds and bodies, unifies them across lines of difference, and empowers them personally in their everyday lives.

Womyn leave the Land knowing that they are returning to their liminal lives in the diaspora, but that the liminal is not all there is. They leave knowing they have built a cultural homeland and family they can return to each year. They also leave feeling a little more materially secure knowing they can call on their family for help. But perhaps the most important thing is that they leave the Land with more confidence in themselves after seeing what womyn are capable of building. They leave feeling stronger and more secure in their own minds and bodies after experiencing the love and healing womyn give each other in a matriarchal culture. Often, this healing and infusion of strength literally means the difference between life and death.

For Kate, one of the young women on my research team, the culture of the Michigan Womyn's Music Festival fundamentally changed they way she viewed herself and the way she moves in the world. I asked Kate to come to Michigan because she was an exceptional student who offered keen insights in class, and I thought her ethnographic skills would benefit this project. At the time, I had no idea that she had grown up in a home with an addict/alcoholic father who verbally and physically abused her. Later, Kate told me how she had looked forward to graduating from high school and going to college because it meant she would leave her situation at home. But her dream of escaping the abuse was crushed in her freshman year of college when she was raped by an acquaintance on campus. These experiences sent her into several years of depression. This young heterosexual womyn had struggled to heal, but in her junior year, her depression grew worse. She said, "There were days that were completely lost. I had a mental breakdown, and I remember thinking that it would benefit everyone I cared about if I just died because I was not worthy to continue to exist." Throughout the summer, Kate battled the thought of suicide, but "as it got closer to August, I began to feel giddy knowing that the festival was just around the corner, even though I had no idea what to expect." During the Festival womyn welcomed her "with open arms." She said, "Although I didn't know the women well, it felt so natural, as though I had a new home and family." Kate also spoke about the sense of peace she experienced, and how she was now able to walk with her head held high. She told me that when she had her body painted, the womyn around her told her how beautiful her body was and that suddenly she was seeing herself through their eyes. For the first time in her life, she realized that she was beautiful, and that experience healed her. "I learned that I am beautiful and that I am not worthless. I also learned to accept, heal and be reborn. I learned that women are much stronger than we are given credit for, and the matriarchal community that can be created in the absence of men is more beautiful than words can express."[443]

This type of experience is common for womyn who experience the power of living in a matriarchal community. After seeing the strength of womyn and what they can accomplish living and working together, womyn leave the Land with a different consciousness, a different way of embodying themselves in the patriarchal world. They often return to their everyday lives with a new confidence in themselves, and even a sense of entitlement to be visible and respected as lesbians and women participating in the everyday social world. For some womyn, this confidence means that their days of masquerading are over. They leave the Land feeling strong enough to endure what might happen if their visibility should cost them their jobs, homes, and families of origin. For most though, their experience of the Festival gives them the strength to endure the liminality of their lives, moving between visibility and invisibility, and the ritual marginalization that continues on a daily basis. Several of the womyn interviewed used the metaphor of "getting their batteries recharged," as a way to describe the strength they receive during the Festival.

Mary: "It's like coming back and getting your batteries recharged for the year. Because, I mean, I say I'm a lesbian. That means I get all my energy from women. I get all my power from women. And this is the most powerful place to come, to get that battery charged. And I'm gonna carry that back with me, back to Miami, and I'm gonna spread it. And we're gonna create that space, that women's space, because we need that. And now we're getting angry,

---

[443] Kate Thom. "Michigan Womyn's Music Festival." Unpublished course paper for American Studies Experiential Learning course, 2005.

cause people are leaving, and we gotta go back out into that world out there, that place that's almost make believe. And we're getting angry. People are getting short tempered just because we have to leave this place."[444]

Colette: "You know, when I go back, I'm gonna be very chilled, and I'm gonna be inside my own kind of rhythm. For me, the Festival gives me a kind of reconnection to my core self, of who I am, who I believe I am, who I know I am. So that when I go back out into the world, I will just observe it. And yeah, I'll see all kinds of craziness, but I will also feel comfortable enough to choose whether I want to address it or not. I mean, I know that's not the only world that exists. I mean, when you are here, you see what's possible. It's like yeah, now we're interacting with other folks, but that's not the only world. And so, that memory, in my mind, is what helps me. And no, I don't think that being lesbian means hating men, because they are part of humanity. I don't go there. I believe we need to fight the oppression, and I hate some of the behaviors, but I don't believe it's a womyn's energy to be hateful. And when a man takes us to that place, he is really taking us outside our womanhood. But the key is not to give them that much power. Sometimes, you just have to work on your own internal self. And yes, I believe we need to fight the oppression, but I'm not going to die for it, because that's not the only reality I experience. So I won't act like his oppression is the only thing I experience."[445]

Akosua: "It's a lot of work to get here, but the year I missed I was devastated. So, it's in my consciousness, not in my subconscious. It's just right up there in my consciousness of what I want to do because it's like filling my cup up. And I can sip little bits of it throughout the year. And it's real important for me to be able to sip from the cup."[446]

Whether they conceptualize the Festival as "recharging their batteries," or "filling their cup," one of the most profound changes in womyn's lives is that they have a source of strength to draw on that they did not have before attending the Festival. Bonnie Morris wrote:

> Perhaps no sentiment is more commonly heard than, "'I live off this week all the rest of the year' or 'I'm here again to have my batteries recharged' or 'Only in festival time do I get to experience total personhood.' Festival season means regeneration as well as recreation. We go because festivals offer the possibility of what our lives *could* be like year-round if we lived each day in a matriarchy actively striving to eliminate racism and homophobia. Living tribally one season per year, all of us share a life together in that concentrated bank

[444] Mary Sims. Personal Interview. August, 2005.
[445] Colette Winlock. Personal Interview. August, 2005.
[446] Akosua. Personal Interview. August, 2005.

statement of time, a wealth of women's culture(s) as the bottom line of accumulated principal."[447]

When Festival is the only time most womyn "experience total personhood," the time between Festivals becomes a long liminal period of feeling incomplete, marginalized, and required to masquerade in order to pass as "normal." This extended liminal period requires womyn to draw on their emotional bank accounts throughout the year, slowly depleting them as they live and work for the *time* they will return to the place they feel at home, safely nestled in the bosom of family and community, on the Land that will replenish them. Thus, one of the things that changes for womyn is their sense of time. During the liminal months, womyn's consciousness shifts from the standard calendar to an emotional calendar that begins and ends in August. This emotional calendar gives womyn a sense of continuity through the liminal year that keeps Michigan centered in their everyday lives.

**Womyn's Emotional Calendars**

For many womyn, their emotional calendar begins on the last day of the Festival as they start breaking down their homes and packing out their gear. Tears fill their eyes as they force their trunk lids closed, and bungee down the last of their plastic bins to the roofs of their vans. They fight back the lump in their throat as they turn to say goodbye to their sisters and mothers, holding them in one last long embrace. For some, the pain of leaving is so unbearable that they break down in the parking lot, sobbing in each other's arms as they invoke promises to "call when you get home so we know you are safe."

Traffic workers see the tears in eyes of womyn as they drive off the Land. Wanting to comfort the womyn, they shout, "See you in 357 days." Womyn are also comforted on their journey when they see other cars with the Festival's bumper sticker, "See You In August." But, these are bittersweet comforts for the hundreds of womyn who experience "withdrawal" symptoms once they hit the pavement. The womyn I spoke with talked about their "withdrawals," and not wanting to leave the womyn they love. They resented having to return to a world where it takes so much energy just to survive; a patriarchal world that begins draining their batteries the moment they leave the Land.

Lorraine: "I actually, literally, go through withdrawals when I leave. Because when you come here it's based on equality. Everybody takes care of one another. You know, like all the good feminist political ideals. So, I literally go through withdrawals because the reality of the outside world starts to dilute out all the good feelings. I really, really looked forward to it every year. And we've come every year. I feel that it's a blessing that I had the opportunity, with Kathy, that we've been able to do it."

---

[447] Morris, xiii.

Kathy: "Whether you want to be here or not, I mean as much as I want to do something different for my vacation – coming here is annoying, it's hard, it's stressful, it's pack this up, it's last minute, let's run. I drive straight through from Jersey to here. And when I get here, it's hurry up and get set up. But once you sit down here, it just becomes something comfortable and relaxing. Where else are you gonna walk around with your shirt off and not feel like there's somebody staring at you or making a comment? And if they do, it's not a derogatory type of comment, because we're all doin' the same thing. It's a very relaxing atmosphere. And then, you don't really want to leave, and go back out there. It's like she says, there is a withdrawal. You find yourself, 'oh, I gotta put my shirt on. I gotta go back and listen to all the crap – listen to men with their bull shit, and stuff like that. It really does get into you, whether you want to be here or not. I mean, just look around! It's so massive! How could it not do something to you? Especially from the beginning. I mean, I never thought this thing would survive. But each year it's progressed to where it's got electricity, running water, hot and cold showers, and every type of support tent you can find. And if there's not one there, somebody will fix something up. So no, no one wants to leave. It's just really hard."[448]

Taz: "I'm leaving on Monday and that will be a sad day. Every year on Monday when I leave, it's just tough. I have some friends leaving today, and it's going to be very sad. But my heart is here. And every year I look forward to coming. The freedom that I feel here is wonderful. It feels like *home*. It's lovely. And I love to see people who love each other, and give each other love, even if they don't know each other."[449]

Van: "It just reaffirms that there's something about a woman's space. Going back out there is always tough."[450]

Veronica: "Last year my recharge wore off so quick. So this year I'm just tryin' to soak in more so I can go at least a couple of months."[451]

Bonnie Morris conceptualizes womyn's emotional calendars beginning in August, when womyn "...fill up their jam jars of inspiration and memory with enough festival preserves to last all winter long. . . . Like the period of weeks between Thanksgiving and New Year, festival time is a packed *family* celebration on which the emotional year turns in heart and memory."[452] When their emotional bank accounts, batteries, and preserves start running low, sometime around June or July (if they've had a good year), some womyn become edgy and even down right cranky. One year I was hitching a ride on the shuttle and I overheard a womyn say, "The guys at my factory always give me shit, but after all these years they know that come June, they had better not fuck with me. They know my batteries are running low, and they won't be

[448] Lorraine Alexis and Kathy Davis. Personal Interview. August, 2002.
[449] Taz. Personal Interview. August, 2005.
[450] Van. Personal Interview. August, 2005.
[451] Veronica Jones. Personal Interview. August, 2005.
[452] Morris, xiii.

recharged until I get back from Michigan." All of the womyn around her laughed because they understood exactly what she meant and they began sharing similar stories about their own coworkers and students.

For musicians and crafts womyn though, the "bank account" analogy is more than a metaphor because the Festival gives them the opportunity to fill up their financial bank accounts selling CDs and pottery that help other womyn maintain their emotional bank accounts throughout the liminal months. For instance, Blanche, a crafts womyn from West Virginia, wrote to *Lesbian Connection*:

> I travel the festival circuit as a crafts womyn. In fact, I am so enthusiastic about being where womyn gather that I arrange my life around these events. . . . Many of us are old Feminist Fogies who got started when the concept of Lesbian Nation was first being kicked around. We felt we were part of a community with values that were evolving in a particular direction, and we figured our Nation would have to have an economy. . . . whatever profit we have made has to last until spring.[453]

But most womyn have to settle for their emotional bank accounts being filled up, and they start marking off days on their emotional calendars; living and working for the next time they will receive the deposits of love they get during the days of Festival. Womyn like Bobbie and I start marking off days the moment we get back, when we clean and repack our camping gear, making sure it is ready to go in August.

More days are marked off as womyn go on line and share their Festival memories with each other on the Bulletin Board. Womyn also mark off days when they pick up their Festival pictures from the drug store, and now a-days print them out from the computer. Still more days are marked off when Festival videos are played at dinner parties for friends who have never been to Michigan before. Days are also marked off when the applications for venders, workshop coordinators, musicians, and workers are sent in on November 1st and February 15th. Still more days are marked off when the holidays bring greeting cards and gifts from Festival families and friends. More days are marked off during the holidays when new tents, lanterns, and sleeping bags are purchased as Christmas and Hanukah gifts.

Days are marked off when Festival friends get together to start counting down the months, weeks, and days before the next Festival. Linda, from Monie, Illinois, wrote to *Lesbian Connection*:

> Recently I got together with my friends at a party to celebrate "six months to Michigan."[454]

---

[453] Blanche. *Lesbian Connection*. Jan/Feb, Vol 21, Issue 4, 1999, 18.
[454] Linda. *Lesbian Connection*. May/June, Vol. 25, Issue 6, 2003, 7.

These types of parties become more frequent as Spring rolls into Summer and womyn find their emotional bank accounts nearly empty. Many womyn announce "reunion parties" on the Festival Bulletin Board, and invite womyn from neighboring states to stay in their homes for the weekend. But as summer kicks in, the Michigan fever really starts to burn. Morris wrote, "It's only June, but I've already started to pack, and all over North America thousands of women are feeling the same hypnotic urge to assemble their tent stakes and bug spray, flashlights and plaid flannel."[455] However, the urge does not always wait for June. For many, the "hypnotic urge" begins the moment they start breaking down their homes and packing their gear out to the parking lot. Because so many womyn "live" during the *one* week of Festival, finding imaginative ways to re-experience Michigan in their everyday realities is a life affirming necessity.

One of the more mundane ways womyn bring Michigan into their everyday lives is to stay in touch with family and friends. For instance, Cindy visits the Michigan Bulletin Board regularly, but she has also called me from Minnesota nearly every Sunday night for the past five years, and although we chat about our week and how things are going in school, we never fail to mention Michigan in one form or another. But Cindy is also an example of how creative womyn can be at bringing the material reality of Michigan into their everyday world through the art of consumerism.

## Consuming For Michigan

Even though consumerism works to maintain the patriarchal institutional of capitalism, womyn use it as a means of bringing Michigan into their everyday lives. Cindy keeps Michigan in the forefront of her mind by incorporating the Festival into her weekly shopping trips. It is not that she buys something for Michigan every week, but she is always on the lookout for something that someone might need, or something fun and unusual that will make our experience more enjoyable. Over the years, some of these items have included paper plates with animal faces, a coffee press, light-up toys to play with at Night Stage, and squirt guns.

During our "festie virgin" year, the 100° heat was so devastating that the Womb was overrun with womyn suffering from heat exhaustion and dehydration. By Wednesday night, Sabrina Matthews, the host of the opening ceremony, worked in a comical warning about dehydration. "The Womb," she said, "has asked me to tell you that if you are not peeing in the daylight, you are not drinking enough. So, just as a reminder, when you see a woman – drink some water." We all laughed, because, on the Land that would mean drowning ourselves. However, the image Sabina planted did help remind us to stay hydrated, and it also reminded Cindy to be on the look out for things to keep us cool during the hot days of August. She purchased the squirt guns shortly after returning to Minnesota that year. "It's the end of the season. They were on

---

[455] Bonnie J. Morris, "At the Michigan Womyn's Music Fest." *The Gay & Lesbian Review.* Sept.-Oct. 2003.

sale!" she retorted when I chided her about her early Michigan purchase. Jokingly, I asked why she had not gotten a kiddy pool. "The store was out of them!" she replied in earnest. But just because summer slipped into fall did not mean that Michigan was on hold for Cindy. For Halloween, she bought her kids flashlights that looked like witches. These were great fun because when squeezed, the witch cackled an evil laugh as her mouth opened to reveal the light. Yet as fun as they were for the kids, as soon as they got back from trick-or-treating, Cindy snagged the flashlights and hid them away in her Michigan bin.

Even when the cold winter months bring the holidays around, Cindy's mind is still on Michigan. One Sunday in December, she called to tell me that she bought Marnie a pair of candle lanterns for Christmas. Beautifully ornamented and mounted on spiraling wrought iron stakes, she was excited because not only would they look good in their yard, but "they would also be great for Michigan!" And, as spring rolled around, she found another way to use the lanterns to experience Michigan.

In late March, Cindy called to tell me about her plans for Marnie's birthday surprise, and of course, the theme was Michigan. "The kids are going to their dad's place for the weekend," she whispered into the telephone, "so I've got it all planned out. I'm going to set up the living room like our campsite at Michigan. I'm going to bring in some potted trees and ferns, and spread them around the living room. I'm gonna spread out our sleeping bags and fill the ice chest with goodies. And of course I'm going to set up the camp-stove and coffee press. I think I'll play Cheryl Wheeler's CD – that'll be fun. It's gonna be great. I just hope I can get it all done before she gets home from work. Oh, and I'm gonna put those candle lanterns that I got her for Christmas in a couple of buckets of dirt. They'll look great at the head of our sleeping bags."

However, other womyn are not quite as creative as Cindy is, so they wait to start marking off the days on their emotional calendars until the spring and summer sales advertisements arrive. Bonnie Morris suggested, these shopping days can even be marked as special initiatory events. "The ritual of accompanying a new partner to buy a sleeping bag, lantern, and waterproof tampon kit for 'her first Michigan' has no Hallmark-card equivalent, yet it is a recognizable rite of passage for many lesbian couples in America."[456]

This type of rite can also work in reverse, as couples break-up and find themselves having to negotiate custody rites over their camping gear. Such was the case for Beth, who lost her tent when she and her partner split up. Trying to cheer her up, Bobbie and I told Beth, "The new Eddie Bauer 10x14 Two-Room Cabin, with louvered windows, LED lighting, and built-in electrical ports that sleeps 9 adults is on sale. We just bought one, so you can stay with us." "Who's having the sale," she asked quickly. When we told her, she said, "Talk to ya later, I've gotta go shopping!" Of course, that year our campsite began to

---

456 Morris, "At the Michigan Womyn's Music Fest," 18.

resemble a small apartment complex rather than a single family home. But it is not just that womyn try to build homes at the Festival, they also try to build the Festival into their homes.

For instance, when they remodeled their basement, Cindy and Marnie dedicated one room to Michigan. The walls of their "Michigan Room" are covered with womyn's art and framed pictures of their Festival *family*. The room also has bookcases loaded with Festival memorabilia (breast castings, programs, photo albums, etc.). And of course, their stereo fills the entire room with women's music. Even within their home in Minnesota, Cindy and Marnie are most at home in the place where they keep their Festival memories. As Jonathan Z. Smith argued, "home is not...best understood as the place-where-I-was-born or the-place-where-I-live. Home is the place where memories are 'housed.'"[457] And for womyn who return to the Festival year after year, their memories are "housed" in Michigan. Even within their own houses, when womyn think of home, their mental maps traverse the geographical landscape and settle in the safety of their Michigan *homes*.

## Conclusion – It's About Building and Belonging to a Community

Michigan changes womyn's lives. It changes the way they experience themselves and their bodies. It changes their consciousness and the way they think about their personal identities and political positions. It changes their temporal and spatial reference points as their emotional calendars and mental maps traverse time and geography. Changes happen when womyn realize that the word "family" invokes mental images of Festival lovers, sisters, mothers, and children rather than biological family members, and the word "home" invokes a mental image of the Land. Womyn experience changes in their thinking about "community" when they find themselves mentally strolling down *Lois Lane* or spending hours each week chatting with friends on the Festival Bulletin Board. Womyn also experience changes in their spiritual lives when they find themselves contemplating the Goddess during their lunch hours or setting up altars in their bedrooms that display pictures of Amazons, Goddesses, and other Michigan memorabilia. They experience changes in their social, political, economic, and spiritual values when they find themselves attending anti-war rallies, becoming vegetarians, or quitting their jobs because their bosses will not give them a week off in August. Joan Rabin and Barbara Slater argued that "creating women's community is an act of validation, a centering of one's experience," and for the womyn I talked with, validating their lives and centering their experience in Michigan gave them the most profound sense of *belonging* they had ever experienced.[458]

---

[457] Smith, 29.
[458] Joan S. Rabin and Barbara R. Slater. "Lesbian Communities Across the United States: Pockets of Resistance and Resilience," *Journal of Lesbian Studies* 9, no. 1/2 (2005): 170.

Kip: "The first time I came, I had just gotten sober and a friend of mine said, 'This is important!' And I said, 'but, I have a job, blah, blah, blah.' She said, 'quit! It's important!' And so I quit. I was twenty-five, [shrugged] who knew better? So I quit. I literally walked out on my job and came here. Plus, my AA sponsor kept telling me to get involved with the community. 'Get involved, it's good for you.' I don't know if she had a sense that this would be important for me, or whether she is just such a staunch Michigan member, Michigan citizen, that she knew it would change my life. And she offered to bring me here, as her assistant – she's a crafts woman. But I said, 'I don't know if I can get off,' and she said, 'come, it'll change your life.' And it did! I had no idea – what a sense – I had never felt at *home* before. I had never felt like I belonged anywhere. And from the minute we came on the property, it was like, Oh! This is what it's about! Oh, this is where I'm supposed to be! Oh, these are my people! Ok!

"And there's been evolution in the practices – in the culture. And some of the young ones kinda have different ideas than we do – kids we raised. What I see here in the *community* is a natural aging of a society. You know, because the kids are growin' up now, and they have different ideas about nose piercing, and gender, and they have all these kind of alternative ideas that we – that go farther than our beliefs. We pushed everything in a direction and the kids are takin' it further, and it makes us nervous. And we go, 'we don't get their music, and we don't know what they want, and we don't know where they're goin' with this.' But they are the ones who are going to take this on. And so I've watched that happen, and that's been really cool – to see the people who are now adult human beings, or semi-adult human beings, who I remember toddlin' after the tractor, in their diapers.

"That's the cool thing. It's the *community*! And everyone takes a piece of it home. You know, on a long winter night I can close my eyes and hear tractors, and as long as I can do that, I remember who I am. It helps me survive out there. Because I remember, Oh that's right, there is someplace I *belong*. My *community* is over there. And that helps me get along in times when I don't know what I would do if I didn't know that, if I didn't have that center. And that's what Michigan gives people. More than the music, more than the games, and everything else. It gives women a sense of where they *belong*."[459]

The Michigan Womyn's Festival "gives womyn a sense of where they belong" because womyn in the 1970s had the courage to stand together against the patriarchy and create a separate homeland and culture of their own, a matriarchal culture that institutionalized socialist, egalitarian, and feminist values. The Festival became a place where womyn built solidarity, and spoke collectively through performance on the stages of Michigan. For instance, at the 2002 Festival opening ceremony, Krissy Keefer passionately called out the powerful words written by Elizabeth Roberts:

---

[459] Kip Parker. Personal Interview. August, 2003.

203

The days of the prison industrial complex are marked. The World Trade Organization and the World Bank are going the way of the dinosaurs. We, justice-loving feminists, anarchists, anti-imperialists; we, Sojourner Truth's children, the children of Emma Goldman, Rosa Luxembourg, Ida B. Wells and Ella Baker, are taking back the power to see another way. We are sitting down in the streets, disrupting your dirty business as usual, building unity and new models, arming ourselves with economic theory and compassion. We are bent on being human, and don't have another minute for your hate, for your greed, for your repression. We are taking the world of white supremacist, capitalist, patriarchy, carefully and absolutely apart.[460]

*Laurie & Bobbie – 2005*

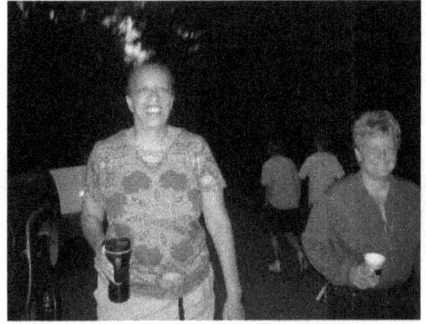

*Stephanie & Laurie – 2006*

On the Land, womyn build a physical environment and they institutionalize their vision of an alternative model to patriarchy. In an article in *Off Our Backs*, Jennie Ruby wrote:

> Ultimately, the fight against patriarchy is a fight of values. Values are developed socially. To create far-reaching and deep social changes, we must create social environments that express our new, feminist values. Women-only and feminist spaces and festivals are an essential step on the way to imagining and ultimately creating a world where there is an alternative to patriarchy.[461]

Womyn on the Land believe they are better situated to see beyond white, middle-class, male, heterosexual, Christian, able-bodied privilege to vision an alternative to patriarchy. In the matriarchal culture of Michigan, values are not based on individual power and privilege, but rather on collective power and

---

[460] Penny Rosenwasser. "Imagine This" *Off Our Backs: The Feminist Newsjournal.* Nov/Dec 2002, Vol XXXII, numbers 11 & 12, 41.
[461] Jennie Ruby. "Women-Only and Feminist Spaces: Important Alternatives to Patriarchy." *Off Our Backs: The Feminist Newsjournal.* March-April, Vol. XXXIII, nos. 5 & 6, 2003, 15.

connection. Womyn on the Land work collectively to accomplice tasks that support the whole community, and they work with a consciousness that recognizes all things are connected in the web of life. This recognition is a differential consciousness that connects the personal to the political to the spiritual to the environmental to the socioeconomic, and so on through the apparatus of love. What womyn on the Land fight for is to transform the matrix of domination into a matrix of love. This type of matrix does not require everyone to conform to social standards that create cookie cutter people, nor does it set a standard of fierce individualism that disconnects individuals from the collective. Rather, it seeks out ways to value individual difference within the whole. For instance, in patriarchal culture an "elderly" womyn with MS might be considered a drain on economic resources. However, in the matriarchal culture of Michigan, Patricia is a valued member of the community who contributed to the whole by painting flags for the opening ceremony and working two shifts as a Night Stage security guard. While the patriarchy might view Patricia as an invalid, at Michigan she is an Amazon priestess preparing a ritual and an Amazon warrior keeping womyn safe on the Land.

Womyn view the Land as a safe place where they heal their patriarchal wounds, transform their consciousness, and envision the world differently. Using symbol, myth, and ritual, womyn transform their marginalized consciousness into an Amazon consciousness. The Amazon is an archetype and cultural hero who unifies womyn and gives them a new sense of personal strength and courage. In song, "Amazon" is the national anthem, and in symbol, myth, and ritual the Amazon provides womyn with a new matrix of meaning, a new meta-ideology, a new narrative template. Using semiotics, womyn deconstruct themselves as oppressed victims of patriarchy, and reconstruct themselves as strong warriors and priestesses who tenaciously fight patriarchal forces. With an Amazon consciousness, womyn write their own histories and literature, orchestrate their own music, carve and paint their own images in art, and create their own families and spiritual traditions in homes and community spaces they build on the Land.

At the Festival, womyn defy the "traditional" definition of "family." Rather than conceptualizing blood as the only binding tie of family membership, womyn see *love* as the tie that binds their "chosen" Festival families. Regardless of what type of biological connections womyn at the Festival might share (mothers, children, grandmothers, sisters, nieces, etc.) Festival families are bound in relationships by the "apparatus of love." Festival families share what Sandoval called a "complex kind of love in the postmodern world, where love is understood as affinity – alliance and affection across lines of difference that intersect both in and out of the body."[462] In Festival families, womyn invest *love* in each other, and that love creates a large network of

---

[462] Sandoval, 170.

support that transcends the borders of the Land. Like the lesbian community Susan Krieger studied, Festival families "exist as a social reality that is, to some extent, independent of anyone's views."[463] At the Festival, whether a womyn called her network a "family" or a "community" had much to do with the degree of marginality she felt in the dominant culture, but for those who had experienced rejection in their families of origin, Festival families became a "social reality" that changed womyn's everyday lives.

*Lauren – 2007*        *Cindy & Marnie - 2005*

Festival families and communities are so important to the womyn who need them that they are willing to spend hours doing backbreaking labor, schlepping wagonloads of "stuff" across the Land so they can, as Jonathan Smith suggests, "bring place into being."[464] On the Land, womyn bring place into being by building homes where they can *experience* familial love and support, and, as Boden Sandstrom argued, experience themselves "in *corpora.*"[465] For womyn who live their everyday lives in emotional and sometimes physical "closets," the Festival is the only time they feel safe enough to embody themselves fully, and experience the full range of their emotional and physical lives. Thus, they pack in as much "stuff" as they can in order to enhance their physical experiences. But they also go to all this trouble because they want to make sure that other womyn have what they need to enjoy their own experience.

Because there is such an ethic of care among womyn at the Festival, and because the Festival producers go to such lengths to provide for *all* womyn's basic physical and emotional needs, Jennie Ruby argued that Michigan is a good economic and social justice model that provides an alternative to patriarchal and capitalist systems.

---

[463] Krieger, "The *Mirror Dance* in Retrospect," 5.
[464] Smith, 26.
[465] Sandstrom, 125.

Your well-being is not at the mercy of what services you can afford to pay extra for during festival. All your basic needs – healthy food, clean water, health care, emotional support – are institutionalized and provided as a matter of course, as a mater of what all of us need from time to time and should not feel ashamed of needing or too poor to afford.[466]

But another way womyn shed "shame" is by building spaces where they experience their bodies differently. In spaces like the Womyn of Color Tent, DART, and Over 40s, as well as in workshops and parades and under the body-painting tree, womyn begin to value their bodies as beautiful and sacred, regardless of their size, shape, color, or scarring.

*Patricia – 2007*

After experiencing themselves and each other as beautiful and sacred, some womyn begin thinking about their religious traditions differently. Like the feminist theological writings Mary Farrell Bednarowski studied, womyn on the Land are ambivalent about organized religions, but they do narrate an emphasis on the ordinariness and immanence of the sacred, as well as relationality as the ultimate reality.[467] During the Festival, some womyn reclaim and redefine their childhood spiritual traditions, while others mix and blend their politics with elements from several traditions to form what they call feminist spirituality. Some even use this same process to form new religions like the Dianic Tradition. And for those with no particular spiritual traditions, the Festival provides an imaginative environment where they create their own rituals to mark the stages of their lives, to heal their minds, bodies, and souls, and even lay their dead to rest.

While the Michigan Womyn's Music Festival does create a model of a matriarchal culture where womyn feel whole and experience themselves as fully participating members of their community, ultimately it does not change the

---

[466] Jennie Ruby. "Michigan Values." *Off Our Backs: The Feminist Newsjournal.* Oct. 2001, Vol XXXI, number 9, 45.
[467] Bednarowski, 1.

fact that womyn return to a patriarchal world that ritually marginalizes them and forces them into liminal ways of living. What changes though, is that womyn leave with a new sense of personal strength, new families they can call on for help, and new cultural traditions that help them survive the patriarchal oppression.

Yet, for most womyn, Michigan is not enough. They want more. They want to share the love of their families year-round, and practice their traditions in community. For womyn like Elana Dykewomon, who want concrete, permanent spaces to call their home, and spaces that institutionalize their values in art, education, policy, and spaces like archives and cemeteries where their memories are kept, one week in August is just not enough. In her call to build permanent space, Dykewomon asked where lesbian cemeteries were located. "My friend SJ says it's in Michigan – but to my knowledge, headstones do not sprout from some partitioned-off section of the Michigan Womyn's Music Festival. Women go to a hill and send the ashes of their lovers off, so that you might have old lover mixed in with the evening tofu and rice – but you would not know the name of the woman whose dust mingles with yours. This is not an idle question. One of the biggest problems of lesbian community is institutional memory."[468] Although Michigan brings a sweet sense of belonging to most womyn, it is also a sharp reminder of just how liminal or invisible their lives are off the Land.

After carefully listening to the womyn who shared their stories with me, and analyzing what they say and *do* on and off the Land, I could not help but see that *where* womyn located the liminal is quite different from where Victor Turner located it. When womyn are ritually marginalized and pressed into interstitial, liminal, and borderland spaces by the institutions and ideologies of the dominant culture, they are deprived of the love, support, and value that other people find in their homes, families, traditions, and cultures of origin.

*Land Art - 2005*

---

[468] Dykewomon, "Lesbian Quarters: On Building Space, Identity, Institutional Memory and Resources," 36.

Again, I would argue that using the term liminal to describe lesbian cultural spaces is counterproductive. It makes *invisible* the actual *culture building* processes taking place at the Festival, and other lesbian and gay cultural spaces like Pride festivals, Gay Rodeo, and the Gay Games. In these times and spaces, lesbian and gay people are building their own matrix of meaning. These are powerful times and places where ideologies and institutions, and even identities are being deconstructed and reconstructed by active agents involved in stabilizing their communities.

Arlene Stein argued that "finding a sense of belonging and membership in a community that is continually changing," and trying to maintain a sense of "stability amid rapid social transformations – are dilemmas of the modern world."[469] For many lesbians, these dilemmas are made particularly difficult when contemporary social theory deconstructs the very identities that womyn claim on the Land. Stein argued that claiming an identity and community were important because, "as long as individuals are defined as different and inferior on the basis of their sexual desires or practices, they will need to develop a sense of collective identity and maintain institutions that counter stigma. This seems particularly true today, as a powerful and well-organized right wing in the United States mobilizes to deny lesbian and gay rights, along with the economic and political rights of other marginalized groups. In the absence of an organized and self-conscious movement, these rights cannot be as adequately defended as they might be. A collective identity requires that boundaries be established by setting forth at least minimal criteria for claiming that identity. The alternative is a vague pluralism that speaks only of 'difference' and views all differences as equal and good. This 'hundred lifestyle' strategy, which calls for 'a pluralism of sexual choice …doesn't represent an adequate response to the one lifestyle that has all the power' – heterosexuality."[470] Framing homosexuality as a "choice" or an "alternative" only creates the illusion of empowerment for lesbians unless heterosexuals also begin seriously conceptualizing their sexuality as a choice or alternative. As long as heterosexuals continue to define their sexuality as "natural" and "normal," they maintain their own institutional power to define and oppress others, and to shape the larger culture according to their desires.

While an argument for a plurality of sexual identities and choices is theoretically possible, the argument itself does not institutionally empower multiple identities to become active participants in the larger culture, nor does it grant all the rights and protections that heterosexuals are given. Bonnie Zimmerman argued that "poststructuralism has made it easy to talk about multiple subject positions, fragmentation, deconstructing identity, and so on. But putting our theories into practice is another story entirely. We all tend to yearn after some kind of consistency, unity, and wholeness. We suffer when we

---

[469] Stein, 4.
[470] Stein, 199.

feel alienated or divided within ourselves. We want the various parts of our lives to flow harmoniously together, to create communities of meaning and understanding."[471]    As easy as poststructuralism has made it to talk about multiple identities, it has neither transformed oppressive patriarchal power structures, nor provided marginalized groups with solid political ground to stand on. Thus, the issue is not whether gender or sexuality is a choice. The issue is power. Who has the power to define themselves and others? Who has the power to grant rights and protections?    Who has the power to institutionalize their ideologies and cultural traditions?    In contemporary American culture that power rests in the hands of the patriarchy.

This power dynamic is the primary reason womyn are determined to build their own separate culture. Within their own culture at the Festival, womyn are claiming the power to define themselves and give meaning to their sexual identities. There is power in claiming an identity and naming the meaning of that identity, as young third wave feminists found when they entered the radical, separatist, lesbian, non-profit women's community of Aradia in western Michigan. In their ethnographic study of Aradia, Jane Dickie and her team found that when womyn label themselves as lesbians and feminists, they build strong and empowering communities. "The option not to label one's sexuality is hailed as one of the greatest benefits of the third wave. Yet, if one refuses to identify it becomes more difficult to create community."[472]

The Michigan Womyn's Music Festival is a place where "women" and "lesbians" claim the power to define themselves as womyn, and build a culture that institutionalizes their definitions and values. Michigan is the solid ground where womyn stand together and fight patriarchal, misogynistic, racist, homophobic, and competitive ideologies by replacing them with feminist ideologies and the "apparatus of love."[473] This love, and the cultural traditions it establishes, helps womyn survive the liminality of their everyday lives outside of the Festival.

*Breast Casting at the WOC Patio – 2007*

---

[471] Zimmerman, "Placing Lesbians," 273.
[472] Dickie, "The Heirs of Aradia, Daughters of Diana: Community in the Second and Third Wave," 104.
[473] Sandoval.

What is the culture of the Michigan Womyn's Music Festival? It is a culture that places womyn's bodies, relationships, and traditions at the *center*. How do womyn make their experience meaningful at the Festival? They begin by hauling in materials to build homes and community spaces where they can experience themselves and each other fully, in corpora, in loving familial relationships of mutual care. They construct symbols, myths, and rituals, and share spiritual traditions that help heal their physical and psychic wounds. They also heal and strengthen themselves by creating the art, music, and literature of their culture. And finally, perhaps the most important way womyn make their experience meaningful is by taking the music, art, and literature of this culture out into their everyday lives. But most importantly, it is by maintaining their relationships across space and time.

This study of the Michigan Womyn's Music Festival demonstrates an alternative way to theorize lesbian cultural spaces. Rather than framing the Festival in Victor Turner's model of liminality, I have inverted the liminal in order to provide a different perspective on lesbian experience and the concrete culture building process they engage in while at the Festival. Theoretically, by conceptualizing the dominant culture as a liminal space and time for marginalized groups, researchers might better understand and articulate the interlocking structures of power and oppression, as well as the "methodologies" that marginalized people use to resist oppressive forces in American culture.

By relocating the experience of liminality in my study, I was able to make visible some of the everyday realities that many lesbians experience and the consciousness that evolved as a result of these experiences. I was able to then theorize an *Amazon consciousness* that uses an "apparatus of love" as a tool for building an Amazon culture at the Festival.[474] For more than 38 years now, womyn have gone to the Michigan Womyn's Music Festival in order to build and embody their own culture. Amazon culture is its own unique culture. It is a concrete culture built by womyn for womyn on the 650 acres they claim as their homeland. It is a culture that narrates its roots in an ancient past with traditions that contemporary womyn revived, reconstructed, and maintain to give their lives meaning and purpose. Therefore, theoretically, Amazon culture is no more or no less an "alternative" culture for womyn than Native American culture is an "alternative" culture for Native Americans. And like Native American culture, Amazon culture does not cease just because womyn leave the Land.

Yet metaphorically speaking, the Michigan Womyn's Music Festival is an island in the sea of patriarchal oppression, a refuge from the patriarchal pollutants that eat away at the fragile lifeboats of womyn's bodies, a sanctuary from the political and religious winds raging off the patriarchal coast. On their island, womyn create their own families, homes, and sacred traditions that help them survive the waves of patriarchal power seeking to grind them into sand on

---

[474] Sandoval.

the beaches of wealthy, white, male, heterosexual, Christian, able-bodied privilege.

This is the Amazon matrix of meaning, and it is why Amazon womyn make their annual pilgrimage from the diaspora to Michigan, from the Liminal to the Land. Womyn who attend the Michigan Womyn's Music Festival are not asking for their slice of the patriarchal pie. They want a different meal entirely. But until that meal is served, they will continue building their kitchens on the Land, stirring their cauldron of ideas, blending their traditions, cooking their relationships, and chopping off the roots of patriarchy one onion at a time.

*Closing Ceremony - 2005*

# Appendix A: Patricia's Web-Journal

Tuesday, August 10, 2004 at 8:30 PM, even though rain was still very much a possibility, 100-150 womyn gathered in the Goddess Grove down on the Night Stage field to ritually celebrate the start of our week together. The ritual included invocations, chants, drumming and the opportunity for each of us to minister to one another. The air signs smudged us with sage. The fire signs rubbed their hands to create heat and offered that heat to each womon. The water signs touched our foreheads, hands and hearts with cleansing water from their water bottles. And the earth signs helped ground us in the earth beneath our feet. In conclusion, we that had no beginning and no end. As sometimes happens, I'd felt a special connection with a womon, whom I later learned was named Laurie. She'd been standing beside me earlier in the ritual and had asked some questions, explaining, "This is my first goddess ritual." Afterwards I asked how it had been for her. She was close to tears and said it had been "lifechanging." We talked as her friends patiently waited, and she told me a bit of her story. As an outgrowth of that conversation, we made a date for her to interview me after lunch on Thursday for her Ph.D. dissertation on women's experience of the sacred. Such a Michigan moment!

Thursday, August 12, 2004; I was ten minutes late for my 12:30 PM appointment with Laurie, whom I'd met at Tuesday's ritual. If you recall, we'd made a date for her to interview me for her Ph.D. dissertation on womyn's experience of the Divine. We sat together under a tree near the DART kitchen tent as I ate my lunch--yummy Waldorf salad and Three Bean salad--and she shared the five questions she wanted me to answer. The ones that stick with me were: 1) Please speak about how you describe and image the Divine; 2) What has been the spiritual journey that has brought you to this place; and 3) How do you see womyn's experiences and definitions of the Divine impacting the world community. As I reflected on and answered her questions, I experienced profound integration and deep healing. Her questions opened doors that had been closed for years. As so often happens at Festival, I was given what I needed before I knew enough to ask for it.[475]

---

[475] Patricia Lay-Dorsey. "Windchime Walker's Journal." [Online]. Accessed 9/23/04. www.windchimewalker.com.

# Appendix B:  First Michigan Womyn's Music Festival Land Map

Sisters-Amazons:
    Welcome to the sacred meadow.  Sure glad you all are here!
Straight ahead at registration, we are asking that you unload
your camping gear and then park your car.
    In order for this weekend to go off, everyone's collective
help is needed.  Food must be prepared, children cared for, cuts
or sunburns treated, security maintained, cars parked, women
registered, etc., etc.  Please think about where you would like
to contribute a few hours so that you can sign up at registration.
    Here are some simple things that will help make this week-
end more pleasant:
        1) Cars be driven only as far as the parking area;
        2) tents be pitched and camp fires made only in the area
           designated for camping;
        3) all fires be treated with considerable caution;
        4) care be taken not to pitch tents over animal holes (a
           little creature may eat a hole in your tent);
        5) everyone show up on time for the work you've agreed to
           do so things run smoothly;
        6) no dogs be in listening area or in camping area; dogs
           be left tied in parking area if unattended.  There's
           camping space in parking area if you want to sleep with
           your dog.
    All women volunteering health care skills will be wearing
red-checked arm bands, and someone will be in the health care
tent every hour on the hour.  Message boards are located near
the food preparation area.  The goddess is smiling on all of us.

                              In sisterhood,
                              We Want The Music Collective

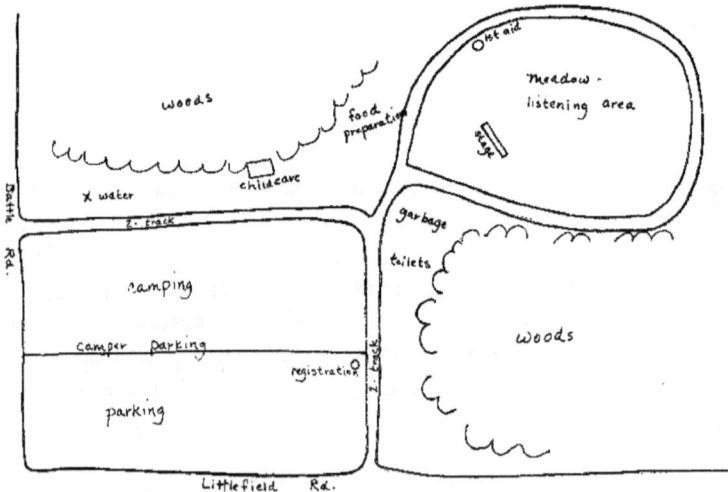

# Bibliography

Abelove, Barale Henry, Michele Aina Barale, and David M. Halperin, eds. *The Lesbian and Gay Studies Reader*. New York: Routledge, 1993.

Abu-Lughod, Lila. *Writing Women's Worlds: Bedouin Stories*. Berkeley: University of California Press, 1993.

Agar, Michael H. *The Professional Stranger: An Informal Introduction to Ethnography*. San Diego: Academic Press, 1996.

Alexis, Lorraine. Personal Interview. August, 2002.

Akosua. Personal Interview. August, 2005.

Anderson, Benedict. *Imagined Communities: Reflections on the Origin and Spread of Nationalism*. London: Verso, 1991.

Ann. Personal Interview. August, 2004.

Anzaldua, Gloria. *Borderlands/La Frontera: The New Mestiza*. San Francisco: Aunt Lute Books, 1999.

Anzaldua, Gloria. "Unnatural Bridges, Unsafe Spaces," in *This Bridge We Call Home: Radical Visions for Transformation*, edited by Gloria E. Anzaldua and Analouise Keating. New York: Routledge, 2002.

*Associated Press*, Aug. 30, 1979, PM cycle, http://www.associatedpress.com/

Atkinson, Ti-Grace. *Amazon Odyssey*. New York: Link Books, 1974.

Avery, Cindy. Personal Interview. August, 2002.

Barrett, Ruth. "Creating Dianic Ritual Workshop." Michigan Womyn's Music Festival: August, 2004.

Barrett, Ruth. "The Dianic Wiccan Tradition." May 7, 2004, http://www.witchvox.com/va/dt_va.html?a=uswi&c=trads&id=8451

Barrett, Ruth. Personal Interview. August, 2004.

Barrett, Ruth. *Women's Rites, Women's Mysteries: Creating Ritual in Dianic Wiccan Tradition*. Bloomington: AuthorHouse, 2004.

Barrett, Ruth. Personal letter in response to trans-activists call for boycotting the Festival. 2013.

Bartholomeu, Asa. Personal Interview. August, 2005.

Bartky, Sandra Lee. "Foucault, Femininity, and the Modernization of Patriarchal Power," in *Feminist Philosophies*, edited by Janet A. Kourany, James P. Sterba, and Rosemarie Tong. Upper Saddle River: Prentice Hall, 1999.

Bechdel, Alison. "Michigan Womyn's Music Festival." *Advocate*, 0001-8996, Nov. 12, 2002, Issue 876.

Beck, Evelyn Torton. *Nice Jewish Girls: A Lesbian Anthology*. Boston: Beacon Press, 1989.

Becker, Penny, and Eiesland, Nancy Edgell, eds. *Contemporary American Religion: An Ethnographic Reader*. Walnut Creek: AltaMira Press, 1997.

Bednarowski, Mary Farrell. *The Religious Imagination of American Women*. Bloomington: Indiana University Press, 1999.

Beemyn, Brett, ed. *Creating a Place for Ourselves: Lesbian, Gay, and Bisexual Communities*. New York: Routledge, 1997.

*Before Stonewall: The Making of a Gay and Lesbian Community*. Videocassette. Directed by Greta Schiller. New York: First Run Features, 1996.

Behar, Ruth. *Translated Woman: Crossing the Boarder with Esperanza's Story*. Boston: Beacon Press, 1993.

Behar, Ruth, and Deborah Gordon, eds. *Women Writing Culture*. Berkeley: University of California Press, 1995.

Bernstein, Mary, and Renate Reimann, eds. *Queer Families/Queer Politics: Challenging Culture and State*. New York: Columbia University Press, 2001.

Bitch and Animal. *The Revolution*. Quoted from their stage performance at the 2002 Michigan Womyn's Music Festival.

215

Blackwood, Evelyn, and Saskia E. Wieringa, eds. *Female Desires: Same-Sex Relations and Transgender Practices Across Culture.* New York: Columbia University Press, 1999.

Blair, Christine E. "Women's Spirituality Empowered by Biblical Story." *Religious Education,* Fall92, Vol. 87:4, 536.

Blanche. *Lesbian Connection,* Jan/Feb, 1999,Vol 21: 4,18.

Birkby, Phyllis, et al. *Amazon Expedition: A Lesbian Feminist Anthology.* New York: Time Change Press, 1973.

Boyer, Paul S., et al. *The Enduring Vision: A History of the American People.* Lexington: D.C. Heath and Company, 1996.

Brown, Karen McCarthy. *Mama Lola: A Vodou Priestess in Brooklyn.* Berkeley: University of California Press, 1991.

Buckmaster, Lynn. Personal Interview. August, 2005.

Budapest, Zsuzsanna. *The Holy Book of Women's Mysteries: Feminist Witchcraft, Goddess Rituals, Spellcasting, and Other Womanly Arts.* Berkeley: Wingbow Press, 1980.

Bunch, Charlotte, and Nancy Morgan. *Class and Feminism: A Collection of Essays from the Furies.* Baltimore: Diana Press, 1974.

Butler, Judith. *Gender Trouble.* New York: Routledge, 1999.

Caputi, Jane. *Goddesses' and Monsters: Women, Myth, Power, and Popular Culture.* Madison: University of Wisconsin Press, 2004.

Caughey, John. "The Ethnography of Everyday Life: Theories and Methods for American Cultural Studies." *American Quarterly,* 34, 1982.

Caughey, John. *Negotiating Cultures and Identities: A Life History Approach.* (Unpublished manuscript used in Caughey's ethnographic methods course, University of Maryland, College Park, MD, 2002).

Cevtkovich, Ann. *An Archive of Feelings: Trauma, Sexuality, and Lesbian Public Cultures.* Durham: Duke University Press, 2003.

Charnas, Suzy McKee. *Walk to the End of the World.* New York: Ballantine Books, 1978.

Chauncey, George. *Gay New York: Gender, Urban Culture, and the Making of the Gay Male World.* New York: Basic Books, 1995.

Chelly. Personal Interview. August, 2005.

Cheney, Joyce, ed. *Lesbian Land.* Minneapolis: Word Weavers, 1985.

Christ, Carol P., and Judith Plaskow, eds. *Womanspirit Rising: A Feminist Reader in Religion.* San Francisco: Harper & Row, 1979.

Christ, Carol P. *Diving Deep and Surfacing: Women Writers on Spiritual Quest.* Boston: Beacon Press, 1980.

Chung, Hyun Kyung. *Struggle to be the Sun Again: Introducing Asian Women's Theology.* New York: Orbis, 1990.

Clifford, James, and George E., Marcus, eds. *Writing Culture: The Poetics and Politics of Ethnography.* Berkeley: University of California Press, 1986.

Clifford, James. *The Perdicament of Culture: Twentieth-Century Ethnography, Literature, and Art.* Cambridge: Harvard University Press, 1988.

Collins, Patricia Hill. "It's all in the Family: Intersections of Gender, Race, and Nation," in *Decentering the Center: Philosophy for a Multicultural, Postcolonial, and Feminist World,* edited by Uma Narayan and Sandra Harding, Bloomington: Indiana University Press, 2000.

Collins, Patricia Hill. *Black Feminist Thought: Knowledge, Consciousness, and the Politics of Empowerment.* New York: Routledge, 2000.

Combahee River Collective. "A Black Feminist Statement," in *Feminist Theory: A Reader,* edited by Wendy Kolmar and Frances Bartkowski. Mountain View: Mayfield Publishing, 2000.

Corwin, Marissa. Personal Interview. August, 2005.

Crowder, Diane Griffin. "Separatism and Feminist Utopian Fiction," in *Sexual Practice, Textual Theory: Lesbian Cultural Criticism,* edited by Susan J. Wolfe and Julia Penelope. Cambridge: Blackwell Publishers, 1993.

Davidman, Lynn. "Truth, Subjectivity, and Ethnography Research," in *Personal Knowledge and Beyond: Reshaping the Ethnography of Religion*, edited by James V. Spickard, J. Shawn Landres, and Meredith B. McGuire. New York: New York: University Press, 2002.
Davis, Kathy. Personal Interview. August, 2002.
D'Emilio, John. *Sexual Politics, Sexual Communities*. Chicago: University of Chicago Press, 1998.
Detweiler, Graig, and Barry Taylor. *A Matrix of Meaning: Finding God in Popular Culture*. Grand Rapids: Baker Academic, 2003.
Dickie Jane R, et al. "The Heirs of Aradia, Daughters of Diana: Community in the Second and Third Wave." *Journal of Lesbian Studies* 9, (2005): 101-102.
Diner, Helen. *Mothers and Amazons: The First Feminine History of Culture*. New York: Anchor Books, 1973.
Deveaux, Monique. "Feminism and Empowerment: A Critical Reading of Foucault," in *Feminist Approaches to Theory and Methodology: An Interdisciplinary Reader*, edited by Sharlene Hesse-Biber, Christina Gilmartin, and Robin Lydenberg. New York: Oxford University Press, 1999.
Duberman, Martin, Martha Vicinus, and George Chancey, eds. *Hidden from History: Reclaiming the Gay and Lesbian Past*. New York: Plume Books, 1990.
Due, Linnea. *Joining the Tribe: Growing Up Gay and Lesbian in the '90s*. New York: Anchor Books, 1995.
Durkin, Red. http://www.change.org/petitions/indigo-girls-and-other-michfest-2013-performers-boycott-mwmf-until-the-organizers-fully-include-trans-women. 2013.
Dykewomon, Elana. "Lesbian Quarters: On Building Space, Identity, Institutional Memory and Resources." *Journal of Lesbian Studies* 9, (2005): 32.
Early, Frances, and Kathleen Kennedy, eds. *Athena's Daughters: Television's New Women Warriors*. Syracuse: Syracuse University Press, 2003.
"Emergency Relief for Mich Workers Affected by Hurricane Katrina." Michigan Forum: http://www.michfest.com/
Emerson, Robert M. *Contemporary Field Research: Perspectives and Formulations*. Prospect Heights: Waveland Press Inc., 2001.
Escoffier, Jeffery. *American Homo: Community and Perversity*. Berkeley: University of California Press, 1998.
Faderman, Lillian. *Odd Girls and Twilight Lovers: A History of Lesbian Life in Twentieth-Century America*. New York: Penguin Books, 1991.
Feldman, Maxine. *Amazon*. (Written by Maxine Feldman but never recorded by her).
Flanigan, Avril. "Womyn's Festival Strikes Harmonic Chord." *Herizons* 9.3, (Fall 95).
Friedan, Betty. "The Feminine Mystique," in *Feminist Theory: A Reader*, edited by Wendy Kolmar and Frances Bartkowski. Mountain View: Mayfield Publishing, 2000.
Frontain, Raymond-Jean. *Reclaiming the Sacred: The Bible in Gay and Lesbian Culture*. New York: Harrington Park Press, 2003.
Frye, Marilyn. "Oppression,." in *Feminist Frontier IV*, edited by Laurel Richardson, Verta Taylor, and Nancy Whittier. New York: McGraw-Hill, 1997.
Futrell, Alison. "The Baby, the Mother, and the Empire: Xena as Ancient Hero," in *Athena's Daughters: Television's New Women Warriors*, edited by Frances Early and Kathleen Kennedy. Syracuse: Syracuse University Press, 2003.
Gandavo, Pedro de Magalhaes de, "History of the Province of Santa Cruz," in *Documents and Narratives Concerning the Discovery and Conquest of Latin America: The Histories of Brazil*, edited by John Stetson. 2 (1922):89-232
Gbadamosi, Maryam. Personal Statement at the Michigan Womyn's Music Festival Opening Ceremony, Hart, Michigan, 2005.
Gearhart, Sally Miller. *Wanderground: Stories of the Hill Women*. Denver: Spinster Ink Books, 1979.
Geertz, Clifford. *The Interpretation of Cultures*. New York: Basic Books, 1973.
Gibbs, Liz, ed. *Daring to Dissent: Lesbian Culture from Margin to Mainstream*. New York: Cassel, 1994.
Gilman, Charlotte Perkins. *Herland*. New York: Pantheon Books, 1979, 57.

Gimbutas, Marija. *Goddesses and Gods of Old Europe, 6500-3500 BC.* Berkeley: University of
   California Press, 1974.
Gimbutas, Marija. *The Language of the Goddess.* San Francisco: Harper and Row, 1989.
Gimbutas, Marija. "Women and Culture in Goddess-Oriented Old Europe," in *Weaving the
   Vision: New Patterns in Feminist Spirituality,* edited by Judith Plaskow and Carol P. Christ.
   San Francisco: Harper and Row, 1989.
Gladstone. A Letter to the "Festival Forum." *Lesbian Connection,* May/June, Vol 17, Issue 6, 1995,
   42.
Goss, Robert E. *Take Back the Word: A Queer Reading of the Bible.* Cleveland: Pilgrim Press, 2000.
Gottlieb, Lynn. *She Who Dwells Within: A Feminist Vision of a Renewed Judaism.* San Francisco:
   Harper, 1995.
Grahn, Judy. *Another Mother Tongue: Gay Worlds, Gay Words.* Boston: Beacon Press, 1984.
Hagedorn, Katherine J. *Divine Utterances: The Performance of Afro-Cuban Santeria.* Washington:
   Smithsonian Institution Press, 2001.
Haraway, Donna. "A Cyborg Manifesto: Science, Technology, and Socialist-Feminism in the Late
   Twentieth Century," in *Feminist Theory: A Reader,* edited by Wendy Kolmar and Frances
   Bartkowski. Mountain View: Mayfield Publishing, 2000.
Haraway, Donna. *Simians, Cyborgs, and Women: The Reinvention of Nature.* New York: Routledge,
   1991.
Haraway, Donna. "Situated Knowledges: The Science Question in Feminism and the Privilege of
   Partial Perspective." *Feminist Studies* 14, no. 3 1988:579.
Hartsock, Nancy. *The Feminist Standpoint Revisited and Other Essays.* Colorado: Westview Press,
   1998.
Heinecken, Dawn. *The Warrior Women of Television: A Feminist Cultural Analysis of the New Female
   Body in Popular Media.* New York: Peter Lang, 2003.
Herdt, Gilbert. *Same Sex, Different Cultures: Exploring Gay & Lesbian Lives.* Boulder: Westview
   Press, 1997.
Hill, Ubaka. Quoted from the Drum Song Orchestra intensive workshop at the Michigan
   Womyn's Music Festival. Hart, Michigan, 2004.
Hill, Ubaka. http://www.afterellen.com/2013/04/fight-about-mich-fest. 2013.
Hoagland, Sarah Lucia, Penelope, Julia. *For Lesbians Only: A Separatist Anthology.* London:
   Onlywomen Press, 1988.
Hoagland, Sarah Lucia. *Lesbian Ethics: Toward New Value.* Palo Alto: Institute of Lesbian Studies,
   1992.
Hockschild, Arlie. "The Second Shift: Working Parents and the Revolution at Home," in *Feminist
   Frontier IV,* edited by Laurel Richardson, Verta Taylor, and Nancy Whittier. New York:
   McGraw-Hill, 1997.
Hollibaugh, Amber. *My Dangerous Desires: A Queer Girl Dreaming Her Way Home.* Durham: Duke
   University Press, 2000.
Hoover, Stewart M., and Lynn Schofield Clark, eds. *Practicing Religion in the Age of the Media:
   Exploration in Media, Religion, and Culture.* New York: Columbia University Press, 2002.
Hunter, Nan D. "Sexual Dissent and the Family: The Sharon Kowalski Case," in *The Social
   Construction of Inequality and Difference,* edited by Tracy E. Ore. New York: McGraw-Hill,
   2003.
Hurtado, Aida. *The Color of Privilege: Three Blasphemies on Race and Feminism.* Ann Arbor: University
   of Michigan Press, 1996.
Inness, Sherrie A., ed. *Action Chicks: New Images of Tough Women in Popular Culture.* Palgrave
   Macmillan, 2004.
Isasi-Diaz, Ada Maria. *Mujerista Theology.* New York: Orbis Books, 1996.
Isherwood, Lisa, and Elizabeth Stuart. *Introducing Body Theology.* Cleveland: The Pilgrim Press,
   1998.
Isherwood, Lisa. *Introducing Feminist Christologies.* Pilgrim Press, 2002.

Isherwood, Lisa, and Dorothea McEwan. *Introduction to Feminist Theology.* Sheffield: Academic Press, 1993.

Janis. A Letter to the "Festival Forum." *Lesbian Connection*, May/June, Vol 16, Issue 6, 1994, 9.

Jay, Karla. *Tales of the Lavender Menace.* New York: Basic Books, 1999.

Johnson, Jill. *Lesbian Nation: A Feminist Solution.* New York: Simon and Schuster, 1973.

Johnson, Jill. "Of This Pure But Irregular Passion." *Village Voice*, July 2, 1970.

Johnson, J. "Return of the Amazon Mother." *Ms.*, 1972, 1:3:90-3, 124.

Johnson, Nedra. "Any Way You Need Her." *Nedra.* © 2005 Nedra Johnson BMI.

Jones, Veronica. Personal Interview. August 2005.

Joslyn. Personal Interview. August, 2005.

Kaiser, Charles. *The Gay Metropolis: The Landmark History of Gay Life in America Since World War II.* New York: Harvest Books, 1997.

Kates, Steven M., and Russell W Belk. "The Meaning of Lesbian and Gay Pride Day: Resistance Through Consumption and Resistance to Consumption." *Journal of Contemporary Ethnography.* Vol. 30 No. 4, August 2001, 403.

Katz, Jonathan Ned. *Gay American History: Lesbians and Gay Men in the U.S.A.: A Documentary History.* New York: Plume Books, 1992.

Keifer, Marnie. Personal Interview. August, 2002.

Kelley, Robin D. G. *Race Rebels: Culture, Politics, and the Black Working Class.* New York: Free Press, 1996.

Kennedy, Elizabeth Lapovsky, and Madeline D. Davis. *Boots of Leather, Slippers of Gold: The History of a Lesbian Community.* New York: Penguin Books, 1994.

Kent, Kathryn R. *Making Girls into Women: American Women's Writing and the Rise of Lesbian Identity.* Durham: Duke University Press, 2003.

Kiki. A Letter to the "Festival Forum." *Lesbian Connection*, May/June, Vol 20, Issue 6, 1998, 53.

Krieger, Susan. "The Mirror Dance in Retrospect," *Journal of Lesbian Studies* 9, no. 1/2 2005: 8.

Kristina. A Letter to the "Festival Forum." *Lesbian Connection*, Nov/Dec, Vol 24, Issue 3, 2001, 10.

Lamos, Colleen. "Sexuality versus Gender: A Kind of Mistake?" in *Cross-Purposes: Lesbians, Feminists, and the Limits of Alliance,* edited by Dana Heller. Bloomington: Indiana University Press, 1997.

Laurel. A Letter to the "Festival Forum." *Lesbian Connection*, Jan/Feb, Vol. 20 Issue 4, 1998, 6-7.

Lay-Dorsey, Patricia. Personal Interview. August, 2005.

Lawlor, Gretchen. Personal Interview. August, 2005.

Lee, L. A., et al. "An Outbreak of Shigellosis at an Outdoor Music Festival," *American Journal of Epidemiology.* Mar 15, 1991; 133 6, 608-15.

Lehr, Valerie. *Queer Family Values: Debunking the Myth of the Nuclear Family.* Philadelphia: Temple University Press, 1999.

*Lesbian Connection*, 2.1 Mar., 1976:7.

LeVey, Simon, and Elisabeth Nonas,. *City of Friends: A Portrait of the Gay and Lesbian Community in America.* Cambridge: MIT Press, 1995.

Levitt, Laura. *Jews and Feminism: The Ambivalent Search for Home.* New York: Routledge, 1997.

Lewin, Ellen, ed. *Inventing Lesbian Cultures in America.* Boston: Beacon Press, 1996.

Lewin, Ellen and William L Leap, eds. *Out in the Field: Reflections of Lesbian and Gay Anthropologists.* Chicago: University of Illinois Press, 1996.

Lewin, Ellen and William L Leap, eds. *Out in Theory: The Emergence of Lesbian and Gay Anthropology.* Chicago: University of Illinois Press, 2002.

Linda. A Letter to the "Festival Forum." *Lesbian Connection*, May/June, Vol. 25, Issue 6, 2003, 7.

Lipsitz, George. *The Possessive Investment In Whiteness: How White People Profit From Identity Politics.* Philadelphia: Temple University Press, 1998.

Lorde, Audre. "Age, Race, Class, and Sex: Women Redefining Difference," in *Feminist Theory: A Reader,* edited by Wendy Kolmar and Frances Bartkowski. Mountain View: Mayfield Publishing, 2000.

Lorde, Audre. "The Master's Tools Will Never Dismantle the Master's House," in *This Bridge Called My Back: Writings by Women of Color.*, edited by Cherrie Moraga and Gloria Anzaldua. New York: Kitchen Table: Women of Color Press, 1981.

Martin, Joel W., and Conrad E. Ostwalt Jr., eds. *Screening the Sacred: Religion, Myth, and Ideology in American Film.* Boulder: Westview Press, 1995.

Mantilla, Karla. "The Michigan Womyn's Music Festival: Another World," *Off Our Backs: The Feminist Newsjournal,* Oct. 2001, Vol XXXI, number 9, 41.

Markko, Mickey. A Letter to the "Festival Forum." *Lesbian Connection,* May/June, Vol 20, Issue 6, 1998, 50.

Maryann. A Letter to the "Festival Forum." *Lesbian Connection,* May/June, Vol. 17, Issue 6, 1995, 41.

Mazur, Eric Michael, and Kate McCarthy, eds. *God in the Details: American Religion in Popular Culture.* New York: Routledge, 2000.

Meyerle, Julianne. Personal Interview. August, 2001.

Michigan Bulletin Board. http://www.michfest.com/

Michigan Womyn's Music Festival Program, 2001.

Michigan Womyn's Music Festival Program, 2002.

Michigan Womyn's Music Festival Program, 2003.

Michigan Womyn's Music Festival Program, 2004.

Michigan Womyn's Music Festival Program, 2005.

Michigan Womyn's Music Festival Program, 2011.

Miller, Neil. *Out of the Past: Gay and Lesbian History from 1869 to the Present.* New York: Vintage Books, 1995.

Mitchem, Stephanie Y. *Introducing Womanist Theology.* New York: Orbis Books, 2002.

Mohnaty, Chandra Talpade. "Crafting Feminist Genealogies: On the Geography and Politics of Home, Nation, and Community," in *Talking Visions: Multicultural Feminism in a Transnational Age,* edited by Ella Shohat. Cambridge: MIT Press, 1998.

Mohnaty, Chandra Talpade. "Genealogies of Community, Home, and Nation." *Feminism Without Borders: Decolonizing Theory, Practicing Solidarity.* Durham: Duke University Press, 2003.

Mohnaty, Chandra Talpade, and Biddy Martin, "What's Home Got To Do With It?" *Feminism Without Borders: Decolonizing Theory, Practicing Solidarity.* Durham: Duke University Press, 2003.

Moon, Dawne. *God, Sex, and Politics: Homosexualities and Everyday Theologies.* University of Chicago Press, 2004.

Moore, Sally F. *Secular Ritual.* Amsterdam: Van Gorcum, 1977.

Moraga, Cherrie, and Gloria Anzaldua, eds. *This Bridge Called My Back: Writings by Women of Color.* New York: Kitchen Table: Women of Color Press, 1981.

Morris, Bonnie J. "At the Michigan Womyn's Music Fest," *The Gay & Lesbian Review,* Sept.- Oct., 16.

Morris, Bonnie J. *Eden Built By Eves: The Cultural History of Women's Music Festivals.* Los Angeles: Alyson Books, 1999.

Morris, Bonnie J. "Negotiating Lesbian Worlds: The Festival Communities," *Journal of Lesbian Studies* 9, no. 1/2 2005: 57.

Moya, Paula M. L. "Postmodernism, 'Realism,' and the Politics of Identity: Cherrie Moraga and Chicana Feminism," in *Feminist Genealogies, Colonial Legacies, Democratic Futures,* edited by Jacqui Alexander and Chandra Talpade Mohanty. New York: Routledge, 1997.

Myerhoff, Barbara. "Life Not Death in Venice: Its Second Life," in *Anthropology of Experience,* edited by Victor Turner and Edward M. Bruner. Chicago: University of Illinois Press, 1986.

Myerhoff, Barbara. "The Transformation of Consciousness in Ritual Performances: Some Thoughts and Questions," in *By Means of Performance: Intercultural Studies of Theatre and Ritual,* edited by Richard Schechner and Willa Appel. New York: Cambridge University Press, 1997.

Narayan, Uma. *Dislocating Cultures: Identities, Traditions, and Third World Feminism.* New York: Routledge, 1997.
Near, Holly. *Fire in the Rain, Singer in the Storm.* New York: Quill, 1990.
Nestle, Joan, ed. *The Persistent Desire: A Femme-Butch Reader.* New York: Alyson Publications, 1992.
Newton, Esther. *Cherry Grove, Fire Island.* Boston: Beacon Press, 1993.
*Off Our Backs: The Feminist Newsjournal,* Vol.XXXII, 11 & 12, November-December, 2002.
Oliver, Melvin L., and Thomas M Shapiro. *Black Wealth/White Wealth: A New Perspective on Racial Inequality.* New York: Routledge, 1997.
Olson, Alix. *Daughter.* http://www.alixolson.com/
Onada-Sikwoia, Akiba. Blessing at the Opening Ceremony of the Michigan Womyn's Music Festival. Hart, Michigan, 1986.
Omi, Michael, and Howard Winant,. *Racial Formations in the United States From the 1960s to the 1990s.* New York: Routledge, 1994.
Oppenheimer, Mark. *Knocking on Heaven's Door: American Religion in the Age of Counterculture.* New Haven: Yale University Press, 2003.
Palmer, Alyson. Personal letter in response to trans-activists call for boycotting the Festival. 2013.
Parker, Kip. Personal interview. 8 Aug. 2003.
Penelope, Julia, and Susan J. Wolfe, eds. *Lesbian Culture: An Anthology.* Crossing Press, 1993.
Penelope, Julia. *Call Me Lesbian: Lesbian Lives, Lesbian Theory.* Freedom: Crossing Press, 1992.
Piercy, Marge. *Woman on the Edge of Time.* New York: Fawcett Crest, 1976.
Pink, Sarah. *Doing Visual Ethnography: Images, Media and Representation in Research.* Thousand Oaks: Sage Publications, 2001.
Planetearthgirrl. "15 yrs + at FEST" thread. Michigan Womyn's Music Festival Discussion Forum. 10-4-01. http://www.michfest.com/
Rabin, Joan S., and Barbara R Slater. "Lesbian Communities Across the United States: Pockets of Resistance and Resilience," *Journal of Lesbian Studies* 9, no. 1/2 2005: 170.
Radicalesbians. "The Woman Identified Woman," in *Feminist Theory: A Reader,* edited by Wendy Kolmar and Frances Bartkowski. Mountain View: Mayfield Publishing, 2000, 195-196.
Randle, Vicki. http://www.epochalips.com/?p=870. 2013.
Rasmussen, Rosemary. Personal interview. 10 Aug. 2002.
Reinfelder, Monika, ed. *Amazon to Zami: Toward a Global Lesbian Feminism.* London: Cassell, 1996.
Rich, Adrienne. "Compulsory Heterosexuality and Lesbian Existence," in *Feminist Theory: A Reader,* edited by Wendy Kolmar and Frances Bartkowski. Mountain View: Mayfield Publishing, 2000.
Richmond-Abbott, Marie. "Women Wage Earners," in *Feminist Philosophies,* edited by Janet A. Kourany, James P. Sterba, and Rosemarie Tong. Upper Saddle River: Prentice Hall Inc, 1999.
Riessman, Catherine Kohler. *Narrative Analysis.* Newbury Park: Sage, 1993.
River, Falcon. Personal Interview. August, 2004.
Roberts, Dorothy. *Killing the Black Body: Race, Reproduction, and the Meaning of Liberty.* New York: Vintage Books, 1997.
Roediger, David R. *The Wages of Whiteness: Race and the Making of the American Working Class.* New York: Verso, 1999.
Rogers, Susan Fox. *Chasing an American Dyke Dream: Homestretch.* San Francisco: Cleis Press, 1998.
Rosaldo, Renato. *Culture & Truth: The Remaking of Social Analysis.* Boston: Beacon Press, 1993.
Rosenwasser, Penny. "Imagine This," *Off Our Backs: The Feminist Newsjournal,* Nov/Dec 2002, Vol XXXII, numbers 11 & 12, 41.
Roth, Benita. *Race, Class and the Emergence of Black Feminism in the 1960s and 1970s.* http://www.uga.edu/~womanist/roth3.1.htm
Ruby, Jennie. "Michigan Values," *Off Our Backs: The Feminist Newsjournal.* Oct. 2001, vol xxxi, number 9.

Ruby, Jennie. "Women-Only and Feminist Spaces: Important Alternatives to Patriarchy," *Off Our Backs: The Feminist Newsjouranl,* March-April, Vol. XXXIII, nos. 5 & 6, 2003, 15.

Rushing, Janice Hocker. "Evolution of 'The New Frontier' in Alien and Aliens: Patriarchal Co-optation of the Feminine Archetype," in *Screening the Sacred: Religion, Myth, and Ideology in American Film,* edited by Joel W. Martin and Conrad E. Ostwalt, Jr. Boulder: Westview Press, 1995.

Russ, Joanna. *The Female Man.* New York: Bantam Books, 1975.

Sandoval, Chela. *Methodology of the Oppressed: Theory Out of Bounds.* Minneapolis: University of Minnesota, 2000.

Schechner, Richard. *Performance Studies: An Introduction.* New York: Routledge, 2002.

Schensul, Stephen L., Jean J. Schensul, and Margaret D. LeCompte, *Essential Ethnographic Methods: Observations, Interviews, and Questionnaires.* Walnut Creek: Alta Mira Press, 1999.

Schulman, Sarah. *My American History: Lesbian and Gay Life During the Reagan/Bush Years.* New York: Routledge, 1994.

Sheffield, Carole J. "Sexual Terrorism," in *Feminist Philosophies,* edited by Janet A. Kourany, James P. Sterba, and Rosemarie Tong. Upper Saddle River: Prentice Hall Inc, 1999.

Shneer, David, and Caryn Aviv. *Queer Jews.* New York: Routledge, 2002.

Sims, Mary. Personal Interview. August, 2005.

Sitkoff, Harvard. *The Struggle for Black Equality.* New York: Hill and Wang, 1993.

Smith, Jonathan Z. *To Take Place: Toward Theory in Ritual.* Chicago: University of Chicago Press, 1987.

Sobol, Donald. *The Amazons in Greek Society.* London: Barns, 1972.

Spradley, James. *The Ethnographic Interview.* Holt, Rinehart & Winston, 1979.

Spretnak, Charlene, ed. *The Politics of Women's Spirituality: Essays on the Rise of Spiritual Power Within the Feminist Movement.* New York: Anchor Press, 1982.

St. Julian, Susi. Personal Interview. August, 2005.

Sandstrom, Boden. "Performance, Ritual and Negotiation of Identity in the Michigan Womyn's Music Festival." Ph.D. dissertation, University of Maryland, 2002.

Starhawk. *The Spiral Dance: A Rebirth of the Ancient Religion of the Great Goddess.* San Francisco: HarperCollins, 1989.

Stein, Arlene. *Sex and Sensibility: Stories of a Lesbian Generation.* Berkeley: University of California Press, 1997.

*Stolen Moments.* Directed by Margaret Westcot. Video Cassette. New York: First Run/Icarus Films, 1999.

Stuart, Elizabeth. *Gay and Lesbian Theologies: Repetitions with Critical Difference.* Burlington: Ashgate Publishing, 2003.

Stokes, Martin, ed. *Ethnicity, Identity and Music: The Musical Construction of Place.* New York: Berg, 1997.

Stone, Merlin. *When God Was A Woman.* San Diego: Harvest/HBJ Book, 1976.

Taylor, Eugene. "Desperately Seeking Spirituality." *Psychology Today.* Nov/Dec94, Vol. 27 Issue 6, 56.

Taz. Personal Interview. August, 2005.

Teresa. Personal Interview. August, 2004.

Thom, Kate. Personal Interview. August, 2005.

Thumma, Scott, and Edward R. Gray. "The Gospel Hour: Liminality, Identity, and Religion in a Gay Bar," in *Gay Religion* edited by Scott Thumma and Edward R. Gray. Walnut Creek, CA: Alta Mira Press, 2005.

Turner, Victor, ed. *Celebration: Studies in Festivity and Ritual.* Washington: Smithsonian Institution Press, 1982.

Turner, Victor. *From Ritual to Theatre: The Human Seriousness of Play.* New York: PAJ Publications, 1982.

Turner, Victor. *Ritual Process: Structure and Anti-Structure.* New York: Aldine De Grauyter, 1995.

Turner, Victor. *The Anthropology of Experience.* Chicago: University of Illinois Press, 1986.

Turner, Victor. *The Anthropology of Performance*. New York: PAJ Publications, 1988.
"V's Healing Thread." Michigan Womyn's Music Festival Discussion Forum. http://www.michfest.com/
Van. Personal Interview. August, 2005.
Vandenburg, Margaret. "Home-phobia," in *Chasing the American Dyke Dream: Homestretch*, edited by Susan Fox Rogers. San Francisco: Cleis, 1998.
Van Gelder, Lindsy, and Pamela Robin Brandt. *The Girls Next Door: Into the Heart of Lesbian America*. New York: Touchstone, 1996.
Villarejo, Amy. *Lesbian Rule: Cultural Criticism and the Value of Desire*. Durham: Duke University Press, 2003.
Vogel, Lisa. *Lesbian Connection*, Nov/Dec, 1999, 5-7.
Vogel, Lisa. http://www.afterellen.com/2013/04/fight-about-mich-fest. 2013.
Wadud, Amina. *Qur'an and Women: Rereading the Sacred Text from a Woman's Perspective*. New York: Oxford, 1999.
Walowitz, Paula. "She's Been Waiting." *She Changes*. Santa Barbara: Heartway Productions, 1991.
Wasserlein, Frances, and Carolynn L Sween,. "Lesquire's Pub – An Essay on Virtual Community Building," *Journal of Lesbian Studies* 9, no. 1/2 2005: 113.
Watson, Natalie K. *Feminist Theology*. Grand Rapids: Wm. B. Eerdmans, 2003.
Wendy. *Lesbian Connection*, Jan/Feb, Vol 25, Issue 4, 2003, 28.
Westenhoefer, Suzanne. "Nothing in My Closet but My Clothes." *Hilarith: The Best of Lesbian Humor*. Audio Cassette. Westlake Village: Uproar Entertainment; 1997.
Weston, Kath. *Families We Choose: Lesbians, Gays, Kinship*. New York: Columbia University Press, 1991.
Whethers, Lauren. Personal Interview. August 2005.
Whethers, Lauren. Personal Statement at the Opening Ceremony of the Michigan Womyn's Music Festival. 2005.
Wilcox, Melissa M. "Dancing on the Fence: Researching Lesbian, Gay, Bisexual, and Transgender Christians," in *Personal Knowledge and Beyond* edited by James V. Spickard, J. Shawn Landers, and Meredith B. McGuire. New York: New York University Press, 2002.
Williams, Delores. *Sisters in the Wilderness: The Challenge of Womanist God-Talk*. New York: Orbis, 1993.
Williams, Walter L. *The Spirit and the Flesh: Sexual Diversity in American Indian Cultures*. Boston: Beacon Press, 1992.
Wilson, Nancy. *Our Tribe: Queer Folks, God, Jesus, and the Bible*. Alamo Square Press, 2000.
Wilton, Tamsin. *Lesbian Studies: Setting An Agenda*. New York: Routledge, 1997.
Winlock, Colette. Personal Interview. August, 2005.
Wittig, Monique. *Les Guerilleres*. Boston: Beacon Press, 1969.
Wolf, D. *The Lesbian Community*. Berkley: University of California Press, 1979.
Wolfe, Susan J., and Julia Penelope, eds. *Sexual Practice, Textual Theory: Lesbian Cultural Criticism*. Cambridge: Blackwell, 1993.
Wright, Janet M. *Lesbian Step Families: An Ethnography of Love*. New York: Harrington Park Press, 1998.
Zimmerman, Bonnie. "Placing Lesbians," in *The New Lesbian Studies: Into the Twenty-First Century*, edited by Bonnie Zimmerman and Toni A. H. McNaron. New York: The Feminist Press, 1996.
Zimmerman, Bonnie. *The Safe Sea of Women: Lesbian Fiction 1969-1989*. Boston: Beacon Press, 1990.

# Index

www.ingramcontent.com/pod-product-compliance
Lightning Source LLC
Chambersburg PA
CBHW031154270326
41931CB00006B/268